"*Introduction to Positive Media Psychology* made me want to go to college again. To learn about all the ways in which media can be used for good, to inspire and connect us as humans, is what I greatly missed back then. This textbook lays out a positive, hope-inspiring media landscape that is firmly grounded in scientific research. It squares the circle of presenting the state of the art of an exciting new research field in plain language with instructive examples. For students and scholars alike, it will serve as the leading authoritative source on the topic."

—**Anne Bartsch**, *University of Leipzig, Germany*

"Probably no other perspective has stimulated media effects and media entertainment research as strongly over the past decade as the advent of positive media psychology. The present textbook provides a dearly needed integration of this fast-developing field. The authors are among the leading scholars who have crucially defined this research area and possess a unique expertise. The volume provides an excellent introduction to media psychology both to advanced undergraduate and graduate students and a well-structured overview to more senior scholars. I am confident that it will leave a lasting footprint and provide fertile ground for future scholarship in this field."

—**Leonard Reinecke**, *Johannes Gutenberg University of Mainz, Germany*

INTRODUCTION TO POSITIVE MEDIA PSYCHOLOGY

Introduction to Positive Media Psychology summarizes and synthesizes the key concepts, theories, and empirical findings on the positive emotional, cognitive, and behavioral effects of media use. In doing so, the book offers the first systematic overview of the emerging field of positive media psychology.

The authors draw on a growing body of scholarship that explores the positive sides of media use, including fostering one's own well-being; creating greater connectedness with others; cultivating compassion for those who may be oppressed or stigmatized; and motivating altruism and other prosocial actions. The authors explore these issues across the entire media landscape, examining the ways that varying content (e.g., entertainment, news) delivered through traditional (e.g., film, television) and more recent media technologies (e.g., social media, digital games, virtual reality) can enhance well-being and promote other positive outcomes in viewers and users.

This book serves as a benchmark of theory and research for current and future generations of advanced undergraduate students, graduate students, and scholars in communication, psychology, education, and social work.

Arthur A. Raney is James E. Kirk Professor of Communication in the School of Communication at Florida State University, USA.

Sophie H. Janicke-Bowles is Assistant Professor in the School of Communication at Chapman University, USA.

Mary Beth Oliver is Distinguished Professor and co-director of the Media Effects Research Laboratory at Pennsylvania State University, USA.

Katherine R. Dale is Assistant Professor in the School of Communication at Florida State University, USA.

INTRODUCTION TO POSITIVE MEDIA PSYCHOLOGY

Arthur A. Raney, Sophie H. Janicke-Bowles,
Mary Beth Oliver, and Katherine R. Dale

Routledge
Taylor & Francis Group

NEW YORK AND LONDON

First published 2021
by Routledge
52 Vanderbilt Avenue, New York, NY 10017

and by Routledge
2 Park Square, Milton Park, Abingdon, Oxon OX14 4RN

Routledge is an imprint of the Taylor & Francis Group, an informa business

Library of Congress Cataloging-in-Publication Data
Names: Raney, Arthur A., author.
Title: Introduction to positive media psychology / Arthur A. Raney, Sophie H. Janicke-Bowles, Mary Beth Oliver, Katherine R. Dale.
Description: New York, NY : Routledge, 2021. | Includes bibliographical references and index.
Identifiers: LCCN 2020032999 (print) | LCCN 2020033000 (ebook) | ISBN 9780367373917 (hardback) | ISBN 9780367373900 (paperback) | ISBN 9780429353482 (ebook)
Subjects: LCSH: Mass media–Psychological aspects. | Mass media–Social aspects. | Well-being.
Classification: LCC P96.P75 R36 2021 (print) | LCC P96.P75 (ebook) | DDC 302.23–dc23
LC record available at https://lccn.loc.gov/2020032999
LC ebook record available at https://lccn.loc.gov/2020033000

ISBN: 978-0-367-37391-7 (hbk)
ISBN: 978-0-367-37390-0 (pbk)
ISBN: 978-0-429-35348-2 (ebk)

Typeset in Bembo
by Taylor & Francis Books

For Laura, Austin, Reed, Mom, and in loving memory of Pop.

—Art

For my sister Romy, Mom, and in gratitude for my better half Rodney.

—Sophie

To John, who is, and always will be, the love of my life.

—Mary Beth

For Mom, Dad, Ryan, Kaitlyn, and Sage, my biggest supporters.

—Katie

Collectively, we also dedicate this book to Dr. Jennings Bryant who left this world much too soon. To Art and Mary Beth, Jennings was a mentor, collaborator, and dear friend. To Sophie, Katie, and countless others, he was a pioneering scholar whose research and writings serve as a foundation for most of media and entertainment psychology. He will be dearly missed, but his brilliance, generosity, and kindness will continue to inspire.

CONTENTS

ILLUSTRATIONS

Figures

Boxes

FOREWORD

For nearly a century, the scientific study of media use has primarily focused on the potential negative consequences on individuals and society: aggression, stereotyping, political divisiveness, knowledge gaps, misinformation, materialism and egocentrism, body dissatisfaction, sleep deprivation, obesity and other health problems, just to name a few. This research—often referred to as media psychology—has been, and continues to be, incredibly important, informative, and socially influential, as it has shined a light on potentially problematic outcomes of media use and in so doing empowered parents, educators, politicians, and consumers to work toward minimizing them. However, over the past decade, a growing body of scholarship has emerged that uses similar approaches and methods to explore the *positive* sides of media use, including creating greater connectedness with others, cultivating compassion for those who may be oppressed or stigmatized, and motivating altruism and other prosocial actions. It has examined how media can be used to foster one's own psychological well-being: enhancing feelings of purpose and meaningfulness, helping to cope with challenges and fears, promoting mindfulness and spirituality, and developing character and empathy. This work joins a few intellectually rich lines of existing media research—entertainment theory, educational and prosocial children's television, narrative persuasion, and entertainment-education initiatives—in examining how media entertainment can be used as a force for social and personal good.

From our perspective, these similar lines of inquiry constitute a growing area in communication, media, and psychology studies: positive media psychology. The purpose of this book is to pull together those lines of inquiry, with the goal of offering a framework for and current overview of this emerging field. For us, positive media psychology is the study of beneficial media use in a broad sense: for pleasure, meaning, transcendence, inspiration, need satisfaction, education, training, physical and mental health, recovery, productivity, information exchange, and coping; such use leads to well-being, social connectedness, contentment, mindfulness, spiritual fulfillment, hope and striving, resilience, tolerance, self-actualization, moral clarity, healthy relationships, civic engagement, community building, longevity, human flourishing, and more. As media psychologists, we do not deny the negative effects of media that have been the focus of our collective work for so long; further, we reject simplistic notions about some media use or content being good and other bad. We embrace the complex roles that media technologies and content play in our lives. Our aim is to unpack those complexities, highlighting beneficial experiences and outcomes in particular.

To that end, the book begins with a broad overview of positive media psychology as an emerging scientific pursuit. The model of positive media use that we offer in Chapter 1—and in truth, the entirety of the text—reflects our perspective as media psychologists within the communication discipline, as we approach this pursuit paying particular attention to three elements of the media communication process: channels/media technologies, messages, and receivers/ audiences. Next, we acknowledge and explore the intellectual roots of positive media psychology by introducing key concepts and theories from the well-established fields of media psychology (Chapter 2) and positive psychology (Chapter 3). Next, we explore how different media contents and technologies can promote our better selves. Three chapters specifically address experiences with entertainment content: hedonic (Chapter 4), meaningful or eudaimonic (Chapter 5) and transcendent (Chapter 6). We also examine how newer technologies can contribute to well-being, specifically social media (Chapter 7) and interactive games and virtual reality (Chapter 8). Three particular types of content are then examined: news and nonfiction (Chapter 9), narrative content designed to persuade (Chapter 10), and children's educational and prosocial programming and games (Chapter 11). To directly address the complexity noted above, differences in processes and effects across individuals and cultures are discussed in Chapter 12. In the final chapter, we offer the reader practical information about how to think about and integrate the content of the text into their daily lives.

In many ways, this book represents the culmination of a journey that the four of us began together in 2015 as the lead researchers on a three-year research project on inspirational media use funded by the John Templeton Foundation. We are indebted to them for entrusting us with the resources to devote time and energy to many of the studies reported herein. We also must recognize the tireless team of students (many now professors) who assisted us with those studies, especially Joshua Baldwin, Winston Connor III, Arienne Ferchaud, Alysia Hendry, Alex Huebner, Laura-Kate Huse, Jacob Lopez, Austin Raney, Abbie Reed, Jerrica Rowlett, Jonmichael Seibert, Cen Wang, and Danyang Zhao. We are incredibly proud of and thankful for you all. The list of mentors and colleagues who continually motivate and humble us is too long to include here (though we must give a quick shout-out to Qihao Ji, Meghan Sanders, and Russell Clayton), but your names can be found throughout the text as references. And finally, this project would not have been possible without the love, support, encouragement, and patience of our family and friends. You inspire and sustain us.

Arthur A. Raney
Sophie H. Janicke-Bowles
Mary Beth Oliver
Katherine R. Dale

1

WHAT IS POSITIVE MEDIA PSYCHOLOGY?

Source: Shutterstock 1577838799

To say that Rex Chapman's life has been a roller coaster would be an understatement. High school basketball phenomenon. Celebrated college player. First round National Basketball Association (NBA) draft choice, leading to a 12-year playing career, front-office management positions, and broadcasting gigs. Along the way came excruciatingly intense pressure from fans, even for an 18-year-old living in a pre-social-media world, followed by numerous basketball-related surgeries, a long-time addiction to pain killers, depression, stints in rehab, ultimately culminating in an arrest for shoplifting $14,000 of merchandise from an Apple Store in 2014. He pawned the stolen goods to pay off gambling debts.

But Chapman persevered. He made amends for his crimes. He says he has been drug-free for several years. He returned to broadcasting as an analyst for college and professional basketball, and even showed up on Cartoon Network's Adult Swim programming block as the host of *Block or Charge*, a program inspired by one of his tweets. Chapman has become a social media influencer, with hundreds of thousands of Twitter followers (@RexChapman), including athletes, celebrities, politicians, and even academics from around the world.

In many ways, Chapman's social media posts have come to reflect what this book is all about. They are funny, thoughtful, and inspiring; more often than not, they reflect how media can be a source of positivity. Chapman explained his social media approach in an interview with ESPN:

> I just think that everybody likes good things … everybody likes to feel good and believe the best in people … if [my Twitter feed is] providing anything, it's just a little laugh during the day, just to remind yourself that we all just have thoughts … We think, we write and we're all people just trying to get along.
>
> *(McGee, 2020)*

TIME magazine proclaimed, "Rex Chapman's Twitter feed is what a COVID-19 world needs" (Gregory, 2020). As the pandemic began to spread across the U.S. in early 2020, Chapman leveraged his online clout to raise money to help families financially devastated by the crisis. Speaking about his followers, Chapman said:

> [T]hese are people who are looking for some good in the world. So it would only seem natural that they would also want to do some good in the world, right? It wasn't so long ago that I was sleeping in my car. If it hadn't been for the kindness of other people, willing to help me, I don't know where I would be. I might be in the ground. So let's make the most of a terrible situation and let's show some of that same kindness.
>
> *(McGee, 2020)*

Understanding how media content like that shared by Rex Chapman and countless others can be a source of goodness—of kindness, laughter, warmth, meaning, education, insight, support, transcendence—is the goal of positive media psychology. More specifically, **positive media psychology** is the field of study devoted to examining processes and relationships associated with media use leading to thoughts, feelings, and behaviors that contribute to individual well-being and flourishing. The field has deep historical roots in scholarship in the disciplines of communication and (positive) psychology, as well as education, sociology, philosophy, economics, political science, information studies, and marketing. However, it is only recently that varying approaches to examining "media for good" have been collectively considered as a separate field of study. The primary goal of this book is to offer an initial framework for the emerging field called positive media psychology.

Historical Roots

In many ways, media use has *always* been associated with positivity, at least from the vantage point of the audience. Media messages are sought as an escape from the frustrations of everyday life, to reduce our uncertainty about the world around us, to fascinate and amaze us. However, the scientific exploration of how media can positively affect our well-being is a new endeavor. This is not to suggest that concern about the effects of media are new. The first documented statement about media's potential influence may have been offered by the Swiss naturalist Conrad Gesner who, in his *Bibliotheca universalis*, decried the "confusing and harmful abundance of books," even in 1545. Thus began a centuries-long fear about the negative effects of media. The Industrial Revolution fueled the rapid development of new and improved mass communication tools. With each new form—from sensationalistic newspapers that seemed to "trade in filth" in the late 1800s to gangster films and comic books that critics argued spawned antisocial behavior in juveniles in the 1930s and 1940s, to the mass adoption of television in the 1960s—researchers repeatedly and increasingly turned their attention to exploring the potential negative impacts on individuals and society, leading to the development of numerous theories and conceptual models of media use and effects (see more in Chapter 2).

But audiences just could not (and cannot) get enough. Why? No doubt, media outlets provide vital news and public affairs information for daily living; they also keep consumers abreast of the latest products and services available. More than anything, though, they entertain. And what many researchers found was that all this informing, persuading, and entertaining could lead to various unintended, negative effects (like stereotyping, aggression, harmful health behaviors, political polarization, etc.). But it also brings us joy, brightens our day, makes us think, helps us cope, and so much more. The beneficial effects of media are numerous and equally worthy of scientific attention. That is the purpose of positive media psychology.

Over the course of this book, the reader will encounter the various ways that researchers have examined positive media effects. A few lines of inquiry—for instance, examining the intended effects of using media to educate, inform, and enlighten adults (Chapters 9 and 10) and children (Chapter 11)—are quite well-established (though they remain fertile fields of inquiry given recent technological developments). The study of media enjoyment also has a rich tradition (Chapter 4). More recent on the scientific scene have been investigations into how media content is used for purposes of reflection, contemplation, recovery, and spirituality (Chapters 5 and 6). Interest in these topics among communication and media scholars coincided with the emergence of the field of positive psychology (Chapter 3) in the early 2000s, which brought new theories and understandings of well-being and human fulfillment. The evolution and ubiquity of online and mobile communication technologies (Chapters 7 and 8) only highlighted the need to better understand how media could be leveraged for personal and social good across vastly different populations (Chapter 12). In short, positive media psychologists operate at the historical and intellectual intersection of media psychology and positive psychology, relying on theories and research from both fields, with the ultimate goal of exploring how audiences can use media technologies and content in the pursuit of beneficial outcomes.

Scientific Examination of Positive Media Use

Positive media psychology is a social science. Like other social sciences—anthropology, political science, sociology, economics, to name a few—positive media psychology applies scientific methods to describe, explore, and understand particular aspects of the human condition. The focus on the human—with our free will, autonomy, advanced symbolization and imagination capacities, self-reflexivity, ability to self-regulate, varying levels of development and maturation, among other characteristics—is what makes the science "social." Natural scientists like physicists, for instance, do not have to consider the varying motivations of an atom; chemists need not worry whether two liquids of different densities might actually mix today just because they wanted to try something new. Because humans are unique and self-determining, the conclusions that can be drawn from social-scientific examinations are (1) necessarily reflective of the population sample expressed in the aggregate, (2) with results not necessarily reflective of each individual. Keeping this in mind throughout your reading of the text will be helpful, especially when you come across something that does not seem to "ring true" for you personally. If (or when) that happens, it does not mean that the finding is incorrect; it is just a reminder that you are not like everyone else in every single way.

The use of the scientific method presumes certain truths or realities about the phenomenon in question. That is, to examine "something" through the lens of science one assumes various things about that "something." Science is not the *only* way to understand our world, media, or well-being; our personal experiences, intuition, traditions and rituals, voices of respect and authority can all provide insight and wisdom for daily living. However, science is the method of examining these phenomena that we employ through this book.

Science assumes that reality is **objective** and can be discovered. In truth, we may never discover everything about the world in which we live, but science contends that all reality can be discovered. Because reality is objective, we can observe it (**empirical**), and we can **measure** it, if we have the right tools. Scientific measurement is most often, but not always, expressed in mathematical or **quantitative** terms. Science is also **deterministic**, which means that it assumes a phenomenon happens for a reason, that everything has a (discoverable, observable, and measurable) cause. In attempting to examine causes and connect them to possible effects, science is governed by rules of **logic**, one of which is **parsimony** (that the simplest solution or explanation is always preferred). Science seeks to yield **generalizable** results, meaning that they can describe, explain, or predict the same phenomenon across various contexts. Science is also **open** in two senses. One is that it is open to modification, as new observations may provide different or more accurate explanations of a phenomenon. But it is also (ideally) open, accessible, transparent, and collaborative, so that methods can be improved, studies replicated with different populations, and analyses verified.

The goal of using science to examine various aspects of a phenomenon is to **describe** (e.g., what is it, what makes it different from something else), **explain** (e.g., what caused it, what does it cause, how is it related to other things), and **predict** (e.g., under what condition should we expect to find it again). The pursuit of those goals yields **evidence** about the particular aspects of interest. Ideally, that evidence can be used as the basis for, or in support of, a **theory**, which is a set of statements that logically lays out a description and explanation of a phenomenon, allowing for the prediction of that phenomenon. Because media content, audiences, and experiences are so diverse and complex, we will introduce numerous theories in the upcoming chapters.

We remind the reader: The word *theory* gets used quite a bit in everyday speech to refer to unproven explanations, guesses, hunches, and even conspiracies. That is not how we will use the term in this context. The theories that are discussed herein have been developed, rigorously tested through the scientific method, and evaluated by leading experts (i.e., **peer reviewed**). As scientists, we acknowledge that some theories end up being refuted and rejected by the scientific community. More often than not this is because better ways to observe a phenomenon have come along or something changes about the nature of the phenomenon in question. In such cases, this does not necessarily mean that science was "wrong" but rather that the scientific process actually worked as intended.

The evidence collected in support of the positive media psychology theories presented in the coming chapters has overwhelmingly come from the use of four specific scientific methods. We briefly describe each now. For a more detailed discussion of research methods in the social sciences, we recommend Babbie (2021); for media-specific research methods, Wimmer and Dominick (2014) is informative.

Content Analysis

Some people complain that news organizations only cover "bad" news, that stories of hope and inspiration are all too rare. If you wanted to scientifically examine such claims, the method you would use is content analysis. As the name suggests, **content analysis** is the method for the "objective, systematic and quantitative description of the manifest content of communication" (Berelson, 1952, p. 18). In other words, it is the application of the scientific method to describe media content. Content analysis tells us what and how much of some predefined category appears in a set of media messages. The method can be applied to any format: text, pictures, audio, moving images, or any combination thereof. You could analyze depictions of heroism in children's cartoons, body positivity messages on Instagram, or words of encouragement in great speeches by U.S. Presidents. To do so, you need to identify what aspect of the content is to be examined (e.g., heroism, body positivity, encouragement), explicitly define how to identify that aspect, and then apply that definition to a sample of content (e.g., cartoons, Instagram posts, presidential speeches).

Content analysis is *objective* and *systematic* in that researchers develop **operational definitions** of content characteristics, which are specific and detailed so that other researchers could (1) reliably produce an identical (or at least an extremely similar) description of the same content, or (2) apply the same definitions to other content, thereby allowing direct comparisons between the two. For example, Dale and her colleagues (2017) examined YouTube videos that had been tagged as "inspirational" for the presence of religiousness and spirituality, among other things. To do so, the researchers operationally defined the presence of religiousness and spirituality in terms of symbols (e.g., crescent and star, Om, crucifix) and rituals (e.g., worship services, prayer, Bar and Bat Mitzvah) depicted onscreen. They then created a **coding manual** that explicitly defined what did and did not count for each category. They then used those definitions to count the number of religious and spiritual symbols and rituals portrayed in the inspirational videos. Because the analysis was objectively and systematically completed, other researchers could take the same coding manual, examine the same YouTube videos as Dale et al. (2017), and find the same number of symbols and rituals. Or they could take the coding manual, examine a different set of YouTube videos (perhaps ones with the most views), and provide results to directly compare with those reported in Dale et al. (2017).

As Berelson (1952) noted, content analysis also yields *quantitative* results. In the example above, the researchers described the YouTube content in terms of the *frequency* of religious and spiritual symbols and rituals depicted. This is a common way to describe content. Content analyses also commonly report *proportions* and *length* of time (or text). Finally, content analysis is generally performed on the *manifest content* of the message, that is, what actually appears (not on the latent content, which is what can be inferred, interpreted, or identified as subtext). The focus on what actually appears underscores the objective nature of the method; interpretations are necessarily subjective.

Content analysis is a powerful tool for media researchers, but it does have limitations. The method permits us to better understand the nature of media messages that people are consuming. However, it does not and cannot allow us to make any statement about the potential effects of seeing, playing, reading, or hearing those messages. Theories may suggest that "if you view more X, then the chance of Y becomes more likely." Content analysis helps us understand what is portrayed and depicted in X, but it cannot specifically or directly tell us anything about Y. Another limitation relates to the generalizability of findings. Randomly selecting 20 Pixar movies to investigate representations of helping behaviors may give insight into the way that Pixar movies overall portray helping. But it would be unwise to assume that those findings represent what is portrayed in all children's movies (even all animated ones), in television programs based on the films, or in digital games featuring characters from the films.

Survey

Most people are at least somewhat familiar with surveys from completing them in the past or seeing results discussed in the news. Generally speaking, surveys can be **descriptive** (e.g., describing current conditions, answering "what?") or **analytical** (e.g., exploring relationships between variables, answering "why?"). In truth, many surveys have both descriptive and analytical components. For example, Raney and colleagues (2018) surveyed more than 3,000 U.S. adults about their use of different media formats for inspiration. They found that music was the format most likely to inspire, followed by film and television; also, most people came across inspiring content by chance, as opposed to having it recommended to them by a friend or relative. These results *describe* the audience of inspirational media content. But the researchers also asked how frequently the respondents performed prosocial actions (e.g., donated to a charity, volunteered time), and then examined the relationship between those behaviors and exposure to inspiring media. They found that more exposure to inspiring media was associated with more prosocial behaviors; this is an example of analytical survey results.

Most of the survey results discussed throughout the book come from **cross-sectional surveys**, which collect data at one single point in time from one single sample. **Panel surveys** collect data at multiple points of time from the same sample; the survey reported in Raney et al. (2018) was from a panel study, with additional results from subsequent waves of data collection reported in Janicke-Bowles et al. (2019). Panel and other types of longitudinal surveys are rarer because of the cost associated with tracking down the same respondents to complete multiple surveys.

Regardless of the type of survey, an important factor in determining the quality of the results is the **sampling** technique used to identify respondents and collect data. Ideally, survey data are collected from a **probability sample** (e.g., random, cluster, multistage) of participants drawn from a known population. Probability samples are drawn by applying mathematical guidelines for the selection of participants, which helps to reduce the error between the observed data and the "true" data. You might be familiar with the term "margin of error" from political polls; using a probability-based approach to select a large number of people to complete your survey shrinks the margin of error. However, probability sampling can be quite expensive. Instead, many positive media psychology surveys are based on data from a **nonprobability sample** (e.g., convenience, snowball, quota). Most of the surveys using college students involve nonprobability samples, as they are often completed by students who volunteer to participate for course or extra credit at the university where the researcher works. Such studies can be extremely valuable for gathering a large amount of information fairly quickly and inexpensively. Some caution must be observed, though, when interpreting the results of a single nonprobability survey in isolation, as one's ability to generalize the findings to the larger population is limited.

An additional limitation to surveys in general is the nature of the conclusions that can be drawn from the results. Analytical surveys attempt to identify how two factors in the same population may be related to one another (i.e., **correlation**). However, just because two factors are correlated with one another does not mean that one causes the other; many otherwise unrelated variables happen to be highly correlated (for some great examples of this, visit https://www.tyler vigen.com/spurious-correlations). Nevertheless, knowing that two or more variables are correlated adds to our knowledge of a phenomenon, knowledge that can be utilized for exploring the phenomenon in different ways.

Experiments

Experiments are the only method used in positive media psychology that can directly examine cause-effect relationships (i.e., **causality**) between factors. Researchers are able to infer causality between two variables when they satisfy three criteria: (1) the two variables are shown to be correlated, (2) the presumed cause precedes the presumed effect in time, and (3) all rival explanations for the presumed effect can be dismissed or rejected. For example, if researchers wanted to explore whether exposure to an educational program caused increased knowledge of a particular concept in children, they would need to demonstrate that (1) exposure to the educational programming and knowledge of the particular concept were correlated (e.g., more viewing was associated with more knowledge, less viewing was associated with less knowledge), (2) that the child did not have knowledge of the concept *before* viewing the program, and (3) that nothing else could reasonably explain how the child acquired the knowledge (e.g., from their parents or peers).

Experiments are able to satisfy these criteria through **control** of various factors. One factor that is controlled is the setting in which the observations take place. **Laboratory (or lab) experiments** are conducted in a setting controlled by the researchers; this allows them to ensure that all observations are made under the same conditions, thereby ruling out (as much as possible) the influence of other factors that can impact the results. Take the previous example for instance, having a child view the educational program by themselves in a room controls the potential influence of other children talking during the program. Other children talking might distract the child, leading to less learning; or, if the talk is about the concept, it might lead to more learning (both of which would be rival explanations). One drawback to lab experiments is artificiality. For the example, children do not normally view television by themselves in a strange place and have questions asked of them afterwards by strangers.

Field experiments, in contrast, are conducted in naturalistic settings, but the researchers do not have as much control over the other possible influences. For the example, researchers might have the child view the educational program in their own home or at their daycare center. This is more natural and less artificial than viewing in the lab. But the researchers might be unable to separate the child from others, which can introduce other possible explanations for whatever outcomes are observed. All experimenters must wrestle with how best to negotiate such trade-offs (e.g., more artificiality but more control, less artificiality but less control).

A second factor that is controlled in an experiment is the presumed cause (also known as the **independent variable**). In the example, exposure to the educational program is the independent variable, which the researchers presume might cause increased knowledge of the concept (i.e., the **dependent variable**). One easy way to control (or manipulate) this particular independent variable would be to show one group of children the educational program and test their knowledge of the concept, while showing a different group of children (which is as similar as possible in every other way) a different (non-educational) program and testing their knowledge of that same concept. In this scenario, the first group is referred to as the **experimental condition** (also sometimes called the **treatment condition**), and the second group is referred to as the **control condition**. Another way to control the independent variable would be to show one group the same episode three days in a row and show another group the episode only once (i.e., manipulate the "dosage"); another way would be to show one group the program and have another group complete a worksheet about the same concept (i.e., manipulate the medium). How the independent variable is controlled ultimately comes down to the precise nature of the question that the researcher is investigating. But some level of control over the presumed cause is a hallmark of an experiment.

A third factor that experimental researchers control is the participants. More specifically, the researchers control which participants receive the treatment (or varying levels of the treatment) and which ones do not. In order to control for rival explanations, this process should be as random as possible. For instance, what if the researcher in our example decided to show the first ten children who showed up to the lab the educational program? Is it possible that *something* might make those children different from the other children? Maybe the children who showed up first were all "only children," which allowed the caregivers to get places more quickly, spend more one-on-one time in general with them, buy them the latest learning technologies, etc. Maybe they were the children who did not get to eat breakfast or maybe they were the children who all lived in the neighborhood closest to the lab. Moreover, what if some of those factors permitted the first ten children who showed up at the lab to learn better (or worse) from the program (i.e., rival explanations)? Because researchers can never know all of the factors that might impact the cause-effect relationship under examination, they randomly assign participants to groups. This way, some of the "only children," some of the no-breakfast bunch, and some of the kids from the same neighborhood show up in each group, thereby distributing the potential influence of those factors across all groups, rendering that influence (statistically) meaningless.

All of this control allows researchers to develop experiments to precisely explore the causal effect of one factor on another. However, this reality also leads to one of the limitations of the method. All that control means that the questions investigated in any one experiment are necessarily quite narrow, with the findings and their generalizability limited in kind. As a result, experiments are ideally replicated with different groups of people in different contexts (often by different researchers) to ensure that the phenomenon observed is reflective of the populations as a whole and not just the initial sample that was examined.

Meta-Analysis

The final method that positive media psychologists rely upon is meta-analysis, which is a "study of studies." Once several studies have been conducted to explore a particular phenomenon—each of which might have slightly different findings—a meta-analysis can be conducted by statistically examining the data across all of those studies to arrive at a combined and synthesized summary estimate of the results. Put another way, meta-analyses help to paint a "big picture" by aggregating the individual "brushstrokes" from similar studies. Because researchers operationally define concepts differently or ask slightly different questions across similar studies, conducting a meta-analysis can be quite challenging (or in some cases impossible). A sufficient number of studies (with a sufficient set of participants) examining the same phenomenon in similar enough ways must be completed before a meta-analysis can be conducted. Given the relative "newness" of the field in general, positive media psychology has had few meta-analyses completed to date (save for some of the more "established" areas, like educational media and children). But the ones most relevant to our discussions are reviewed in the coming chapters.

Positive Media Use

For the regular media user, the formula seems fairly straightforward: Watch a funny YouTube clip and laugh. Play a fast-paced video game and feel excited. View a sad movie and cry. Listen to a podcast and think. Tune in to a science program and learn. Although all of these scenarios might ring true, they ignore the complex set of psychological, biological, situational, content, and context factors and processes at play when we use media. To understand how media use can lead to beneficial outcomes, one must first appreciate the complexity of the media-use phenomenon. To that end, we offer a **model of positive media use** (Figure 1.1), which is inspired by similar models of the entertainment experience (e.g., Raney & Ji, 2017; Vorderer, Klimmt, & Ritterfeld, 2004).

Broadly speaking, media use as a communication phenomenon—regardless of delivery medium, format, genre, or content—involves six basic processes: motivation, selection, reception, response, appraisal, and effects. Although we identify each as a distinct process, in reality the boundaries are quite fluid and the processes interdependent. In the model, we attempt to highlight specific aspects and subprocesses that are important to positive media use. To be clear, in using the term *positive media use* we are not attempting to define some media content or technology as positive and others negative. Nor are we offering a prescription: "If you do this, this, and that, then you will experience these benefits." Rather, we offer the model, to a certain extent, as a summary of the existing literature. That is, based on research findings and theoretical considerations, positive media psychologists have come to identify a host of factors that are salient and active during media experiences associated with beneficial outcomes. The specific factors, characteristics, and subprocesses identified in the model are not intended to be exhaustive but rather representative. Furthermore, they serve as a broad preview of the issues that will be discussed and expanded upon in the following chapters.

Media use is typically conceptualized as a leisure activity. Humans are motivated to seek out such activities for a variety reasons, with most associated with some sort of need satisfaction. Much of that **motivation** is intrinsic; that is, we pursue media experiences because they are satisfying in and of themselves.

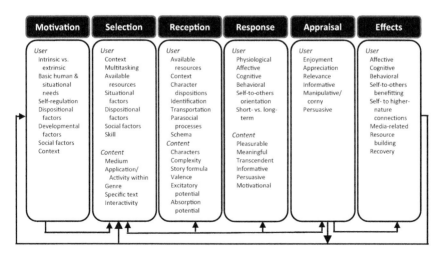

FIGURE 1.1 Model of Positive Media Use

However, extrinsically motivated media use (e.g., parents limiting a child's screen time to particular educational content) can also result in positive outcomes. Additionally, media use may be pursued to meet needs that are foundational and universal to all humans (e.g., belonging, autonomy), that differ across people (e.g., dispositional, personality-trait-dependent, developmental), and that are personal, idiosyncratic, and situational (e.g., boredom, context). Rarely is media use motivated by a single need but rather by a host of factors spanning all of these categories.

Selection involves an interaction between user needs and desires and the technological and content offerings available. The goal of selection is to match the various needs and expected gratification of those needs with a particular content, learned through past experiences (e.g., via classical conditioning, implicit memory). Selection is a multi-layered process. We first select a medium: radio, television, film, book, magazine, social media, video game, etc. Then, we choose the specific channel, activity, or application to use on that medium. Next, we must select the genre or type of content within that channel or app, followed by a selection of the specific title and even the specific elements or portions within that specific title. Further, the process of selection itself may influence the in situ motivation to use media, based on the availability of, or access to, a choice on any one layer. For instance, sitting down to binge watch the next season of a particular show only to find that it is not available on the streaming service could influence one's motivation to select a different program, channel, medium, or activity altogether. The selection of any one media message does not ensure positive benefits; the media-use process is dynamic and situationally dependent such that perfectly predicting positive outcomes is impossible.

In many respects, media use is a demanding activity. As is discussed in several upcoming chapters, the use of media involves the engagement of many cognitive, emotional, physiological, and even behavioral processes. Also, as with selection, **reception** involves an interplay between user and content. Much of the interaction mirrors the social and psychological experiences in the material world, as the user engages both directly and vicariously with characters, settings, plots, situations, challenges, fortunes, and disappointments. No specific constellation of user or content factors guarantees positive outcomes; again, the media-use process is dynamic and situationally dependent such that perfectly predicting positive outcomes is impossible.

The results of media reception include emotional, cognitive, physiological, and behavioral **responses** to the content; these responses are detailed in several upcoming chapters. The specific reactions are generally tied to specific content but emerge as subjective experiences via the interpretive lens of the individual user. Furthermore, most media experiences lead to a variety of responses, some of which seem contradictory on their surface (e.g., "enjoying" a sad film). Some responses are fleeting; others are long-lasting. Also, as the model suggests, responses can impact both the reception and possibly even the selection processes;

for instance, a depiction that strongly resonates with a past life event may lead a user to reflect on that event (impacting reception) and, if too painful, may lead to stopping the program (selection).

One factor that is particularly important to beneficial outcomes is the orientation of the response in relation to the self. We respond to stimuli in our environment that are perceived (either consciously or not) to be *relevant* to us. In this way, all responses to media are necessarily self-oriented to a degree. But some emotions and cognitions (and resulting motivations and behaviors) direct us beyond our self-interest to the interest of others. Consider, for example, the difference between joy and admiration, both of which can be experienced while watching an online video of a music performance. Joy is self-referential; it is the viewer's pleasure. Admiration, which is also experienced by the viewer, is oriented toward the musician. To be clear: We are not arguing that one response is "better" than the other. Both joy and admiration play roles in human fulfillment and flourishing. Rather, different media content can lead to different responses that orient us more or less toward ourselves and others. Understanding this reality helps us better understand the complex ways that media can benefit users.

Ultimately, at the conclusion of (but in reality, throughout) any media-use experience, audiences evaluate or appraise the content and the overall experience, through the lens of the motivation, selection, reception, and response processes. *Enjoyment* is the term we most often use as an **appraisal** of media experiences, but it is surely not the only one that audiences make. At times the appraisal is explicit ("Wow! That was awesome!"); at other times it is not. Similarly, sometimes the appraisal is immediate, whereas other times it requires reflection and contemplation. Also, as the model implies, the results of the appraisal process have important implications on subsequent media use, potentially reinforcing or weakening motivations and selection factors on various levels (e.g., medium, channel, genre, particular title).

Finally, the great variability that is intrinsic to each of these processes assures subjective media-use experiences across technologies and content, resulting in different **effects** on individuals. The sole interest for positive media psychology is outcomes that are beneficial to the media user. However, similar to the response process, those effects may be characterized along a continuum of self- to others-benefitting; they may also be content-specific or more content-agnostic and abstract. For example, viewing the film *Hidden Figures*, in which the lead characters overcome gender and race barriers to contribute immeasurably to NASA and the U.S. space program, can elicit feelings of hope. As a result, hope may lead the viewer to donate money to a local charity that provides scholarships for children in low-income families to attend math and science summer camps (others-oriented, content-specific) or to recommit to finish a difficult home-improvement project started months earlier (self-oriented, content-agnostic). Again, we do not mean to suggest that one effect of hope is better than the next. Both are beneficial for different reasons.

One beneficial outcome of positive media use is positive reinforcement for consuming such content, which can lead to changes in motivation and media selection. It can also lead to changes in cognitive schema, message processing, and interpretations in support of beneficial responses, which should lead to positive appraisals and outcomes. Thus, we contend that positive media use can lead to an upward spiral of emotional, cognitive, and behavioral responses and effects leading to greater mindfulness, purpose, and agency when considering media use as a leisure activity (see similar ideas about positive emotions in general in the broaden-and-build theory; Fredrickson, 2001 and Chapter 3). The following chapters offer evidence for these claims.

Challenges and Opportunities for Positive Media Psychology

As noted previously, the focus of positive media psychology is the beneficial outcomes from media use. But positive media use rarely occurs in a vacuum; along with the use of media for good comes the possibility of less-than-ideal or even detrimental, unintended consequences. Over-reliance on mobile and other digital technologies, even for seemingly positive purposes, can lead to problematic use (see Chapter 13). Turning to fun and light-hearted entertainment for the sake of pleasure (Chapter 4) often brings exposure to stereotypes, glamorized portrayals of violence, unhealthy behaviors, and other content associated with negative effects. Even some forms of meaningful (Chapter 5) and transcendent (Chapter 6) content—like the films *The Blind Side* (2009) and *The Help* (2011)—can trigger feelings of hope and gratitude on one level but can oversimplify and ignore serious, systematic racial problems on another (for a critique of White savior films, see Hughey, 2014). Online videos that many people find touching and moving can leave others feeling manipulated, which can actually reinforce negative outcomes. "Inspiring" stories and videos about disability can leave people with those disabilities feeling exploited (for a discussion of "inspiration porn," see Grue, 2016). Simply liking or re-posting a social media message about a social problem or political cause can make some users feel like they are "doing their part," despite the desperate need for more meaningful action (i.e., slacktivism). These few examples are intended to highlight the complex set of factors that are involved in the selection, reception, and appraisal of (positive) media use. Untangling and understanding this complexity—with the myriad, often contradictory potential outcomes for users—is a chief challenge for positive media psychologists.

At the same time, one of the real opportunities that positive media psychologists have is to communicate and translate the potential benefits of media use to a large audience. A goal of media psychology in general is media literacy (see Chapter 2), or education and training in the evaluation, analysis, interpretation, criticism, and creation of media content and technologies. Many positive psychology scholars (see Chapter 3) have written popular-press books that convey the science of well-being and human flourishing in non-jargony, easily accessible language for the mass audience. **Positive media literacy** is a movement that merges these two approaches. The purpose is to communicate the scientific knowledge emerging from the field of positive media psychology to the larger public so that people can strategically use media in mindful and purposive ways for their own benefit. In this way, positive media psychology aims to bring meaningful social change through media one user at a time.

BOX 1.1 REWIRE HAPPINESS

The goal of positive media literacy is to transfer academic research into practical knowledge for everyone. The same is true for media psychology (e.g., various research centers and initiatives at the University of Southern California's Annenberg School for Communication and Journalism) and positive psychology (e.g., University of California, Berkeley's Greater Good Science Center). For example, knowing that indulging in online videos or gaming at work can benefit employees stress levels and feelings of recovery, especially when they receive little support from their employers (e.g., Reinecke, 2009), can be influential for the development of organizational policies about social media use in the workplace. Another important application area is in the sector of children and youth educational and entertaining programming. Common Sense Media (https://www.commonsensemedia.org) is an independent, research-based nonprofit organization committed to providing age ratings of popular programming and apps, aided by a positive media psychological perspective.

One positive media psychologist leading the positive media literacy charge is co-author Sophie Janicke-Bowles through her website and blog, *Rewire Happiness* (https://www.rewirehappiness.com). One of her early blog posts was an introduction to the field. Here is an excerpt from "Positive Media Psychology – What Is It?":

> I call myself a positive media psychologist because I study media's role in human happiness. I apply theories from positive psychology to the context of media. I think that we cannot understand human happiness in the world we live in now without regarding media and the technologies we interact with on a constant basis. Now, there is no division of positive media psychology, nor is there a journal specifically devoted to this kind of work (even though our work does find a home in journals related to media psychology). However, I think it is important to brand the term Positive Media Psychology and demand such a discipline to foster scholastic progress in this field.
>
> About 20 years ago, some forward-thinking communication scholars arrived at a dead end when explaining entertainment experiences that seemed to be more than merely joyful ... We all understand that media

> makes us laugh and we often seek it out to feel entertained, escape our distressing environment, and manage potential dysphoric mood, or alleviate boredom ... However, media can also create more complex feelings such as laughter and sadness at the same time, elevation, compassion or even lead to self-reflection, reflection about life's purpose, altruistic behavior and connectedness towards humanity ...
>
> Right now, the research on inspiring media effects on prosocial behavior, well-being, character development and the role new communication technologies play in the "good life" is just at the beginning: The beginning of a discipline that I think can have an enormous impact on finding solutions for many of the deep problems our society is facing today, including empathy deficiency, loneliness, aggression, and materialism. What role does media play in personal and humanity's well-being? Positive Media Psychology is here to find out.

Summary

Positive media psychology is an emerging field that applies the scientific method to investigate how media use can lead to well-being and human flourishing. Theories and concepts from media and positive psychology provide an intellectual background to the field, with content analyses, surveys, experiments, and meta-analyses offering empirical support for those theories and concepts within the positive-media-use context. The various processes of selection, reception, response, and appraisal that occur during media use can support beneficial effects. But the way that those processes play out during any one media-use experience is complex and highly dependent upon motivations, situations, personality variables, technologies, and, of course, content.

References

Babbie, E. R. (2021). *The practice of social research* (15th ed.). Boston, MA: Cengage Learning.

Berelson, B. (1952). *Content analysis in communication research*. Glencoe, IL: Free Press.

Dale, K. R., Raney, A. A., Janicke, S. H., Sanders, M. S., & Oliver, M. B. (2017). YouTube for good: A content analysis and examination of elicitors of self-transcendent media. *Journal of Communication*, 67, 897–919. doi:10.1111/jcom.12333.

Fredrickson, B. (2001). The role of positive emotions in positive psychology: The broaden-and-build theory of positive emotions. *American Psychologist*, 56, 218–226. doi:10.1037//0003-066X.56.3.218.

Gregory, S. (2020, April 6). 'It takes my mind off this crazy world.' A quarantined world is here for Rex Chapman's Twitter feed. *TIME*. https://time.com/5815792/rex-chapman-twitter/.

Grue, J. (2016). The problem with inspiration porn: A tentative definition and a provisional critique. *Disability & Society*, 31, 838–849. doi:10.1080/09687599.2016.1205473.

Hughey, M. (2014). *The white savior film: Content, critics, and consumption.* Philadelphia, PA: Temple University Press.

Janicke-Bowles, S. H., Raney, A. A., Oliver, M. B., Dale, K. R., Jones, R. P., & Cox, D. (2019). Exploring the spirit in U.S. audiences: The role of the virtue of transcendence in inspiring media consumption. *Journalism & Mass Communication Quarterly.* Advanced online publication. doi:10.1177/1077699019894927.

McGee, R. (2020, March 26). Rex Chapman is a comeback story and a Twitter feed for our time. *ESPN.* https://www.espn.com/mens-college-basketball/story/_/id/28958919/rex-chapman-comeback-story-twitter-feed-our.

Raney, A. A., Janicke, S. H., Oliver, M. B., Dale, K. R., Jones, R. P., & Cox, D. (2018). Profiling the sources of and audiences for inspiring media content: A national survey. *Mass Communication & Society,* 21, 296–319. doi:10.1080/15205436.2017.1413195.

Raney, A. A., & Ji, Q. (2017). Entertaining each other? Modeling the socially shared television viewing experience. *Human Communication Research,* 43, 424–435. doi:10.1111/hcre.12121.

Reinecke, L. (2009). Games and recovery: The use of video and computer games to recuperate from stress and strain. *Journal of Media Psychology: Theories, Methods, and Applications,* 21, 126–142. doi:10.1027/1864-1105.21.3.126.

Vorderer, P., Klimmt, C., & Ritterfeld, U. (2004). Enjoyment: At the heart of media entertainment. *Communication Theory,* 14, 388–408. doi:10.1111/j.1468-2885.2004.tb00321.x.

Wimmer, R. D., & Dominick, J. R. (2014). *Mass media research: An introduction* (10th ed.). Boston, MA: Wadsworth.

2

KEY THEORIES AND CONCEPTS FROM MEDIA PSYCHOLOGY

Source: Shutterstock 693103318

Since the early 20th century, psychology as an academic discipline and public fascination has experienced tremendous growth, such that much of the way that we go about our day has been informed by the field. Pumping yourself up for a work out. Identifying as an introvert. Taking a deep breath to calm down. Trying to figure out why someone is acting "out of character." Thinking happy thoughts to feel better. Wondering if someone who is being nice to you has an ulterior motive. These few examples demonstrate how the concepts and interests of psychology are truly all around us.

One reason for the growth in the field has been the development of numerous branches and subfields, each with a particular interest and concern. **Media psychology** emerged as one of those branches, with a particular focus on the relationship between media use and human thoughts, feelings, and behaviors. Although the American Psychological Association acknowledged media psychology as an official subfield in the 1980s, in truth, the scientific study of the effect of media content and technology on individuals dates back to the late 1920s, when scholars in Chicago began exploring whether gangster films were contributing to juvenile delinquency. In this chapter, we outline the major concepts and theories related to well-being that have emerged over the past 100 and more years of media psychology research. These concepts and theories lay an important foundation for the issues that are discussed throughout the book.

Media Psychology: A Broad Overview

The subfield of media psychology is exceedingly broad, but the vast majority of the research and writings fall into three primary lines of inquiry, which to some extent have emerged chronologically. First, media psychology involves the study of **media effects**. More specifically, media psychologists investigate the effect of media technology and media content on individuals. Media *technology* effects are related to the use of specific devices, forms, and formats, such as dependency on media during crises, problematic smartphone use, media use instead of or displacing other behaviors, and the immersiveness of virtual reality compared to 2D or 3D displays, to name just a few. Comparatively speaking, media psychologists have generally paid greater attention to media *content* effects, especially to the potential negative impacts of violent, stereotyped, and sexual portrayals on audiences (for a recent overview, we recommend Oliver, Raney, & Bryant, 2020). Furthermore, media effects are often categorized as either cognitive (media's impact on what we think and believe), emotional (media's impact on what and how we feel), or behavioral (media's impact on what we do). We return to this typology below in our discussion of key theories and concepts.

Secondly, media psychology involves the study of **media processes**. This term refers to various psychological mechanisms that are active during and in relation to media use. These include *motivation* to select, *attention* to, *perception* of, *learning* from, and *emotions* elicited by media, to name a few. Many media psychologists take an approach informed by evolutionary theory to studying media processes, focusing on how certain patterns of thinking, feeling, and behaving that are adaptive and functional for human survival are present and active during media use. This approach has led to increasing interest in neuroscientific, psychophysiological, and other biological markers and indices that can be measured during media use, such as eye tracking, changes in arousal and hormone levels, and brain activity. Some disagreement exists among media psychologists as to the precise dividing line between a media process and a media effect, as it appears that some experiences during media use—like emotional reactions—are both processes and effects. Because of this, we will typically use and discuss the terms together: media processes and effects.

Thirdly, media psychology involves the exploration, development, and promotion of **media literacy** awareness and skills. This aspect of the subdiscipline is perhaps most akin to approaches used in clinical psychology as it involves understanding how to combat, overcome, and "treat" potential negative effects of media and, more to the aims of the current text, to value, harness, and strategically utilize media technology and content for the sake of well-being and human flourishing, as well as training others how to do so. The final chapter in this book deals with issues related to (positive) media literacy.

In media psychology, as with all other sciences (see Chapter 1), research is conducted with an agreed-upon set of philosophical assumptions about the objects of inquiry: those objects exist, they can be observed and measured, they are caused by something else that exists which can also be observed and measured, etc. Furthermore, each area of scientific research is guided by additional assumptions about the specific phenomenon in question, based on the current understanding and body of knowledge shared by researchers. Several such assumptions undergird media psychology research. A basic understanding of these assumptions will be useful as we explore specific research findings.

1. **Media audiences are active**. "Vegging out" or "chilling" with media—passively and inattentively relaxing while watching or listening—is an activity that most of us can relate to. We all, from time to time, use media in this way. But when we do, we are actually *making a choice* to do so. You could just as easily "veg out" in your bed or on the couch without media. Media psychologists view the various aspects of media selection—which medium, what genre, what title, at what time, for how long—as evidence of an active audience. Furthermore, though you might not think about it in this way, the processing and comprehending of media narratives actually requires a lot of cognitive resources, as you must access memories to understand plots, settings, storytelling devices, and characters, while simultaneously updating and evaluating the facts and scenes presented in the unfolding story (see Box 2.1). In this way, audiences are actively processing, interpreting, and making meaning from the content (and the medium, the settings, etc.) they are using at any given moment.

BOX 2.1 LIMITED CAPACITY MODEL OF MOTIVATED MEDIATED MESSAGE PROCESSING

The **limited capacity model of motivated mediated message processing** (LC4MP) (Lang, 2000) explains the complex and dynamic interactions that occur in real-time during media use between an audience member's cognitive processing system and mediated content. The cognitive processing of media content requires three subprocesses: encoding (selection of information from the message to process), storage (activation and linking of new information from the message to existing information in memory), and retrieval (recalling of information previously stored). Each of these subprocesses requires cognitive resources. However, as the name of the model implies, our cognitive resources are ultimately limited; that is, humans have a finite and invariable pool of resources available to process our environment. If we dedicate some of those resources to one task (e.g., watching a video), we have fewer to allocate to another task (e.g., studying for an exam).

Humans are able to consciously and intentionally allocate resources to the processing of a media message; in layperson's terms, we do this when we "pay attention" to a message. However, our brains automatically (and without our control) allocate resources as well. Why? Because our phylogenetically old biological motivational systems activate in response to relevant stimuli in our environment that are potential threats and potential opportunities, preparing us to either avoid or approach the stimuli. These systems activate whether we want them to or not; they evolved for our survival. The LC4MP explains that structural and content features of media messages—camera changes, pacing, new voices, emotional words, music, special effects, pop-up advertisements, etc.—automatically trigger orienting responses (OR) in viewers, which demand some of our limited processing resources. The more demanding these features, the fewer resources we have remaining to intentionally allocate toward the message. As a result, the consumption of many media products can be extremely demanding (for an extended discussion in relation to video games, see Bowman, 2018).

Media psychologists generally accept that all of our active use of media is **functional** in some way. That is, we use media because we have psychological, sociological, and biological needs that we are constantly striving to meet: companionship, sense of belonging, fulfillment, purpose, safety, self-esteem, life balance, to name just a few. At times, we are conscious of the media-use–needs connection. You check Instagram to see how your out-of-town sister's birthday went. You check the weather to see if you should wear a jacket. You tune in to Twitch to watch your favorite game stream. But at other times, we are unaware of the specific need—or, more likely, the set of needs—that we seek to have met through media use. We turn on the radio out of habit; we routinely check social media before we go to sleep. Of course, we perform a lot of other nonmedia-related behaviors and strategically arrange the rest of our environments to also meet our needs. Further, despite our best efforts, our needs are often unsuccessfully met. And, even when they are, more needs arise. Nevertheless, media use serves a purpose; it has a function. Audiences actively make choices and use media in line with those purposes, sometimes consciously and at other times not.

2. **Media audiences are complex**. One of the big take-away revelations from the knowledge accumulated by the field of psychology over the century past is that humans are complicated. Though it may seem a bit naïve to us today, early studies of media effects were largely blind to this reality. Scholars generally assumed that the effect of media technology and content on individuals was direct, powerful, and uniform. That is, everyone—except a group of educated elites—was thought to be vulnerable to and imminently threatened by the influence of media. Over time, though, studies revealed that people differ in the ways they select, use, and interpret media. The differences are based on a variety of factors: past experiences, socialization, gender identity, age, personality traits, moral and religious values, political orientation, culture, general interests, and on and on. Chapter 12 deals specifically with these differences in relation to media use for well-being.

   The **differential susceptibility to media effects model** (DSMM) (Valkenburg & Peter, 2013) explains well in general and comprehensive terms how differences across individuals can lead to varying types and levels of media effects. Of particular note, the model explains that not all users will respond to or be affected by all technologies or content in the same way. Instead, *developmental* (differences in cognitive, emotional, and social development), *dispositional* (differences based on stable personal traits and transient situational states), and *contextual* (differences based on interpersonal, societal, and institutional relationships) factors influence the selection and processing of media content, with implications on subsequent media effects. For instance, young children are frightened by images that do not frighten adults (developmental factors). Introverts and extroverts seem to use social media differently (dispositional factors). Films containing nudity are more restricted in the United States than they are in other countries (contextual factors). These are just a few examples, but because of these variations, people are not uniformly affected by media but rather differentially so. Consequently, audiences—and the ways individual audience members process and are affected by media—are seen as complex phenomena.

3. **Media content is varied**. Not only are audiences diverse, but so is content. TV and books are not the same, neither are video games and in-theater films. However, such differences are not nearly as stark as they used to be. Today you can watch TV, read a book, play a video game, and screen a film all on a smartphone. Despite that fact, each of these media forms can be and generally are categorized as **mass communication**. The basic model of mass communication is a single source communicating a message to many receivers (or one-to-many). Traditionally, mass communication has been examined differently than other forms of communication—such as interpersonal or small-group forms—because the messages are necessarily more generalized and less personalized, in order to appeal to as large and as heterogenous an audience as possible. Also, direct and immediate feedback

from the audience to the source, such that messages are altered as a result, is quite difficult. The term "mainstream media" originally reflected the reality that mass communication aims to appeal to the greatest number of people by offending the least. Nevertheless, across mass communication, content is still incredibly varied, in terms of genres, topics, themes, age-appropriateness, complexity, suspense, valence, length, etc. Further, with increased delivery capabilities, the sources of mass-produced content—TV networks, streaming services, websites, film and gaming studios—have never been more numerous. The sheer amount of mass communication content available is incredible.

With the widespread adoption of internet-supported devices such as smartphones and tablets, a blurring of the lines between mass and other forms of communication has occurred. Without a doubt, smart devices support one-to-many mass communication messages, such as TV shows, books, and films. But they also make possible new forms of communication, in particular social media, which support content that is both mass and interpersonal in nature. In fact, social media platforms are often categorized as **masspersonal communication**. Take Twitter for example. A local music venue uses their official Twitter account to send out information about upcoming shows (one-to-many). You can send a reply and ask a specific question about parking at one of the events (one-to-one). Other users can see your reply (one-to-many), and several may send you a note giving their suggestions for parking (many-to-one), which may lead to several people joining the conversation to agree or disagree with their suggestions (many-to-many). Thus, one of the important innovations introduced by masspersonal forms of media is the capacity for audience members— previously, just the *receivers* of mass communication messages—to now also be content creators and mass communicators themselves. As a result, the volume, diversity, and reach of media content has never been greater; consequently, the need for examinations of media processes and effects has never been more important.

4. **Our brains process media content as real**. From an evolutionary perspective, you are reading this right now because your ancestors some 200,000 years ago fled when they were confronted by a menacing animal or enemy; they found, gathered, and consumed food for energy and survival. When they saw, heard, smelled, or felt something, it was *real*, and they reacted accordingly. The ones who did so survived; the ones who did not or did not react quickly enough perished. The human brain has evolved considerably since that time, but the parts of our ancestors' brains that guided them in such decisions long ago are the ones that still guide those decisions in us today. This fact matters for the current discussion because human brains treat media content—scenes, settings, characters, portrayed events, emotions—as real, just as our ancestors treated everything in their

surroundings. That is, your brain (and the rest of your body) reacts emotionally and cognitively to media content as if it were actual and present; it does not experientially differentiate between mediated and nonmediated events, situations, and people. Thus, we cry after watching certain YouTube videos, and we jump and get scared during horror movies. Communication scholars Byron Reeves and Clifford Nass (1996) identified this phenomenon as the **media equation**, in that humans equate their experiences with media technologies and content with reality. This assumption is important to understanding many of the theories that explain media processes and effects.

Types of Media Processes and Effects

As noted earlier, the field of media psychology is organized around three broad categories of processes and effects: cognitions, emotions, and behaviors. Admittedly, these three psychological domains are interdependent: our thoughts influence our behaviors, our emotions influence our thoughts, etc. Therefore, to speak of these categories as mutually exclusive would be impossible and improper. Nevertheless, the categories reflect the nature of *primary* outcomes of interest, which point to underlying psychological mechanisms presumably responsible for those outcomes. Following chapters will introduce numerous theories and concepts that describe, explain, and predict specific aspects of those outcomes and underlying mechanisms, especially as they are observed in different contexts and with various content. But some concepts and theories are foundational to the field. These are introduced now.

Cognitive Processes and Effects

In order to discuss the ways that media content can affect how and what we think, we must first introduce some basic information about thoughts and memory. First, humans have several types of memory, including short- and long-term memory. Our concern is the latter. Furthermore, humans have several types of long-term memory, which entail memories of the things that have happened to you (episodic memory), how to do things (procedural memory), and the facts, concepts, and ideas that you know about the world and social living (semantic memory). Our primary interest will be semantic memory.

Second, although neuroscientists have discovered a tremendous amount about the brain over the past few decades, we still cannot produce a roadmap of memories; unfortunately, there are no billboards in the brain that point out where knowledge about the Grand Canyon or the Industrial Revolution resides. Instead, several theoretical models of memory have been proposed. Media and communication scientists have generally adopted and relied upon **network models of memory** when discussing media's effect on cognitions (Anderson, 1983; Wyer, 2004).

All network models of memory—and there are a few—share two basic assumptions. First, all memory is organized, with concepts represented in memory as **nodes**. What you know about animals is stored in your "animal node," what you know about beaches is in your "beach node," and what you know about Kenya is in your "Kenya node." Nodes remain in a resting state unless something in the environment triggers the related concept. Furthermore, nodes have activation thresholds. Some nodes, such as those we access often in our daily lives, have a lower threshold than others and are more easily triggered. If the environmental trigger is sufficient for the node to reach its threshold, then the node is activated; if not, then it remains at rest. Activated nodes do not (necessarily) mean that you are consciously thinking about a concept, but it means that your brain is *ready* for you to think about it. Once activated, a node will return to its resting state, assuming no other environmental input (or related cognitive activity on your own part).

Consider this example: You are walking through a park. As you do so, you encounter countess environmental stimuli: grass, trees, other people, dogs, birds, play equipment, a fountain. You have a node representing all of these concepts in your semantic memory. As you encounter them on your walk, you are most likely not consciously contemplating each one. That would be impossible (and cognitively taxing). But your brain is set up in a way to prepare you to think about them if you need to, for example if a dog breaks free from its owner and runs toward you. Once you leave the park, those concepts will return to resting, assuming you do not encounter (or intentionally think about) them again.

As noted above, resting thresholds differ across nodes. Moreover, a concept's threshold can change over time, based on how frequently you encounter the concept, how recently you encountered the concept, and how much cognitive effort you spend processing the concept (among others). The ease by which a concept is activated is referred to as **accessibility**. Think back to something you studied in middle school, like the names of all the rivers in your home region or the stages of mitosis. You studied hard and aced the exam, back in the day. Your studying made those concepts more readily accessible in memory, so that when you saw the words on the exam (which activated the corresponding node) you were able to recall the information quickly. But now you remember little, if any, of that information. Activation thresholds weaken across time, such that concepts become less accessible. But concepts that we access all the time, that are triggered by our environment repeatedly, that we think about consistently can become **chronically accessible**.

The second major assumption that network models of memory share is that all memory is interconnected via **associative pathways**. Your animal node is connected to your dog node, your cat node, your elephant node, etc. Your animal node may also be connected to your beach node (because of seagulls, dolphins, and crabs). But "animal" as a concept is more related to "dogs" than "beaches" (at least for most people). That is, the *strength* of the associative pathways between concepts varies. Pathways between nodes become stronger for the same reasons that nodes become more accessible: frequency, recency, and effort of processing. For instance, the more often we encounter two concepts related in our environment—peanut butter and jelly, doctor and nurse, yellow bus and school—the stronger the associative pathways become between those nodes. This is important because the energy that activates a node also spreads to other related nodes. Stronger pathways allow for more energy to spread. As a result, when one concept is activated in your environment (doctor), then highly related ones (nurse, hospital) can also be activated, which means that you are *more ready* to think about or act on those related concepts simply because you encountered the first (doctor). The process of spreading activation from one concept to highly related ones is called **priming**. The result of priming is that semantically related concepts can be activated thereby increasing the likelihood of related thoughts for a short period of time (i.e., until the nodes return to resting).

Media content is one environmental stimulus we encounter nearly every day. Because our brains process media as real, what we encounter therein influences our semantic memory in a number of ways. First, we encounter information about concepts in media content, which, if sufficiently encoded to be stored in long-term memory, gets added to the existing related node. That is, media content helps us develop the nodes in our semantic memory, adding to the information about a concept that we have learned from other sources. For some concepts, media content may be the *only* source of information; for instance, the only thing you know about the Andes Mountains may have come from watching a travel show or nature documentary.

One important media theory describes the long-term impact of encountering information about concepts in media: **cultivation theory** (Gerbner, 1969; Gerbner & Gross, 1976). The theory was originally developed in the late 1960s and 1970s to explain the potential impact of television viewing on perceptions of social reality. Over time, many researchers have presumed that the same processes and effects can be experienced with other forms of media, though the vast majority of the work still focuses on television. In short, cultivation theory explains how people learn about the world through media. The information we acquire then impacts how we subsequently perceive the world, with the effects being stronger among persons who spend more time with media (i.e., "heavy users").

On its surface and based on the earlier discussion, this should seem perfectly logical and nonproblematic. All of our environment—including what we find in media—provides information about concepts, which our brain processes and stores in related nodes. Persons who use media a lot acquire more such information through media than persons who use it less, in the same way that students who regularly attend class and faithfully read the assigned textbook acquire more of the course content than those who attend and read less. This is simply the way our brains work. Potential problems arise, though, based on the way that media content often portrays reality. Studies consistently reveal that, for instance, the proportion of Latinx persons shown on television is far lower than the actual proportion of Latinx persons in the U.S. Persons of color are disproportionately shown in news as the "face of poverty," as compared to real-world poverty levels. The murder rate on primetime TV is astronomically higher than anywhere on the planet. The average body size of women in fashion magazine advertisements is much smaller than the average body size of women in the real world. Because the media world is not equivalent to the real world in countless ways, it follows that the more time people spend acquiring information about the world via media, the more their perceptions of the real world will be skewed toward the version of the world portrayed in media. For example, one finding from the cultivation literature is that because of the ubiquity of crime and violence on television, heavy viewers are more likely than lighter viewers to perceive the real world to be a mean and scary place, a place where others cannot be trusted, a place where they are more likely themselves to be a victim of a crime. Cultivation researchers called this effect the **mean–world syndrome**. More to our purposes, logic would dictate that repeated consumption of media that presents a different view of the world—one in which people are kind, helpful, tolerant, decent, and connected—could likewise result in a more pleasant view of the planet, leading to a **kind–world syndrome** (see Oliver, Krakowiak, & Tsay, 2012).

Second, media content can influence the accessibility of a concept. The more frequently and recently we encounter a concept in media, the more easily it is activated in our memories. This reality is at the heart of the **agenda–setting effect** of news (McCombs & Shaw, 1972; see also Chapter 9), because the more news outlets cover certain topics, the more readily audiences think about those topics (i.e., increased accessibility) and consequently the more audiences think those topics are the most important ones facing the world today.

Third, media content presents concepts in relation to one another. Television programs set in hospitals always have doctors and nurses. Sitcoms routinely show children boarding yellow buses to go to school. As a result, media content can strengthen the associative pathways between concepts. Typically, this effect is not problematic. But this neurological process also explains how media content creates and perpetuates **stereotypes** (for a recent summary, see Dixon, 2020). If news programs routinely (and disproportionately) report on crimes allegedly committed by African American males, then the "crime" and "African American male" concepts become necessarily more strongly related in an audience member's brain (e.g., Dixon & Linz, 2000). If films routinely show persons of the Islamic faith as terrorists, those two concepts also become more strongly associated (e.g., Ahmed & Matthes, 2017). However, if YouTube videos show African American males and Muslims living in harmony with others, making music, sharing meals, acting kindly, then the associations between *those* concepts can likewise be strengthened.

Fourth, media content can trigger concepts leading to spreading activation, which means that semantically related concepts are now more accessible as well, which increases the likelihood of related thoughts. Earlier, we described this phenomenon as priming; when media content serves as the trigger, the phenomenon is called **media priming**. A great deal of research has examined how media content can prime violent and political concepts as well as various stereotypes, influencing thoughts and attitudes for a short period of time thereafter (see Ewoldsen & Rhodes, 2020). The role of media priming positive thoughts and attitudes is an area needing more attention.

Emotional Processes and Effects

Despite the centrality of emotions in our daily lives and overall well-being, the relationship between media use and emotions has not received nearly the scholarly attention historically as cognitions. Thankfully, though, over the past few decades this has started to change (for a great overview, see Nabi, 2020). In many ways, greater attention to emotional processes and effects of media has led to the growth of positive media psychology as a field, as the later chapters will reflect.

Psychologists cannot seem to agree on one "perfect" definition of an emotion. Nevertheless, most agree that an emotion is an internal state experienced as a reaction to and evaluation of some relevant stimulus in the environment. Emotions vary in valence (positive to negative) and intensity. Emotions arise and dissipate quickly and can generally be tied to a specific cause. Emotions differ from moods. Moods also vary in valence and intensity, but they are thought to be less intense than emotions, more enduring and stable over time, more cognitively oriented, and less tied to a specific cause. Also, the term *affect* is routinely used by psychologists to refer to the general experience of feeling; thus, emotions and moods are both considered affective states.

One leading and widely accepted approach to emotions is the **component process model** (Scherer, 1984), which contends that all emotions consist of five components that are associated with basic biological and psychological human subsystems. First is a *cognitive* component; all emotions result from an appraisal or evaluation of an environmental stimulus as being relevant to our major concerns. Of course, this should not imply that emotions begin with lengthy contemplation; stimulus relevance is appraised quickly through a complex series of automatic and implicit evaluation processes.

Second, emotions all involve a *physiological* component, most often referred to as **arousal** of the central nervous system, autonomic nervous system (which includes the sympathetic and parasympathetic systems), and/or neuro-endocrine systems. Arousal is a nonspecific, physiological response to a stimulus. As a result, emotions are not thought to have unique arousal "signatures." For instance, your heart rate can increase if you are experiencing love, anxiety, or fear; that is, you do not have a special "love heart rate." Cognitive appraisals guide you to interpret the meaning of the physiological arousal—that is, what emotion you are feeling—based on the nature and context of the stimulus. Also, because our bodies are constantly trying to maintain or return to homeostasis for the sake of survival, the experience of arousal—and thus, an emotion—is fleeting. Third, all emotions have a *subjective feeling* component, which is the state of feeling that most of us associate with having an emotional experience. Fourth, all emotions have a *motor expression* component, which includes facial (e.g., smile, raised eyebrows, quivering lip) and vocal (e.g., "Oh no!," "Wow!") expressions. These are thought to have evolved as a way for emotions to be communicated to others.

Finally, all emotions involve a *motivational* component. This component involves the preparation of the body for appropriate action. Two schools of thought among emotion researchers have emerged that differ in how the motivational component is conceptualized (among other ways). Dimensional emotion psychologists see all emotions as motivational states that vary by arousal and valence and that are associated with activation of the broadly conceived appetitive (approach) or aversive (avoid) motivational systems. In contrast, discrete emotional psychologists argue that different emotions involve *particular* motivational action tendencies. By and large, the discussions of emotions in the following chapters will reflect the discrete emotion perspective.

In media psychology, affective states are thought to play a variety of roles. For one, emotions and moods can drive media selection. Mood management theory (Zillmann, 1988; for more, see Chapter 4) and the Selective Exposure Self- and Affect-Management model (SESAM; Knobloch-Westerwick, 2015) are two important examples of this work. Secondly, emotions are studied as a response to media, including joy (enjoyment), suspense and anxiety, fear, sadness, hope, awe, to name a few. Many of these emotional responses to media are discussed in subsequent chapters. Third, emotions can serve to influence other effects and outcomes of media, such as the role of fear in the persuasiveness of certain advertisements and health campaigns or the role of positive emotions in the motivation to share a meaningful online video.

Behavioral Processes and Effects

An enduring assumption held by many politicians, religious leaders, educators, and members of the public is that media content causes people to act in certain ways. Mass shootings, offensive language, drug and alcohol use among minors, and unprotected sexual activity are all routinely blamed on TV, films, video games, books, and social media. The scientific record supports the claim that media technology and content *can* affect behavior, though the process is much more complicated than most people suspect. Without a doubt, at times, we act directly on messages we encounter in media: we take an umbrella to work based on the weather report; we show up at the polls before the announced 7:00 p.m. closing time; we preheat the oven to 350° to try the recipe. Furthermore, we can learn a great many *new* behaviors—how to patch a bicycle tube, change our hairstyle, create charts in Microsoft Excel, salsa dance—from watching TV shows and YouTube videos. All of these examples demonstrate that media content *can* affect our behavior. But, of course, many other factors affect it as well, like past experiences, intentions, goals, mood, upbringing, values, personality traits, context, hormone levels, etc. And given our free will and personal agency, we can change our behaviors, even in similar situations, from minute to minute, day to day. As a result, isolating a single cause (for instance, playing *Grand Theft Auto*) for most behaviors (like getting into a fight at a club) is incredibly difficult and typically inaccurate.

One of the foundational theories in media psychology—or rather, in psychology as a whole—that seeks to explain many of these processes is **social cognitive theory** (SCT; Bandura, 1986). On a simple level, SCT explains how humans learn about behaviors—how to perform them, in which situations they are acceptable, what consequences might result—by observing others. The theory contends that people have agency with regard to their actions and their environments; that is, behaviors reflect active choices made based on goals, motivations, presumed consequences, ruminations on past behaviors, and communal interests. Much of the input for those choices has been learned by observing other people acting. Further, because human brains do not readily differentiate between mediated and nonmediated situations, this learning can be accomplished by observing others in our daily lives and in the world of media. The famous Bobo doll studies conducted by psychologist Albert Bandura and his colleagues in the 1960s provided initial evidence of this fact (see Box 2.2).

BOX 2.2 ALBERT BANDURA AND THE BOBO DOLL EXPERIMENTS

In the 1960s, psychologist Albert Bandura at Stanford University conducted a set of studies that serve as the basis for our understanding of how behaviors observed in media may be modeled by audience members. The so-called Bobo doll experiments involved researchers playing and interacting with an inflatable doll weighted at the bottom so that it automatically returned to an upright position when knocked over. Across the set of studies, preschool children watched same- and opposite-sex adults act in a physically and verbally abusive manner toward the doll or ignore the doll altogether; a control group witnessed no adult model. In some studies, the adult played with the Bobo doll in the same room as the children; in other studies, the children watched the adult play with the doll on videotape. In each study, the children were subsequently given an opportunity to also play with the Bobo doll, as well as with other toys, while researchers observed them.

When children were given an opportunity to play with the doll, those who chose to do so played somewhat roughly, often pushing or punching it. This was the case for all children, whether they had observed an adult play with the doll that way or not, though the ones viewing the aggressive models did so significantly more often. This is unsurprising because, given the toy itself, pushing and punching seems like a natural way to play with it. However, the adult models had also displayed behaviors that were not so natural: they hit the Bobo doll with a mallet; they pushed it over, held it down, and struck it repeatedly; they made specific aggressive remarks, like "Pow!" when hitting the doll. These novel behaviors were the ones of real interest to the researchers. Would the children model them? The answer was a resounding "Yes." A vast majority of the children who observed the novel behaviors modeled them. Furthermore, they picked up on the aggressive language as well, repeating it while playing with the dolls. Moreover, the children displayed the process of abstract modeling as well, with those viewing the aggressive models being significantly more likely to play with a toy gun that was also present in the room, many of whom used the gun to threaten and hit the Bobo doll. The adult models never played with the gun. It was through these and similar studies that Bandura and other scholars began developing our current understanding of the process of observational learning, modeling, abstract modeling, and ultimately our ability to learn new behaviors through media.

One primary outcome of observing others can be the development of new behaviors, a process SCT refers to as **modeling**. In order for a behavior to be modeled, four processes must be completed by the person observing the behavior. Cooking, home decorating, and other DIY content assume that modeling can and does occur in media audiences; because of this, a related example might be helpful to understand how modeling can occur.

You've just returned from a new restaurant where you had some great guacamole. You decide it is time to learn to make it yourself. So, you go to the Tasty channel on YouTube and search for a video recipe. You find one liked by thousands of people and start watching. In order for you to model the behavior you are about to observe (i.e., guacamole making), you must first pay attention to the behavior (*attentional process*). This seems obvious. But it is also a process that is quite complex, dependent upon the salience, complexity, and perceived functional value of the behavior (among others), as well as your cognitive capacity, existing knowledge, and interest (among others). Given that you searched for the video, you are likely prepared to pay attention, but if your friend texts you that you left your jacket at the restaurant, then you might be distracted and your ability to ultimately model the behavior is compromised.

Thankfully you have your jacket and you are able to attend to the video. The second process that must be accomplished for you to ultimately model the behavior is that you must remember the behavior (*retentional process*). Again, this seems obvious, but you cannot model a behavior that you do not remember.

The retentional process is also more complex that it initially appears. It involves symbolically encoding and decoding the words and actions and building new, or adding to existing, knowledge structures. Thirdly, to learn to make guacamole from watching the video you must be capable of reproducing the behaviors you witnessed (*production process*), which involves not only your physical skill set and capabilities but also cognitive ones related to trial enactments and self-correction.

You make it through the video, having paid strict attention, remembering how to make the recipe, and feeling pretty confident that you can replicate the series of actions that you observed. The final step that must be completed to model the behavior is that you must be sufficiently motivated to actually do so (*motivational process*). Reflecting the agentic perspective mentioned above, you will not model the making of guacamole unless you choose to do so. As you might expect by this point, the motivational process involves a variety of factors as well. One key element of motivation is the perceived rewards (or punishments) you expect to receive from performing the behavior (*outcome expectations*). Several forms of incentives can influence those perceptions: the people in the video eating the recipe looked super happy (vicarious incentives), you are hungry and learning to cook for yourself is really important to you (self-incentives), and you know your roommate also loves guacamole (external incentives). Another factor influencing the motivational process is *self-efficacy*, or the extent to which you are confident that you can perform the behavior. Persons with high levels of self-efficacy toward a particular behavior are much more likely to actually try to perform it; they are also more likely to try again if the outcome is not completely beneficial or rewarding.

With the four processes of modeling accomplished, you head to the grocery store to buy the supplies. According to SCT, the evidence that you observationally learned how to make guacamole is that you actually make it; that is, you model the behavior. The various forms of reward–punishment feedback you receive—Did it taste good? Was it difficult to make? Was the avocado too expensive? Did your roommate take one bite and leave the rest? etc.—all influence your motivation to repeat the behavior or not in the future.

SCT also explains that observing others can lead to more than direct modeling or mimicry of a behavior. We also learn information about the context, motivation, rules, and other factors that seem to influence, govern, lead to, and result from behavior that we observe. Consequently, innovative thoughts about behaviors can be generated, potentially leading to adaptations to the observed behaviors or even the introduction of novel behaviors that are similarly motivated or more contextually appropriate. This process is known as **abstract modeling**. For instance, the guacamole recipe may include chopped red onion, which you dislike; so, you leave it out. Or your roommate notices the joy that cooking seems to bring to you, and she decides to try a new dish as well.

Furthermore, the higher-order learning of contextual, motivational, and outcome information continues throughout our lives, for all behaviors, even the ones we regularly perform. That new information can influence how, when, where, and why we act in certain ways. For example, many people who grew up in a world before smartphones—your parents, perhaps—learned to write personal letters in a formal way. When many of them started texting, they followed the same rules: full sentences, proper punctuation, capitalized letters, etc. But as they received more texts—that is, they observed others texting—they learned that different rules apply. As a result, they changed their own texting behavior. Similarly, for some people, telling certain types of sexual jokes in the workplace used to be commonplace, but the #MeToo movement has led many of those people to change that behavior as well. The broader point is that SCT explains how humans are *constantly* learning information about behaviors from their environment, both directly and vicariously, and how that information *continues* to shape how we act throughout our lives. Furthermore, because our brains process observations in media the same way they do in the real world, information impacting our behaviors come from both sources.

Given the breadth of description and explanation about observational learning, social cognitive theory is fundamental to our understanding of how media content can positively impact our behaviors. However, SCT is not the only theory of behavioral effects of media. Two others that are particularly important when it comes to health-related content are worthy of mention. The **health belief model** (Janz & Becker, 1984; Rosenstock, 1974) identifies various factors that influence the likelihood that someone will perform a health-related behavior, including the perceived threat (involving severity and susceptibility) of the ill-health condition, perceived benefits of and barriers to performing the behavior, and one's perceived self-efficacy. Media messages that demonstrate the benefits of performing the behavior, communicate ways to overcome any barriers preventing the behavior, and emphasize the threat of not performing the behavior are thought to encourage healthy actions. Similarly, messages that bolster the audience member's self-efficacy can also be beneficial. Such messages can be explicitly persuasive in nature, such as a public service announcement (PSA) or advertisement, or less obviously so, like storylines in a film or videogame. We discuss these issues in Chapter 10.

A third relevant behavioral effects theory is really a set of theories referred to as the **reasoned action approach** (RAA), which includes the theory of reasoned action (Ajzen & Fishbein, 1980), the theory of planned behavior (Ajzen, 2011), and the integrated behavioral model (Head & Noar, 2013). The RAA contends that the best predictor of a behavior is one's intention to perform that behavior. Behavioral intentions are influenced by three primary factors: attitudes about the behavior, perceived social norms about the behavior, and perceived behavioral control over the behavior (self-efficacy). Furthermore, each of those factors is also impacted by related beliefs. Media messages have been shown to potentially influence all three predictors of behavioral intentions, as well as the beliefs that undergird them.

Summary

The history of media psychology research is surprisingly long. For nearly a century, scholars have been investigating how audiences select, process, react to, and critically consume media content. Moreover, a tremendous amount of research has been conducted into the ways that media technologies and content can affect an individual's thoughts, attitudes, beliefs, emotions, moods, and behaviors. This research, especially over the past few decades, has formed a picture of how audiences and media interact. In the hands of scholars today, this picture, along with a basic understanding of human psychology, constitutes the subfield that is known as media psychology.

References

Ahmed, S., & Matthes, J. (2017). Media representation of Muslims and Islam from 2000 to 2015: A meta-analysis. *International Communication Gazette*, 79, 219–244. doi:10.1177/1748048516656305.

Ajzen, I. (2011). The theory of planned behaviour: Reactions and reflections. *Psychology & Health*, 26, 1113–1127. doi:10.1080/08870446.2011.613995.

Ajzen, I., & Fishbein, M. (1980). *Understanding attitudes and predicting social behavior.* Englewood Cliffs, NJ: Prentice-Hall.

Anderson, J. (1983). *The architecture of cognition.* Cambridge, MA: Harvard University Press.

Bandura, A. (1986). *Social foundations of thought and action: A social cognitive theory.* Englewood Cliffs, NJ: Prentice-Hall. Bowman, N. D. (2018). *Video games: A medium that demands our attention.* New York, NY: Routledge.

Dixon, T. L. (2020). Media stereotypes: Content, effects, and theory. In M. B. Oliver, A. A. Raney, & J. Bryant (Eds.), *Media effects: Advances in research and theory* (4th ed., pp. 243–257). New York, NY: Routledge.

Dixon, T. L., & Linz, D. (2000). Race and the misrepresentation of victimization on local television news. *Communication Research*, 27, 547–573. doi:10.1177/009365000027005001.

Ewoldsen, D., & Rhodes, N. (2020). Media priming and accessibility. In M. B. Oliver, A. A. Raney, & J. Bryant (Eds.), *Media effects: Advances in research and theory* (4th ed., pp. 83–99). New York, NY: Routledge.

Gerbner, G. (1969). Toward "cultural indicators": The analysis of mass mediated public message systems. *A V Communication Review*, 17, 137–148. doi:10.1007/BF02769102.

Gerbner, G., & Gross, L. (1976). Living with television: The violence profile. *Journal of Communication*, 26, 172–199. doi:10.1111/j.1460-2466.1976.tb01397.x.

Head, K. J., & Noar, S. M. (2013). Facilitating progress in health behaviour theory development and modification: The reasoned action approach as a case study. *Health Psychology Review*, 8, 34–52. doi:10.1080/17437199.2013.778165.

Janz, N. K., & Becker, M. H. (1984). The Health Belief Model: A decade later. *Health Education Quarterly*, 11, 1–47. doi:10.1177/109019818401100101.

Knobloch-Westerwick, S. (2015). *Choice and preference in media use: Advances in selective exposure theory and research.* New York, NY: Routledge.

Lang, A. (2000). The limited capacity model of mediated message processing. *Journal of Communication*, 50, 46–70. doi:10.1111/j.1460-2466.2000.tb02833.x.

McCombs, M. E., & Shaw, D. L. (1972). The agenda-setting function of mass media. *Public Opinion Quarterly*, 36, 176–187. doi:10.1086/267990.

Nabi, R. (2020). Media and emotions. In M B. Oliver, A. A. Raney, & J. Bryant (Eds.), *Media effects: Advances in research and theory* (4th ed., pp. 163–178). New York, NY: Routledge.

Oliver, M. B., Krakowiak, K. M., & Tsay, M. (2012, May). *Elevating entertainment and the 'kind-world' syndrome.* Presented at the annual meeting of the International Communication Association, Phoenix, AZ.

Oliver, M. B., Raney, A. A., & Bryant, J. (2020). *Media effects: Advances in research and theory* (4th ed.). New York, NY: Routledge.

Reeves, B., & Nass, C. I. (1996). *The media equation: How people treat computers, television, and new media like real people and places.* New York, NY: Cambridge University Press.

Rosenstock, I. M. (1974). Historical origins of the Health Belief Model. *Health Education and Behavior, 2,* 328–335. doi:10.1177/109019817400200403.

Scherer, K. R. (1984). On the nature and function of emotion: A component process approach. In K. R. Scherer & P. Eckman, *Approaches to emotion* (pp. 293–317). Hillsdale, NJ: Lawrence Erlbaum Associates.

Valkenburg, P. M., & Peter, J. (2013). The differential susceptibility to media effects model. *Journal of Communication, 63,* 221–243. doi:10.1111/jcom.12024.

Wyer, R. S. (2004). *Social comprehension and judgment: The role of situation models, narratives, and implicit theories.* Mahwah, NJ: Lawrence Erlbaum Associates.

Zillmann, D. (1988). Mood management through communication choices. *American Behavioral Scientist, 31,* 327–340. doi:10.1177/000276488031003005.

Additional Readings

Appiah, O. (2008). Stereotyping and the media. In W. Donsbach (Ed.), *The international encyclopedia of communication.* Hoboken, NJ: John Wiley & Sons.

Bandura, A., Ross, D., & Ross, S. A. (1961). Transmission of aggression through imitation of aggressive models. *The Journal of Abnormal and Social Psychology, 63,* 575–583. doi:10.1037/h0045925.

Bandura, A., Ross, D., & Ross, S. A. (1963). Vicarious reinforcement and imitative learning. *The Journal of Abnormal and Social Psychology, 67,* 601–607. doi:10.1037/h0045550.

Bargh, J. A., Bond, R. N., Lombardi, W. J., & Tota, M. E. (1986). The additive nature of chronic and temporary sources of construct accessibility. *Journal of Personality and Social Psychology, 50,* 869–878. doi:10.1037/0022-3514.50.5.869.

Beedie, C., Terry, P., & Lane, A. (2005). Distinctions between emotion and mood. *Cognition and Emotion, 19,* 847–878. doi:10.1080/02699930541000057.

Lang, A. (1990). Involuntary attention and physiological arousal evoked by structural features and emotional content in TV commercials. *Communication Research, 17,* 275–299. doi:10.1177/009365090017003001.

Ramasubramanian, S., & Banjo, O. O. (2020). Critical media effects framework: Bridging critical cultural communication and media effects through power, intersectionality, context, and agency. *Journal of Communication, 70,* 379–400. doi:10.1093/joc/jqaa014.

Sanders, M. S., & Ramasubramanian, S. (2012). An examination of African Americans' stereotyped perceptions of fictional media characters. *Howard Journal of Communications, 23,* 17–39. doi:10.1080/10646175.2012.641869.

3

KEY THEORIES AND CONCEPTS FROM POSITIVE PSYCHOLOGY

Source: Shutterstock 425547400

Everybody wants to be happy. The 5-year-old crying for an ice-cream, the 20-year-old sharing a meal or YouTube clip with their friends, the 40-year-old who succeeds in their career or builds sand castles with their kids at the beach, as well as the 70-year-old who volunteers at an animal shelter or chats with the neighbor on their morning walks. Happiness is a universal thriving force of life. Yet, it is defined and achieved in many different ways. The science of positive psychology provides a framework to investigate what happiness is and how to achieve it in a systematic way.

What Is Positive Psychology?

For the better part of the 20th century, the field of psychology focused on the negative aspects of the human experience: mental illness, violence, overcoming adversities, racism, self-esteem management, and the like. In 2000, psychologists Martin Seligman and Mihaly Csikszentmihalyi published an article arguing for the study of what makes life worth living. **Positive psychology** is an umbrella term for theories and research that focus on the positive aspects of life, that strive to reveal what makes societies and individuals thrive. More specifically, it deals with positive subjective experiences (i.e., feelings of well-being), positive traits (i.e., character strengths), and positive institutions that enable experiences and traits (e.g., family, workplaces), which ultimately enable optimal functioning or flourishing. In doing so, it seeks to understand what "makes people happy."

Happiness, as it is called by the general public, is generally referred to as **well-being** in the scientific community. The term well-being captures various aspects of happiness that will be outlined in this chapter. Defining well-being in a straightforward fashion has been shown to be difficult, as the concept is multifaceted and understood from various philosophical and cultural angles. During the period between the 8th and the 3rd centuries BCE, at least 12 different conceptions of happiness were already being debated around philosophy roundtables. Today, at least seven times as many conceptualizations of happiness and well-being exist. The most prominent ones are discussed in this chapter, particularly as they relate to the study of media psychology.

Types of Well-Being

The different conceptualizations of well-being can broadly be categorized into two philosophically distinct approaches: hedonic and eudaimonic (Ryan & Deci, 2001; see also Waterman, 1993). The hedonic–eudaimonic distinction has been made for centuries, first popularized by Aristotle in *Nicomachean Ethics* in the 4th century BCE. A contemporary philosopher named Aristippus had proposed that the highest good in life was to seek pleasure and avoid displeasure, a perspective known as *hedonia*. In contrast, Aristotle proposed in his now-famous essay that happiness goes beyond seeking pleasure; it also comes from a person acting virtuously and nobly (*eudaimonia*). Ever since, disagreements about the "true" nature of well-being have persisted. Some scholars have argued for only one conception, either hedonic or eudaimonic. However, most researchers have embraced the idea that both hedonic and eudaimonic well-being are needed for an optimal existence, a state also referred to as flourishing (Keyes, 2002), optimal human functioning (Ryff, 1989b; 2016), or living the full or good life (Seligman, 2002).

Hedonic Well-Being

Most positive psychologists today refer to hedonia as **subjective well-being**, a term coined by Diener and his colleagues (e.g., Diener, 1984). Subjective well-being includes an affective and cognitive component. A relatively high frequency and presence of positive emotions, coupled with a relatively low presence and frequency of negative emotions, characterize the affective component. The cognitive component primarily involves the assessment of one's satisfaction with life.

Subjective well-being is best thought of as an assessment of one's *overall* level of happiness; that is, it is not thought to be bound to one particular source, such as family, occupation, or religion (Ryan & Deci, 2001). To illustrate, a person with high subjective well-being would typically indicate that within the last week (or month) they often felt enthusiastic, inspired, active, and strong, and rarely afraid, scared, distressed, or upset. They would also typically report that they felt generally quite satisfied with and positive about their life. The character Joy from the Pixar movie *Inside Out* (2015) illustrates high subjective well-being.

Subjective well-being is related to a multitude of positive outcomes on the individual and societal level, including greater income, more friends, better marriages, better self-control, self-confidence, more helpfulness, creativity, better problem solving, more resistance to stress, stronger social support, more meaning in life, better physical health (on a genetic level), and even longer life (for a review, see Lyubomirsky, King, & Diener, 2005). Subjective well-being theories emerged when study after study revealed that objective variables like demographics, positive life events (e.g., winning in the lottery), and traumatic life events (e.g., becoming paralyzed) were only weakly correlated with feelings of happiness. As such, one's subjective experience of happiness is an important component for actual flourishing.

Eudaimonic Well-Being

As an approach to well-being, eudaimonia takes into account complexity, adversity, and the search for meaning: aspects of life which may not necessarily be perceived as pleasant or associated with life satisfaction. Instead, the focus is on one's strengths and on how to live in accordance with one's true nature. Eudaimonia is less a momentary state of being and more a way of living a good and fulfilled life. As a result, happiness is understood in an Aristotelian sense as the "pursuit of excellence, virtue and self-realization" (Waterman et al., 2010, p. 42), including having a purpose in life, feeling autonomous in one's actions, experiencing personal growth, and looking at life from a bigger picture, among others. An exemplar of living a eudaimonic life would be the animated movie character Ferdinand in the Fox Entertainment movie *Ferdinand* (2017).

Some research suggests that eudaimonic well-being, compared to hedonic well-being, has more long-term benefits and may foster well-being in oneself as well as others (Fredrickson et al., 2015; Huta, Pelletier, Baxter, & Thompson, 2012; Huta & Ryan, 2010). That is, when considering hedonic well-being—"Am I happy?"—we typically think of ourselves at that particular moment, with the hope that the answer is "Yes!" On the other hand, when considering eudaimonic well-being, we tend to think about what will make us happy in the long run. A happy feeling from any one activity is not the main focus with eudaimonic well-being. Instead it is the activity itself which enhances one's quality of life and provides meaning, accomplishment, and self-realization. Moreover, it also includes being motivated to help others become happy. For example, pursuing the goal of creating a meditation club on campus is not only pleasurable for me but also gives me a feeling of meaning and self-expression, which can benefit me in the long run. The establishment of the club, in turn, might also raise the well-being of members in the club, which would be further meaningful to me.

Although it is tidy to discuss hedonic and eudaimonic well-being as two separate concepts, in truth, the latter is often thought to include aspects of the former (see Box 3.1). For example, Fredrickson and colleagues (2008) found that when people experience more positive emotions (hedonic well-being) in their daily lives they also felt more purpose in life, environmental mastery, self-acceptance, and positive relations with others (eudaimonic well-being; Ryff 1989b). Other studies also show a correlation between hedonic and eudaimonic orientations for life satisfaction, vitality, and self-esteem (for an overview, see Huta, 2016). Taken together, hedonic and eudaimonic well-being share a dynamic interrelationship, with both components vitally important for flourishing.

BOX 3.1 HEDONIC AND EUDAIMONIC WELL-BEING AS SYSTEMS OF THINKING

The distinction between hedonic and eudaimonic well-being can also be conceptualized as two systems of thinking (Steger & Shin, 2012). In his widely influential 2011 book *Thinking, Fast and Slow*, Nobel-Prize-winning psychologist and economist Daniel Kahneman described what he calls System 1 and System 2 thinking. System 1 is based on fast judgment-making in response to a stimulus, often with reliance upon heuristics (or mental short-cuts) to make decisions about how to engage in a situation. The older and subcortical brain structures are involved in such decision-making, following instincts of safety and security. System 2 thinking involves the newer developed cortical areas of the brain that allow for self-regulation, abstract thinking and deliberation and, therefore, are slower in their judgment-making.

Applying this distinction to well-being, Vittersø (2016) argued that subjective well-being (SWB)—which conceptualizes happiness as a subjective and heuristic assessment of one's quality of life—is closely related to System 1 thinking. Hence, SWB could be called Happiness 1. It includes the component of being happy *in* one's life, based on the pleasant feelings experienced (high positive affect and low negative affect), and being happy *with* one's life, based on the cognitive evaluation of one's life (life satisfaction). In contrast, eudaimonic well-being (EWB) can be thought of as Happiness 2, as it relates to System 2 thinking. EWB conceptualizes happiness as a more complex and deep state of being. It includes *having* a happy life, with "happy" based on the agreed-upon criteria espoused by one of the theories of eudaimonic well-being discussed in the chapter. In addition, because eudaimonic activities are sought out because they are themselves pleasurable (and not because they necessarily lead to a pleasurable outcome), Happiness 2 also, in part, relies upon System 1 thinking in terms of being happy in the process of *fulfilling* one's life. This occurs through "activities and experiences included in, or resulting from, the development of valuable individual potential and social relations" (Vittersø, 2016, p. 19). Thus, it can be thought that SWB is related to System 1 thinking leading to Happiness 1, whereas EWB is related to both System 1 and 2 thinking leading to Happiness 2.

Theories of Eudaimonic Well-Being

Because eudaimonic well-being is a more complex concept than hedonic well-being, a variety of theories have been developed to explain it. Below we introduce three theories that have most influenced the study of eudaimonic well-being within positive psychology and that have also been explored in media psychology. The three theories have been derived from and are based on existential and clinical psychology research, and all present well-being as the ultimate fulfillment of an optimally functioning life. In addition, we introduce a newly developed theory that carries interesting potential in the positive media psychology context.

Eudaimonic Well-Being Theory

According to Waterman (1993), the subjective state of eudaimonia is achieved by self-realization, which comes about through personal expressiveness. The feeling of being able to express oneself fully evolves through "the fulfilment of personal potentials in the form of the development of one's skills and talents, the advancement of one's purpose in living, or both" (Waterman, 1993, p. 679). Pursuing life goals that fit with one's innate nature is what gives life purpose. These are the basic tenets of **eudaimonic well-being theory**.

Any activity that is perceived to be pleasant and satisfies intrinsic needs can lead to hedonic happiness. But eudaimonic well-being comes from engaging in activities that are self-determined and effortful, provide a balance between challenges and skills, and which can lead to a state of flow (see p. 46). For example, learning a new skill or volunteering at a homeless shelter (personally expressive activities) can bring about eudaimonic happiness but can also be considered pleasant (hedonic happiness); in contrast, many activities can be considered pleasant (hedonic happiness) but not lead to eudaimonic happiness. Thus, eudaimonic happiness is a sufficient but not necessary condition for hedonic happiness to occur. Further, hedonic happiness is sought out as an end in itself. On the other hand, eudaimonic happiness is a byproduct that is only experienced when pursing activities that foster self-realization and intrinsic goal pursuit; that is, it is sought out as a means to an end.

The theory conceptualizes eudaimonic well-being along six interrelated dimensions: self-discovery, perceived development of one's potential, purpose and meaning in life, investment of significant effort in pursuit of excellence, intense involvement in activities, and enjoyment of personally expressive activities. To measure the concept, Waterman and colleagues (2010) developed the Questionnaire for Eudaimonic Well-Being (QEWB), which has proven to be universally applicable (as it reveals no demographic differences in eudaimonic well-being). Further, the scale measures aspects related to identity formation (e.g., personal expressiveness, self-esteem, internal locus of control) and thus represents a unique contribution to positive psychological functioning.

Psychological Well-Being Theory

As a counter to Diener's (1984) subjective well-being, Ryff (1989a) proposed the concept of **psychological well-being**, a competing multidimensional model that went beyond the mere seeking of pleasure and life satisfaction. Instead, Ryff focused on being well psychologically, which meant living a life that is full of optimal experiences (Ryff, 1989b). Derived from a range of humanistic, clinical, and developmental psychological theories (e.g., maturity, individuation, self-actualization, personal development), six dimensions of psychological well-being were identified that support optimal human functioning (or positive functioning; Ryff, 1989b; 2016).

The first dimension is *autonomy*, which refers to the feeling of behaving independently, self-determined, and with self-regulation. Autonomous individuals are free from external influences and are guided by an internal locus of control. *Environmental mastery* refers to one's ability to manipulate the environment in accordance with one's needs and values. It refers to the ability to successfully manage one's daily affairs and the ability to change the surrounding environments, either through a change in viewpoints (mental activity) or actual physical manipulation. *Personal growth* refers to the individual's concern with self-realization, that is realizing one's highest potential. It involves constant growth and development, which becomes realized over time and can be expressed in successfully overcoming challenges, change of attitudes and behaviors, more self-knowledge, and effectiveness. *Positive relations with others* is the fourth dimension of psychological well-being, referring to one's ability to empathize, love, and care for close others and humanity overall. People high in this dimension are concerned about the welfare of others, have strong and trusting relationships, and embrace intimacy. *Purpose in life* refers to the clear understanding of one's life purpose and meaning. People high in this dimension hold beliefs that give their life meaning; they live with intention, direction, and goals in mind, which in turn contribute to a sense of meaningfulness. The sixth dimension of psychological well-being is *self-acceptance*, referring to one's positive conception of the self. This includes having a positive attitude toward oneself and relating positively to one's past, strengths, and weaknesses.

A variety of health benefits are associated with psychological well-being, including reduced mortality risk, greater general health, and lower risk for disease, particularly among people high in purpose in life. Purpose in life and positive relations with others also appear to lead to reduced levels of comorbidity (i.e., having multiple illnesses at one time) in later life, reduced risk for health problems based on social inequality, and reduced risk for mental illness (see Ryff, 2013). Additionally, people with high psychological (but not hedonic) well-being demonstrated downregulated pro-inflammatory gene expression and increased expression of antibody synthesis genes (Fredrickson et al., 2013), which are genetic indicators for good health; high levels of self-acceptance, autonomy, positive relations, and purpose in life seem to be of particular importance for these positive genetic benefits. Psychological well-being is also associated with positive affect, quality of sleep, and other health-promoting behaviors.

In terms of measurement and universality, Ryff and Keyes (1995), using a nationally representative sample, demonstrated the relative independence of the six dimensions in supporting the construct of psychological well-being. The resulting scale has now been translated into more than 30 languages and used in more than 500 publications (Ryff, 2016).

Self-Determination Theory

A third theory of eudaimonic well-being is actually based on Ryff's work on psychological well-being. **Self-determination theory** (SDT; Deci & Ryan, 1985; 2000; Ryan & Deci, 2001) conceptualizes human flourishing as the satisfaction of three intrinsic psychological needs. The first basic need is *autonomy*, which refers to having a sense of control (or volition) and freedom when engaging in an activity. *Competence* refers to perceiving oneself to be effective in manipulating the environment in a way that results in valued outcomes. The final need is *relatedness*, or the sense of connection, care toward others, or feeling cared for by others. Deci and Ryan (2000) argued that individuals do not seek out behaviors primarily to satisfy these needs because of a perceived deficit caused by a disruption in homeostasis. Instead, we are intrinsically motivated to seek out activities with autonomous regulation and awareness in order to come closer to our true selves. As a result, the satisfaction of the three basic needs is a secondary result, which ultimately contributes to well-being and psychological growth.

The pursuit of intrinsic aspirations—such as meaningful relationships, personal growth, and community engagement—has repeatedly been shown to lead to greater well-being than the pursuit of extrinsic aspirations (e.g., financial success, social recognition). In fact, the pursuit of extrinsic goals can actually lead to ill-being; for instance, materialism has been found to be negatively related to well-being around the world (e.g., Niemiec, Ryan, & Deci, 2009). In contrast, psychological need fulfillment mediates the relationship between poor economic conditions and physical and mental health (Di Domenico & Fournier, 2014).

As will be seen in several upcoming chapters, self-determination theory is relevant in media psychology as media use is often conceptualized as an intrinsically motivated activity, autonomously sought out and providing opportunities for self-awareness. Indeed, numerous studies have shown how videos, social media, and digital games can satisfy the needs of autonomy, competence and relatedness, in turn contributing to human flourishing.

Self-Centeredness and Selflessness Happiness Model

The relatively newer **self-centeredness and selflessness happiness model** (SSHM) (Dambrun & Ricard, 2011) brings together many of the assumptions underlying eudaimonic well-being and self-determination theories. According to SSHM, hedonic and eudaimonic happiness are based on the way individuals perceive themselves. The self can be perceived as seemingly rigid, permanent, and independent, which supports a *self-centered* psychological functioning (e.g., how we feel, think, and behave). On the other hand, the self can be perceived as a permeable, interdependent, and flexible entity, which favors a *selfless* psychological functioning. Self-centered psychological functioning predicts hedonic happiness and fluctuating forms of well-being, whereas selfless psychological functioning predicts long term, stable well-being (Dambrun 2017; Dambrun & Ricard, 2011).

Self-centered functioning is related to egoism, biased self-interest, and more generally an exaggerated importance of the self, which then favors experiences that maximize personal pleasures and minimize pains. The experience of these hedonic objectives leads to momentary joy and pleasure. However, because the pleasurable experiences are based on the availability of certain conditions or stimuli, the cessation of the conditions or stimuli leads to displeasure; in cases where the conditions or stimuli persist (e.g., getting a new car) the outcome is hedonic adaptation (see Lyubomirsky, 2011). The inability to obtain a desirable object can also lead to afflictive affect such as frustration, anger or jealousy, which hampers well-being. Thus, the self-centered hedonic approach to happiness is characterized by a constant fluctuation between pleasure and displeasure (Dambrun & Ricard, 2011).

Selfless functioning does not see the self as a completely separate entity from others but rather as closely connected to others and the environment as a whole. The driving force of selflessness is to live in harmony with the different elements of the environment and is expressed in values such as benevolence and universalism (or self-transcendent emotions; see Chapter 6). Selfless psychological functioning is related to authentic and durable happiness, which is defined as a durable state of contentment, emotional balance, and inner peace that is independent of circumstances (Dambrun, 2017; Dambrun & Ricard, 2011).

Research has successfully demonstrated that self-centeredness and selflessness are separate constructs and predict happiness in distinct ways via distinct processes

(Dambrun, 2017). Whereas self-centered psychological functioning predicts fluctuating happiness, mediated by negative affect (or afflictive affects), selflessness psychological functioning predicts durable authentic happiness, mediated by feelings of harmony and emotional stability.

Compared to other theories of well-being, the SSHM argues that happiness is dependent on our understanding of the self rather than psychological qualities that foster happiness (e.g., intrinsic need satisfaction; Ryan & Deci, 2000) or focusing on activities that make oneself fulfilled, engaged, and alive (e.g., Waterman, 1993). Dambrun and Ricard (2011), however, warn of a prescriptive approach in which people strive for selflessness as a means to attain authentic, durable happiness. Such an approach/avoidance approach underlies the hedonic principle of attaining pleasure (or selflessness) and avoiding pain (self-centeredness) and would likely only lead to fluctuating happiness. Instead, engaging in activities that naturally lead to selflessness, such as mediation or mental training, is more likely to lead to a happiness that is free from hopes and fears about attaining desirable and avoiding undesirable objects. It can be argued that media could be another unobtrusive means to change people's perception about their selves.

Determinants of Well-Being

Having conceptualized the different forms of well-being, it is important to understand the determinants of well-being. Within the framework of positive psychology, we assume that well-being levels can be changed. But how much influence do we really have over our well-being?

Prominent positive psychologist Sonya Lyubomirsky, along with her colleagues, argued that an individual's genetic composition (referred to as happiness set point) accounts for 50% of their **chronic happiness level**, which refers to a person's happiness level during a particular period of their life (not just the fleeting, momentary shifts that may occur from day-to-day). An additional 10% is thought to be attributable to one's specific circumstances, like the culture or region one is living in or the life events or traumas one experiences. The final 40% of a person's happiness level is thought to be associated with intentional activities (Lyubomirksy, Sheldon & Schkade, 2005). Although these specific proportions are only theoretical proxies, they give us a good overview of the potential determinants of well-being. What readily becomes apparent is that you have a large amount of influence on your own level of happiness. This influence comes not only from the activities you intentionally choose to participate in (e.g., physical exercise, having a positive mindset, striving for important life goals), but also from the genetic composition of one's happiness set point, which as was mentioned above, is now understood to be more malleable than once thought.

In the remainder of the chapter, we focus on three theories—broaden-and-built, PERMA, and Virtues in Action—that identify specific, core elements of well-being that one can personally address and influence, and when focused upon, can lead to high levels of hedonic and eudaimonic well-being.

Broaden-and-Build Theory

As was discussed in Chapter 2, emotions are a primary focus of psychology, in large part because they are thought to be functional for human survival as they motivate us to act in response to the emotion-eliciting cause in our environment. **Positive emotions** are of particular interest to positive psychologists because of their connection to subjective well-being. Positive emotions include joy, gratitude, serenity, interest, hope, pride, amusement, inspiration, awe, and love.

All emotions are assumed to carry actions tendencies with accompanying physiological changes which, from an evolutionary point of view, prepare humans to adapt to survival. Negative emotions, such as anxiety or anger, narrow the focus of a person's thought-action repertoire to act quickly and in a way that maximizes survival (e.g., fight or flight). According to the **broaden–and–build theory**, positive emotions *broaden* a person's thought-action repertoire (Frederickson, 2001). The broadening benefit then *builds* personal resources, which can be cognitive (e.g., greater mindfulness, widened spatial attention), psychological (e.g., mastery of environmental challenges, resilience, increased self-efficacy), social (e.g., giving and receiving emotional support, trust, oneness, acting prosocially) or physical (e.g., decreased likelihood of illnesses, cardiovascular health, health supportive genetic expression, longevity; see Fredrickson, 2001, Fredrickson, Cohn, Coffey, Pek, & Finkel, 2008).

Additionally, positive emotions can be useful to anticipate future threats and explore the environment; therefore, in the evolutionary sense, they too are adaptive for survival (Fredrickson, 2001). In a positive affective state, one becomes more open and receptive to things in the environment, which in turn can increase one's chances to experience even more positive emotions, leading to an **upward spiral of human flourishing**. Media can be a powerful source for eliciting positive emotions; after all, one of the main reasons why people consume media content is to modulate their emotional makeup (see Chapter 4). As such, one key part of what positive media psychologists study is how media can be part of the upward spiral of positive human flourishing, as identified in the broaden-and-build theory.

PERMA

Psychologist Martin Seligman identified five central components to well-being in his highly acclaimed and influential book *Flourishing: A Visionary New Understanding of Happiness and Well-Being* (2011). The five components are easily communicated with the acronym PERMA, which stands for (p)ositive emotions, (e) ngagement, positive (r)elationships, (m)eaning, and (a)ccomplishment. More specifically:

- *Positive emotions* refer to the trait or state of feeling joyful, vital, or pleasant. Related outcomes and processes are discussed in the broaden-and-build theory.
- *Engagement* refers to the act of being absorbed in activities with a high level of interest and focus; one concept most often associated with engagement is **flow** (Csikszentmihalyi, 1988). Flow describes a state in which one is completely immersed in an activity; the state involves a distorted sense of time and a loss of self-awareness. To achieve a state of flow, an activity must challenge one's skills but not to the point of frustration and despair; the activity can be mastered. Engaging activities are perceived to be highly enjoyable and are therefore done for their own sake, not for any particular result (i.e., they are intrinsically motivating). Examples of situations in which flow states might be achieved include a musician playing a highly demanding piece, an athlete training for a competition, and friends getting lost in a good conversation. Flow experiences have been shown to promote well-being in a variety of contexts, including one's work life through increased job satisfaction and sociability. As discussed in Chapter 8, digital games have been found to be a great elicitor of flow and, as such, have been found to contribute to well-being as well.
- *Positive relationships*, or relating to others in a positive way, have been found to be an innate need for humans (e.g., relatedness in self-determination theory) and therefore highly important for well-being and physical health across the world (Diener & Oishi, 2000). Research indicates that people with strong, high-quality social relationships are significantly less likely to die prematurely or even to catch the common cold when exposed to the virus. Further, people who feel lonely and less satisfied with the quality of their social relationships are more likely to die prematurely, have high blood pressure, have higher levels of depression, and experience social anxiety. It comes as no surprise then that treating others with kindness—instead of treating oneself to a treat or enjoying a massage—can lead to greater subjective and psychological well-being (Nelson, Layous, Cole, & Lyubomirsky, 2016). Ultimately, positive relationships are not only good to have but are also a necessary component of positive functioning. And as we will discuss in coming chapters, feeling positively connected with media characters and consuming media content that facilitates feelings of connectedness with others are also powerful forces to foster feelings of relatedness, at least in the short run.
- *Meaning* is understood as making sense out of one's life, in particular the nature of one's existence in relation to something larger than the self. In many ways, then, meaning in the PERMA framework is similar to purpose

in life as identified in the psychological well-being concept. Having a sense of purpose and meaning in life has been shown to be strongly related to psychological and subjective well-being, and negatively related to health-risk behaviors (e.g., alcohol consumption, cigarette smoking, unsafe sex) and mental health problems (Brassai, Piko & Steger, 2011). As will be discussed in Chapter 5, meaningful entertainment can be an effective tool for promoting well-being through media.

- *Accomplishment* is the result of achieving something through effort for its own sake. Having the desire to accomplish something by being determined, having self-discipline, and working hard to achieve a goal can lead to a feeling of accomplishment, independent of the actual goal being achieved (Seligman, 2011). Thus, relating accomplishment to well-being is best done by assessing the individual's attitude to strive for achievement. Research has shown that a persevering attitude predicts academic accomplishments beyond IQ and the personality trait of conscientiousness (Duckworth, Peterson, Matthews, & Kelly, 2007). Additional correlations between achievement attitudes and grade point average and life-satisfaction have been observed. Achievement attitudes are also often found in inspirational social media content, often in portrayals of perseverance and the successful overcoming of obstacles (see Chapter 6). Media consumption, as well as user-generated productions (e.g., filming one's accomplishments, DIY videos), provide ample opportunities for individuals to engage in and (vicariously) experience accomplishment as a means to foster flourishing.

Whereas some of these aspects may sound similar to previously discussed concepts from hedonic and eudaimonic well-being theories, the fundamental difference is that PERMA constitutes the *building blocks* of well-being rather than representing well-being itself (Seligman, 2018). As a result, then, people who strive to increase the positive emotions in their lives, create opportunities for engaging experiences, invest in intimate and strong relationships, search for and find meaning, and work to achieve a sense of accomplishment will *feel happier* overall (in particular in terms of subjective well-being; Seligman, 2018), compared to people who invest little effort in those PERMA elements. In addition to increased subjective well-being, people with high PERMA aspects in their lives have better physical health. The PERMA framework has also found great application in institutional settings (e.g., school, work environments) through programs that support people's flourishing, including physical health, life satisfaction, job satisfaction, organizational commitment, and academic performance.

Virtues in Action and Character Strengths

The PERMA model provides a framework for individuals to strategically work on their well-being by increasing the states of PERMA in their everyday life.

Another approach to increase well-being has been outlined by Peterson and Seligman (2004), which focuses more on the personality of the individual, specifically, their **character strengths**. Until recently, psychologists thought that personalities, as well as happiness set points, were rigid and almost not changeable. This view changed with the scientific discoveries of epigenetics (i.e., the idea that genes for certain traits can become active by environmental input) and neuroplasticity (i.e., the idea that the brain is malleable even in adulthood). Today, we know that personality traits and happiness set points can, in fact, be altered (Damian, Spengler, Sutu, & Roberts, 2019; Layous, 2018; Luhmann & Intelisano, 2018). In this vein, Peterson and Seligman's (2004) **Virtues in Action** (VIA) framework identifies six key human virtues with 24 corresponding, trait-like character strengths that one can develop, providing more opportunities for increased flourishing (see Figure 3.1).

Based on a sweeping historical survey of religious thinkers and moral philosophers in China, South Asia, and Western societies, Peterson and Seligman identified six basic human virtues: wisdom, courage, humanity, justice, temperance, and transcendence. These virtues are thought to be universal, grounded in biology as a way of providing an evolutionary advantage to survival through striving toward moral excellence. Whereas the virtues reflect a more abstract understanding of ways to live a good life, the related character strengths are the concrete psychological expressions that define each virtue.

Character strengths are trait-like dispositions that guide a person's thoughts, emotions, and actions (Park, Peterson, & Seligman, 2004). They are stable in that they are enacted across different situations and time, but they are also thought to be malleable. The character strengths appear to be universal, in that have been found to be present in and valued by individuals of various cultures (Park, Peterson, & Seligman, 2006). Kindness, fairness, authenticity, gratitude, and open-mindedness have been found to be most strongly endorsed across 40 different analyzed countries (Seligman, Steen, Park, & Peterson, 2005).

Numerous studies have shown how character strengths are related to indicators of positive functioning, including successfully overcoming adversities (e.g., illness, work stress), maintaining positive relationships, and exemplary work performance. Character strengths are also highly related to subjective and psychological well-

FIGURE 3.1 Virtues in Action (VIA) Framework: Virtues and Character Strengths (Based on Peterson & Seligman, 2004)

being (see Harzer, 2016); they are also strongly related to all five PERMA dimensions (Wagner, Gander, Proyer, & Ruch, 2020).

Some character strengths seem to be particularly beneficial for well-being, including zest, hope, curiosity, gratitude, and love (see Park et al., 2004). Harzer (2016) argued that what the three top strengths have in common with both hedonic and eudaimonic well-being is that they foster a proactive way to live, one where the individual is energized to do something (zest), believes they can do something (hope), and has a reason for why they do something (curiosity). This aligns well with the argument that increasing well-being requires effort and endorsement by the individual (Lyubomirsky, Dickerhoof, Boehm, & Sheldon, 2011); it does not just fall into place. For what it is worth, the least often correlated strengths with subjective and psychological well-being are modesty, spirituality, prudence, and appreciation of beauty (for a detailed outline, see Harzer, 2016).

Within the media context, the depiction of character strengths within media characters—for example, the protagonists in the movie *Avengers: Endgame* portraying bravery and social intelligence—can portray powerful modeling of exemplary behaviors for viewers to learn from (see Chapter 6; also for a list of movies portraying different character strengths, see Niemiec & Wedding, 2014).

Summary

The field of positive psychology seeks to scientifically understand what makes life worth living and has been systematically exploring the concepts of happiness and well-being for more than 20 years. Well-being can generally be divided into two main approaches: hedonic and eudaimonic well-being. Subjective well-being is the most referenced theory in the context of hedonia. Three theories—eudaimonic well-being, psychological well-being, and self-determination theory—are most often referenced within the context of eudaimonic well-being. The broaden-and-build theory helps explain how the experience of positive emotions can facilitate the development of personal resources that promote flourishing. The PERMA approach identifies five avenues (positive emotions, engagement, positive relationships, meaning, and accomplishment) through which we can pursue well-being. And the Virtues in Action framework helps to classify human strengths, which can then illuminate specific interventions and behaviors (e.g., random acts of kindness, counting one's blessings, reflecting on positive experiences, affirming one's most important values, savoring positive experiences) to promote optimal living and the good life.

References

Brassai, L., Piko, B. F., & Steger, M. F. (2011). Meaning in life: Is it a protective factor for adolescents' psychological health? *International Journal of Behavioral Medicine*, 18, 44–51. doi:10.1007/s12529-010-9089-6.

Csikszentmihalyi, M. (1988). The flow experience and its significance for human psychology. In M. Csikszentmihalyi & I. Csikszentmihalyi (Eds.), *Optimal experience: Psychological studies of flow in consciousness* (pp. 15–35). New York, NY: Cambridge University Press.

Dambrun, M. (2017). Self-centeredness and selflessness: Happiness correlates and mediating psychological processes. *PeerJ*, e3306. doi:10.7717/peerj.3306.

Dambrun, M., & Ricard, M. (2011). Self-centeredness and selflessness: A theory of self-based psychological functioning and its consequences for happiness. *Review of General Psychology*, 2, 138–157. doi:10.1037/a0023059.

Damian, R. I., Spengler, M., Sutu, A., & Roberts, B. W. (2019). Sixteen going on sixty-six: A longitudinal study of personality stability and change across 50 years. *Journal of Personality and Social Psychology*, 117, 674–695. doi:10.1037/pspp0000210.

Deci, E. L., & Ryan, R. M. (1985). *Intrinsic motivation and self-determination in human behavior.* New York, NY: Plenum.

Deci, E. L., & Ryan, R. M. (2000). The "what" and "why" of goal pursuits: Human needs and the self-determination of behavior. *Psychological Inquiry*, 11, 227–268. doi:10.1207/S15327965PLI1104_01.

Di Domenico, S. I., & Fournier, M. A. (2014). Socioeconomic status, income inequality, and health complaints: A basic psychological needs perspective. *Social Indicators Research*, 119, 1679–1697. doi:10.1007/s11205-013-0572-8.

Diener, E. (1984). Subjective well-being. *Psychological Bulletin*, 95, 542–575. doi:10.1037/0033-2909.95.3.542.

Diener, E., & Oishi, S. (2000). Money and happiness: Income and subjective well-being across nations. In E. Diener & E. M. Suh (Eds.), *Culture and subjective well-being* (pp. 185–218). Cambridge, MA: MIT Press.

Duckworth, A. L., Peterson, C., Matthews, M. D., & Kelly, D. R. (2007). Grit: Perseverance and passion for long-term goals. *Journal of Personality and Social Psychology*, 92, 1087–1101. doi:10.1037/0022-3514.92.6.1087.

Fredrickson, B. (2001). The role of positive emotions in positive psychology: The broaden-and-build theory of positive emotions. *American Psychologist*, 56, 218–226. doi:10.1037//0003-066X.56.3.218.

Fredrickson, B. L., Cohn, M. A., Coffey, K. A., Pek, J., & Finkel, S. M. (2008). Open hearts build lives: Positive emotions, induced through loving-kindness meditation, build consequential personal resources. *Journal of Personality and Social Psychology*, 95, 1045–1062. doi:10.1037/a0013262.

Fredrickson, B. L., Grewen, K. M., Algoe, S. B., Firestine, A. M., Arevalo, J. M., Ma, J., & Cole, S. W. (2015). Psychological well-being and the human conserved transcriptional response to adversity. *PloS One*, 10(3), e0121839. doi:10.1371/journal.pone.0121839.

Fredrickson, B. L., Grewen, K. M., Coffey, K. A., Algoe, S. B., Firestine, A. M., Arevalo, J. M., Ma, J., & Cole, S. W. (2013). A functional genomic perspective on human well-being. *Proceedings of the National Academy of Sciences*, 110, 13684–13689. doi:10.1073/pnas.1305419110.

Harzer, C. (2016). The eudaimonics of human strengths: The relations between character strengths and well-being. In J. Vittersø (Ed.), *International handbooks of quality-of-life. Handbook of eudaimonic well-being* (p. 307–322). Cham, CH: Springer International Publishing.

Huta, V. (2016). An overview of hedonic and eudaimonic well-being concepts. In L. Reinecke & M. B. Oliver (Eds.), *The Routledge handbook of media use and well-being* (pp. 14–33). New York, NY: Routledge.

Huta, V., Pelletier, L. G., Baxter, D., & Thompson, A. (2012). How eudaimonic and hedonic motives relate to the well-being of close others. *The Journal of Positive Psychology*, 7, 399–404. doi:10.1080/17439760.2012.705318.

Huta, V., & Ryan, R. M. (2010). Pursuing pleasure or virtue: The differential and overlapping well-being benefits of hedonic and eudaimonic motives. *Journal of Happiness Studies*, 11, 735–762. doi:10.1007/s10902-009-9171-4.

Kahneman, D. (2011). *Thinking, fast and slow*. New York, NY: Farrar, Straus and Giroux.

Keyes, C. L. (2002). The mental health continuum: From languishing to flourishing in life. *Journal of Health and Social Behavior*, 207–222. doi:10.2307/3090197.

Layous, K. (2018). Malleability and intentional activities. In E. Diener, S. Oishi, & L. Tay (Eds.), *Handbook of well-being* (pp. 741–753). Salt Lake City, UT: DEF Publishers.

Luhmann, M., & Intelisano, S. (2018). Hedonic adaptation and the set point for subjective well-being. In E. Diener, S. Oishi, & L. Tay (Eds.), *Handbook of well-being* (pp. 219–243). Salt Lake City, UT: DEF Publishers.

Lyubomirsky, S. (2011). *Hedonic adaptation to positive and negative experiences*. In S. Folkman (Ed.) *Oxford handbook of stress, health, and coping* (pp. 200–224). New York, NY: Oxford University Press. Lyubomirsky, S., Dickerhoof, R., Boehm, J. K., & Sheldon, K. M. (2011). Becoming happier takes both a will and a proper way: an experimental longitudinal intervention to boost well-being. *Emotion*, 11, 391–402. doi:10.1037/a0022575.

Lyubomirsky, S., King, L. A., & Diener, E. (2005). The benefits of frequent positive affect. *Psychological Bulletin*, 131, 803–855. doi:10.1037/0033-2909.131.6.803.

Lyubomirsky, S., Sheldon, K. M., & Schkade, D. (2005). Pursuing happiness: The architecture of sustainable change. *Review of General Psychology*, 9, 111–131. doi:10.1037/1089-2680.9.2.111.

Nelson, S. K., Layous, K., Cole, S. W., & Lyubomirsky, S. (2016). Do unto others or treat yourself? The effects of prosocial and self-focused behavior on psychological flourishing. *Emotion*, 16, 850–861. doi:10.1037/emo0000178.

Niemiec, C. P., Ryan, R. M., & Deci, E. L. (2009). The path taken: Consequences of attaining intrinsic and extrinsic aspirations in post-college life. *Journal of Research in Personality*, 43, 291–306. doi:10.1016/j.jrp.2008.09.001.

Niemiec, R. M., & Wedding, D. (2014). *Positive psychology at the movies 2: Using films to build character strengths and well-being* (2nd ed.). Boston, MA: Hogrefe Publishing. Park, N., Peterson, C., & Seligman, M. E. P. (2004). Strengths of character and well-being. *Journal of Social and Clinical Psychology*, 23, 603–619. doi:10.1521/jscp.23.5.603.50748.

Park, N., Peterson, C., & Seligman, M. E. P. (2006). Character strengths in fifty-four nations and the fifty US states. *The Journal of Positive Psychology*, 1, 118–129. doi:10.1080/17439760600619567.

Peterson, C., & Seligman, M. E. P. (2004). *Character strengths and virtues: A classification and handbook*. Washington, DC: American Psychological Association.

Ryan, R. M., & Deci, E. L. (2000). Self-determination theory and the facilitation of intrinsic motivation, social development, and well-being. *American Psychologist*, 55, 68–78. doi:10.1037/0003-066X.55.1.68.

Ryan, R. M., & Deci, E. L. (2001). On happiness and human potentials: A review of research on hedonic and eudaimonic well-being. *Annual Review of Psychology*, 52, 141–166. doi:10.1146/annurev.psych.52.1.141.

Ryff, C. D. (1989a). Beyond Ponce de Leon and life satisfaction: New directions in quest of successful aging. *International Journal of Behavioral Development*, 12, 35–55. doi:10.1177/016502548901200102.

Ryff, C. D. (1989b). Happiness is everything, or is it? Explorations on the meaning of psychological well-being. *Journal of Personality and Social Psychology*, 57, 1069–1081. doi:10.1037/0022-3514.57.6.1069.

Ryff, C. D. (2013). Eudaimonic well-being and health: Mapping consequences of self-realization. In A. S. Waterman (Ed.), *The best within us: Positive psychology perspectives on eudaimonia* (pp. 77–98). Washington, DC: American Psychological Association.

Ryff, C. D. (2016). Beautiful ideas and the scientific enterprise: Sources of intellectual vitality in research on eudaimonic well-being. In J. Vittersø (Ed.), *Handbook of eudaimonic well-being* (pp. 95–107). Cham, CH: Springer International Publishing.

Ryff, C. D., & Keyes, C. L. M. (1995). The structure of psychological well-being revisited. *Journal of Personality and Social Psychology*, 69, 719–727. doi:10.1037/0022-3514.69.4.719.

Seligman, M. E. P. (2002). Positive psychology, positive prevention, and positive therapy. In C. R. Snyder & S. J. Lopez (Eds.), *Handbook of positive psychology* (pp. 3–9). New York, NY: Oxford University Press.

Seligman, M. E. P. (2011). *Flourish*. New York, NY: Free Press.

Seligman, M. E. P. (2018). PERMA and the building blocks of well-being. *The Journal of Positive Psychology*, 13, 333–335. doi:10.1080/17439760.2018.1437466.

Seligman, M. E. P., & Csikszentmihalyi, M. (2000). Positive psychology: An introduction. *American Psychologist*, 55, 5–14. doi:10.1037/0003-066X.55.1.5.

Seligman, M. E. P., Steen, T., Park, N., & Peterson, C. (2005). Positive psychology progress: Empirical validation of interventions. *American Psychologist*, 60, 410–421. doi:10.1037/0003-066X.60.5.410..

Steger, M., & Shin, J. Y. (2012). Happiness and meaning in a technological age: A psychological approach. In P. Brey, A. Briggle, & E. Spence (Eds.), *The good life in a technological age* (pp. 110–126). New York, NY: Routledge.

Vittersø, J. (2016). The most important idea in the world: An introduction. In J. Vittersø (Ed.), *Handbook of eudaimonic well-being* (p. 1–24). Cham, CH: Springer International Publishing.

Wagner, L., Gander, F., Proyer, R. T., & Ruch, W. (2020). Character strengths and PERMA: Investigating the relationships of character strengths with a multidimensional framework of well-being. *Applied Research in Quality of Life*, 15, 307–328. doi:10.1007/s11482-018-9695-z.

Waterman, A. S. (1993). Two conceptions of happiness: Contrasts of personal expressiveness (eudaimonia) and hedonic enjoyment. *Journal of Personality and Social Psychology*, 64, 678–691. doi:10.1037/0022-3514.64.4.678.

Waterman, A. S., Schwartz, S. J., Zamboanga, B. L., Ravert, R. D., Williams, M. K., Bede Agocha, V., Kim, S. Y., & Brent Donnellan, M. (2010). The Questionnaire for Eudaimonic Well-Being: Psychometric properties, demographic comparisons, and evidence of validity. *The Journal of Positive Psychology*, 5, 41–61. doi:10.1080/17439760903435208.

Additional Readings

Chida, Y., & Steptoe, A. (2008). Positive psychological well-being and mortality: a quantitative review of prospective observational studies. *Psychosomatic Medicine*, 70, 741–756. doi:10.1097/PSY.0b013e31818105ba..

Csikszentmihalyi, M. (2008). *Flow: The psychology of optimal experience*. New York, NY: Harper Perennial Modern Classics.

Diener, E. (2000). Subjective well–being: The science of happiness and a proposal for a national index. *American Psychologist*, 55, 34–43. doi:10.1037/0003-066X.55.1.34.

Diener, S., Oishi, E., & Tay, L. (2018). *Handbook of well-being*. Salt Lake City, UT: DEF Publishers.

Gable, S. L., & Haidt, J. (2005). What (and why) is positive psychology?. *Review of General Psychology*, 9, 103–110. doi:10.1037/1089-2680.9.2.103.

Isham, A., Gatersleben, B., & Jackson, T. (2019). Flow activities as a route to living well with less. *Environment and Behavior*, 51, 431–461. doi:10.1177/0013916518799826.

Kahneman, D. (1999). Objective happiness. In D. Kahneman, E. Diener, & N. Schwarz (Eds.), *Well-being: The foundations of hedonic psychology* (p. 3–25). New York, NY: Russell Sage Foundation.

Kern, M. L., Waters, L. E., Adler, A. & White, M.A. (2015). A multidimensional approach to measuring well-being in students: Application of the PERMA framework, *The Journal of Positive Psychology*, 10(3), 262–271. doi:10.1080/17439760.2014.936962.

Krok, D. (2018). When is meaning in life most beneficial to young people? Styles of meaning in life and well-being among late adolescents. *Journal of Adult Development*, 25, 96–106. doi:10.1007/s10804-017-9280-y.

Layous, K., & Lyubomirsky, S. (2014). The how, why, what, when, and who of happiness: Mechanisms underlying the success of positive interventions. In J. Gruber & J. Moscowitz (Eds.), *Positive emotion: Integrating the light sides and dark sides* (pp. 473–495). New York, NY: Oxford University Press.

Ryan, R. M., & Martela, F. (2016). Eudaimonia as a way of living: Connecting Aristotle with self-determination theory. In J. Vittersø (Ed.), *Handbook of eudaimonic well-being* (p. 109–122). Cham, CH: Springer International Publishing.

4

HEDONIC ENTERTAINMENT

Source: Shutterstock 401699047

It comes as no great shock to anyone that one of the most basic benefits of media use is the pleasure it provides. Without a doubt, the primary goal of most entertainment is for the audience to be entertained, to enjoy, to be satisfied. But what exactly does that mean? How does media content lead to enjoyment? And how does media enjoyment contribute to our overall sense of health and well-being? In this chapter, we will try to answer those and similar questions. To begin, though, we must first come to an understanding of what positive media psychologists mean by the terms *entertainment* and *enjoyment*.

Entertainment and Enjoyment

Often people use the word entertainment to refer to a category of media content, distinguishing things like dramas and video games from news and advertisements. But in truth, for decades many viewers have tuned into the National Football League's Super Bowl simply because they love watching the advertisements. News programs routinely include humorous and other human-interest stories because viewers enjoy them. Even the super-serious Twitter feed of the U.S. government's North American Aerospace Defense Command tracks and tweets out the location of Santa Claus on Christmas Eve. Thus, *any* media source, format, or content can potentially be entertaining. Furthermore, not everything that gets called entertainment is entertaining to everyone. Ultimately, entertainment is in the eyes of the beholder, which helps explain why great variance exists in the appeal of media content across populations.

But this does not mean that entertainment cannot be defined. Most media scholars adopt the perspective offered by Dolf Zillmann and Jennings Bryant, two pioneers of media entertainment research: **Entertainment** can be defined as "any activity designed to delight and, to a smaller degree, enlighten through the exhibition of the fortunes or misfortunes of others, but also through the display of special skills by others and/or self" (Zillmann & Bryant, 1994, p. 438). This definition is helpful because it (1) conceptualizes entertainment in a broad sense ("any activity," implicitly acknowledging that entertainment is not solely found in media), (2) identifies intent by the creators ("designed to"), (3) focuses our attention on the primary, though not only, outcome ("delight"), and (4) helps to identify aspects of the activity that are responsible for that outcome ("fortunes and misfortunes of others," "special skill"). We will explore those aspects in more detail later in the chapter.

As the definition suggests, feelings of delight (or pleasure) are central to entertainment. In fact, many people would say that those feelings are how they know they have been entertained in the first place. Typically, we refer to those feelings as enjoyment. **Enjoyment** can be defined as the pleasure derived from the consumption or use of media entertainment. It is primarily examined by researchers as a positive emotional reaction to media, associated with the activation of neurotransmitters in the "pleasure centers" of the limbic system in the brain. A large part of the research on entertainment has focused specifically on how audiences get pleasure from media use. However, scholars also understand that enjoyment involves more than positive emotions, with simple and complex thoughts and reflection, behaviors, and social interactions also important dimensions of the entertainment experience. Specifically, media psychologists also explore the ways that audiences use media to make better sense of their lives, to pursue meaningfulness and insight, and to explore the beautiful complexity of the human condition; we discuss those perspectives in Chapters 5 and 6. In this chapter, we focus solely on **hedonic** entertainment.

BOX 4.1 WHY *HEDONIC* ENTERTAINMENT?

In Greek mythology, Hedone, the daughter of Eros and Psyche, was the goddess of sensual pleasure and delight. In fact, her name is virtually the same as the Greek word for pleasure: *hêdonê*. Philosophers in various cultures have for millennia mused about the relationship between pleasure and virtue, contentment, and well-being. As a result, hedonism developed as a school of thought emphasizing, in simplistic terms, that the seeking of pleasure and the avoidance of pain are foundational to life and happiness. You may recall from Chapter 3 that positive psychologists adopted the term *hedonic* to refer to subjective well-being and happiness, primarily characterized in terms of positive and negative affect. This is often in contrast to psychological or eudaimonic well-being, which focuses more on meaningfulness. Media scholars have done the same in discussions of entertainment experiences, differentiating those that primarily elicit and involve positive emotions as *hedonic* from *eudaimonic* ones that feature mixed affect, contemplation, and meaning-making (see Chapters 5 and 6).

The study of hedonic entertainment has developed along two primary lines of inquiry: (1) what motivates people to seek out media use and to select particular content (or "entertainment selection processes"), and (2) how content and audience factors interact in the reception process to facilitate enjoyment (or "entertainment theory"). We dedicate a section to each below.

Entertainment Selection Processes

Much of positive media psychology is based on a functionalist perspective. Therefore, it is assumed that hedonic media entertainment serves various social and psychological functions in the lives of audience members. Over the past half century, studies of media-use motivations and selection have largely fallen under two broad research traditions: uses and gratifications and selective exposure. These traditions share a basic assumption about all humans: that we are pleasure seekers (see Box 4.1). Our experiences show us that media content can help us in our pursuit of pleasure. The uses and gratifications approach and selective exposure research help explain how that is the case.

In 1944, social psychologist Herta Herzog explored why people listened to daytime radio serials (like soap operas), finding that females in particular reported tuning in to more programs when they were experiencing more difficulties in their daily lives. Most scholars consider hers to be the first study to take the approach that would eventually be called **uses and gratifications** (U&G). Blumler and Katz (1974) outlined the basics of the approach: People have social and psychological needs that they presume media can meet. As a result, people seek out different content at different times depending on those needs, with the expectation that the specific content selected will gratify those needs. Thus, the approach assumes that people are motivated to select (and avoid) particular media content at different times. Further, the approach assumes that people are aware of and can accurately report their motivations for selecting media at different times for different need-related reasons. The U&G approach gained widespread acceptance and popularity in media studies in the 1970s and 1980s.

The roots of selective exposure theory also date back many decades. In the mid-1950s, social scientists began to understand that people typically seek information that is consistent with their prevailing attitudes, beliefs, and thoughts (for more information, see balance theory, Heider, 1958; and cognitive dissonance, Festinger, 1957). Furthermore, people tend to avoid information they know will contradict their existing attitudes and belief structures. These perspectives led to the understanding that when people encounter information incongruent with existing beliefs, they experience psychological and cognitive distress, which leads them to seek out ways to alleviate the dissonance and distress. One way to avoid this problem is to seek out information that *is* congruent with existing attitudes and to avoid information that would produce dissonance. When such choices are made within the context of media use, the behavioral process is referred to as **selective exposure** (Zillmann & Bryant, 1985). Individuals most often intentionally—but usually unconsciously—choose media content that is presumed to be, by and large, consistent with their existing attitudes, beliefs, values, personality traits, moods, and thoughts. For entertainment scholars, selective exposure naturally extends to include the selection of media content that not only fits with our basic sense of self and prevailing circumstances but that also presumably brings pleasure.

In many ways, selective exposure theory sounds like the uses and gratifications perspective. In fact, the basic premise of U&G is that people selectively expose themselves to certain content in order to gratify certain perceived needs. One key difference though is selective exposure scholars argue that the motivation to use specific media content is typically beyond conscious consideration; in contrast, U&G scholars see media selection as more of a conscious process, with individuals considering needs and making choices accordingly. More differences exist between the two perspectives, but for our purposes this distinction is enough. Both perspectives have decades of research findings supporting their basic arguments. Therefore, both perspectives offer valid ways of thinking about media choice and need: At times, it is likely a conscious decision, and at other times not. Because of this, the various findings from the two perspectives are discussed together below.

The motivations to select entertainment are, in large part, directly related to enjoyment. Selective exposure theory argues that media users come to learn to associate particular content with positive outcomes. Thus, people generally select entertainment because of the positive outcomes anticipated (and desired) from doing so, with those expectations based on past experiences with similar content.

Some of those motivations are consistent and persistent among audiences and across time. Other motivations for media selection vary across situations and individuals. Furthermore, the needs discussed below should not be thought of as mutually exclusive from each other; in other words, media content is rarely selected for only one reason or to meet only one need. Hedonic media selection is a complex phenomenon, motivated by numerous factors simultaneously.

Foundational Needs

The drive for hedonic media entertainment can, on one level, be tied to persistent basic or foundational human needs arising from evolutionary, biological, or core psychological processes. All of these, in one way or another, are tied to the ongoing pursuit of pleasure.

Need for "Play"

All mammals participate in play activities. And they do so for similar reasons. In general, play helps to promote the development of skills that serve important adaptive functions: hunting, predator avoidance, learning of social ranks, and social communication, among others. Across millennia, humans also developed the ability to play imaginatively; think back to the make-believe games you used to play on the playground. Imaginative play allows us to create and interact within safe, secondary realities where we can try on new roles, expand our usual sense of self, act and think in ways that we usually wouldn't, and learn to cope with and compensate for constraints and limitations that we encounter in our physical and social worlds. Play is often thought of as just a child's activity, but adults continue to play sports, board games, online games, and many others throughout their lifetime. In fact, a 2019 study by the American Association for Retired People (AARP) found that nearly 40% of people 70 years and older regularly play some sort of video game.

Communication scholar Peter Vorderer, another pioneer in the study of media entertainment, argued that media entertainment offers a similar alternate reality as imaginative play. That is, media entertainment facilitates temporary shifts in perceptions of reality during which audience members access narrative worlds filled with jubilant, disappointing, suspenseful, challenging, and rewarding situations. By "playing" in these safe and controlled secondary environments, individuals learn how to cope with and compensate for their material and existential problems and shortcomings (Vorderer, 2001). For example, narratives featuring antihero protagonists like HBO's *The Sopranos* have been shown to provide viewers with a "moral sandbox" in which they can ponder morally questionable responses to social situations (Eden, Daalmans, van Ommen, & Weljers, 2017). And doing so is pleasurable. Ultimately, because of opportunities to explore these and countless other possible realities, humans today are intrinsically motivated to frequently seek out various forms of (media) entertainment as "play."

Life Balance

The human body is equipped with internal systems that automatically try to keep it regulated for optimal functioning and survival. For example, the sympathetic and parasympathetic nervous systems work together to regulate heart rate, returning the body to a state of balance (or homeostasis). Over time, as social and physical environments became more complex, humans developed nonautomated systems, like decision-making and reasoning, to support the struggle for a balanced life and well-being. These systems allow us to manipulate and arrange our environments, when necessary, to promote positive emotions, moving ourselves back toward life balance. One environmental input that can achieve this goal is the selection of media entertainment. That is, entertainment can function as one of the many means through which humans govern the balance of their lives for well-being and survival.

Autonomy, Competence, Relatedness

According to self-determination theory (Deci & Ryan, 2000; see also Chapter 3), all people are intrinsically motivated to pursue goals and activities that help to satisfy three basic needs essential for psychological growth, well-being, and happiness: autonomy, competence, and relatedness. In other words, everyone shares the need do things that allow them to act in a way that is in keeping with their own sense of self (autonomy), to feel challenged by but also effective in their environment (competence), and to feel connected to others (relatedness). Media entertainment use is thought to be one such intrinsically motivated activity. Individuals are free to select media content that is in keeping with their sense of self (autonomy), they can choose content that they can comprehend or master (competence), and they can choose media experiences that involve others (such as going to the movies with a friend) or that contain characters with whom they can relate (relatedness). As a result, increased happiness, pleasure, and well-being are experienced. For example, Ryan and colleagues (2006) showed that playing video games alone can help the player meet autonomy and competence needs, through game and in-play selection and through mastery of the challenges presented in the game respectively. Further, the researchers found that playing games with others online can also help satisfy relatedness needs, meaning that playing multiplayer online games can assist with the satisfaction of three basic needs that all humans possess.

Situational Needs

In addition to these persistent needs that all people have, audience members are motivated to select hedonic media entertainment based on situational needs. Many of these needs are the ones consistently identified in U&G and selective exposure studies with various media, including television, music, games, social media, and other online content.

Mood Regulation

Negative moods—like boredom, stress, and frustration—are unavoidable. We all experience them from time to time. Mood management theory (Zillmann, 1988) explains how individuals as pleasure-seekers and dissonance-avoiders often select media content to disrupt and overcome negative mood states, as well as to maintain and prolong positive ones. Moods differ from one another in a variety of ways, including arousal level (e.g., stress vs. calm) and hedonic valence (e.g., pleasant vs. sad). Zillmann argued that media contents also differ from one another along similar dimensions: excitatory (or arousal) potential, hedonic valence, and absorption (or engagement) potential. In other words, media content varies in terms of how arousing (*Fast & Furious* vs. *Little Women*), positive or negative (*Dora the Explorer* vs. *Ex Machina*), and absorbing (*Inception* vs. *Ed, Edd n Eddy*) they are. Furthermore, content can either match or not match an audience member's current mood (particularly in terms of valence); that is, content can have a high or low semantic affinity with one's current mood state.

Mood management theory states that media users come to learn associations between content and its impact on mood through experience. As a result, when people are in negative mood states, they tend to seek out content that they have come to associate with positive moods, and when they are already in a positive mood, they seek out content that they think should maintain it. For instance, bored individuals (low arousal) are more likely to choose to listen to fast-paced music (high excitatory potential) to increase their arousal, whereas stressed individuals (high arousal) are more likely to select slow and soothing music (low excitatory potential). Similarly, an angry person (negative state) might select more engaging fare like a complex mystery (high absorption potential) to interrupt their thoughts about and ruminations on the event or situation that caused their anger in the first place, thereby overcoming the negative mood. Also, someone saddened by a romantic breakup might pass on the somber love story (high semantic affinity) and instead choose a light-hearted film or show (low semantic affinity) for the evening's viewing.

The predictions of mood management theory have received extensive research support over the years, with a variety of media content and formats. However, it should be noted that mood optimization concerns do not *always* drive media selection. Other situational factors—like the need for information ("I know it will make me mad, but I really should watch this presidential debate") or ritual ("I always watch this show every Sunday night")—can and often do override such concerns. Also, mood is often just one of the needs that influences media selection (or, for that matter, your general behavior) at any given time.

Escape

Another often-cited motivation for selecting hedonic entertainment across a variety of media platforms is escape (or diversion, or to pass time). In general, the term describes an "escape from" (motivation to avoid) some current unsatisfying real-world circumstance, although it can also refer to an "escape to" a media world (motivation to approach). With regard to the former, Henning and Vorderer (2001) identified three escape motivations: sociological, social-psychological, and individual-psychological. Sociological escapism is driven by stresses and problems arising from work or from work–life imbalance. Social-psychological escapism is motivated by negative (non-work-related) social interactions and situations. Individual-psychological escapism is driven by situations not socially caused, like "having nothing to do." Individuals seek out media for all three purposes from time to time, but individual-psychological factors may be the most prevalent motivation for selecting media for escape. Regardless, the ability for media to take us away from the pressures and stresses of our daily lives is surely (almost always) experienced as pleasurable.

Recovery

Related to both mood and escape, recovery is another need motivating media use and selection. In this context, recovery is conceptualized as the replenishing of physical and psychological resources following their depletion through work or stress (Sonnentag & Zijlstra, 2006). Sleep can lead to recovery, but increasingly evidence suggests that media use can as well.

The process of recovery is thought to involve four dimensions: psychological detachment (from the stressor), relaxation, control (over one's activities), and mastery (of challenges, which helps to build internal resources). In a series of studies, Reinecke and colleagues (2009; 2011) demonstrated that video game play can address all four dimensions of recovery. Similarly, Rieger and her colleagues (2014) showed that hedonically oriented film clips can promote psychological detachment and relaxation. Furthermore, media-induced recovery experiences can lead to positive and pleasurable outcomes like self-reported feelings of vitality.

Learning

Although some people dismiss media entertainment as trivial and frivolous, it is indisputable that entertainment use can be motivated by learning. A prime example of this is prosocial children's television, which we discuss at length in Chapter 11. In fact, many immigrants claim to have learned the languages and cultural tokens of their adopted countries through children's programming, which often is designed to be both universally accessible and intellectually and culturally enriching. The documentary film and podcast industries leverage the learning motivation for entertainment consumption, as do sports and live game streaming platforms like Twitch.

Social Utility

A lot of entertainment content centers on the inner thoughts and social lives of characters. Because of this, audiences encounter a never-ending stream of social information. At times, we are specifically motivated to consume entertainment to wade through that stream. Katz, Haas, and Gurevitch (1973) argued that media use can meet needs related to one's self (e.g., confidence, credibility) and needs related to others (e.g., strengthening contact with family, friends, the world). At times, we select entertainment to satisfy a wide range of social needs: watching a popular show to be prepared for conversations that everyone will be having at the office the next day, binging reality television to feel better about ourselves (often through feeling sorry for the contestants), adolescent boys viewing horror films to perform behaviors related to social constructions of masculinity (e.g., laughing, not appearing scared), or viewing a drama to cope with the loss of a loved one, just to name a few.

Beyond these various needs that we seek to meet through media use, patterns of hedonic entertainment selection can also be observed along other lines, such as cultural, demographic, and personality characteristics. We discuss these issues at length in Chapter 12.

Reception and Enjoyment of Media Entertainment

The second major line of entertainment research—often referred to as **entertainment theory**—explores how content and audience factors interact during the media reception process to facilitate enjoyment. We highlight a few prominent theories and concepts now.

Importance of Characters and Narrative Resolutions

Affective disposition theory (ADT) explains how and why we enjoy media narratives (Zillmann & Cantor, 1976). More specifically, ADT describes (1) how viewers take emotional sides with (or "form affective dispositions toward") media characters, (2) how doing so triggers hopes and fears (or "anticipatory emotional reactions") toward the unfolding events in the story that involve those characters, and (3) how those emotional responses, along with the outcomes portrayed, result in enjoyment.

According to ADT, the emotional affiliations that audiences form and hold toward characters in a media narrative play a primary role in the process of enjoyment. Most entertainment centers on the clash between good and evil: superheroes and super villains, law enforcement and criminal, young lovers battling life's unfairness, Link and Ganon (for *Zelda* fans). Because humans are by nature social creatures, we generally side with the forces of good because of moral considerations tied to evolutionary concern for safety and longevity. This is true in the real world and in mediated worlds. As a result, audience members morally monitor and evaluate the behaviors and motivations of characters, leading to the formation of dispositions along an emotional continuum, from extremely positive through indifference to extremely negative. Of course, other factors can influence feelings toward characters—attitudes about the actor, attractiveness, dialogue, subject matter, etc.—but studies consistently demonstrate that moral considerations (especially ones related to empathy) are central to liking a character. Given variability in values, beliefs, and norms, it is unsurprising, then, that people differ on the characters they love and hate and, as a result, on the narratives they enjoy the most.

The more we like characters, the more we feel *for* them by empathizing with their pain and struggles, as well as their joy and victories. Further, the more we like them, the more we feel *with* (or against) them: sharing in the hope that good will triumph over evil and fearing that the opposite will come to pass. These hopes and fears are called **anticipatory emotions**. Over the course of a story, audiences ride an "emotional roller coaster" with the characters, ultimately leading to an outcome or resolution. According to ADT, enjoyment is experienced as the pleasure that we experience in relation to the resolution. If the story outcome lines up with the one anticipated and desired by the audience member, then pleasure is experienced (relative to the intensity of those anticipations as guided by the intensity of the dispositions held toward the characters). If the story outcome in some way does not line up with the one anticipated and desired, then less pleasure is experienced. Therefore, according to ADT, enjoyment is a function of the affective dispositions held toward characters and the outcomes associated with those characters as revealed in the unfolding narrative. More specifically, enjoyment increases when liked characters experience positive outcomes and/or when disliked characters experience negative ones. Conversely, enjoyment suffers when liked characters experience negative outcomes and/or disliked characters experience positive ones. The intensity of enjoyment is in large part dependent upon the intensity of the affective dispositions held toward those characters. To be clear: Other factors beyond dispositions toward characters and narrative resolutions influence enjoyment. But the basic ADT formula has been shown to explain well a significant portion of enjoyment across a variety of media contents: humor, drama with traditional heroes as well as antiheroes, sports, horror, action films, reality TV, video games, and even news. In other words, support for the ADT explanation of the enjoyment process is widespread.

Content Features

In addition to characters and story outcomes, many other content features are associated with increased enjoyment, including frightening depictions, interactivity, moral complexity, and aesthetics. A detailed review of all of these issues is impossible in this chapter. But we do offer a brief discussion of two important and common narrative elements linked with enjoyment: violence and suspense.

People often criticize media content for being "too violent." In response, media content providers say that they are just giving people what they want. Do we find violence enjoyable? The easy answer for many people is "yes." But the questions "why?" and "for whom?" are more complicated. Only a handful of studies have directly examined the enjoyment of the same content with and without violence. As one example, Bryant, Comisky, and Zillmann (1981) varied the degree of violence in clips from a professional football game. Male viewers reported more enjoyment as the degree of roughness in the play increased. A similar pattern was observed with female viewers but was not statistically significant. But not all violence is equally enjoyable. Numerous factors such as who is the perpetrator and who is the victim, the justifiability of the violence, the centrality of the violence to the plot, and many others impact the enjoyment of violent content. Further, most explanations for why we enjoy violent content typically place less importance on the violent acts themselves and more on the outcomes resulting from the violence, like the restoration of justice or the defeat of evil.

With regard to suspense, why should audience members enjoy the distress associated with witnessing a beloved media character struggle against terrible odds and imminent threats of harm or even death? This "paradox of suspense" has been explored extensively by entertainment theorists. Carroll (1990) described suspense in fiction as the emotional apprehension and anticipation experienced during a scene or event critical to the resolution of a narrative that offers the conflict between two potential outcomes: one morally superior but in doubt, the other evil and likely. When a beloved character is facing certain suffering and defeat, viewers experience suspense via empathic concern; suspense is greater when the feared evil outcome seems more likely to occur than not. Furthermore, more suspense generally leads to more enjoyment, especially when a hoped-for outcome is revealed. That is, you can enjoy a thrilling, back-and-forth basketball game between your favorite team and its biggest rival no matter the outcome, but enjoyment should be much greater if your favorite team actually wins. **Excitation transfer theory** (Zillmann, 1971) explains why this is the case (see Box 4.2 for more details).

Reception Processes

Several additional processes contribute to the joy experienced during hedonic media reception. These occur situationally to a varying degree, based on the content and the audience. As a result, they differentially impact enjoyment at different times.

BOX 4.2 ENJOYING SUSPENSE

What is the most suspenseful movie you've ever seen? Alfred Hitchock's *Psycho* is an oldie, but for many people the shower scene in the film is still incredibly suspenseful (we encourage you to Google it if you have never seen it). When we encounter disruptions in our environment—like the suspenseful moments in a movie—our bodies, through the sympathetic nervous system, automatically react: our palms sweat, our heart races, our muscles tense. As discussed in Chapter 2, collectively, these reactions are called **arousal**. When aroused, our bodies naturally start trying to get us back to homeostasis, a state of balance that promotes optimal health and survival. But when we encounter another suspenseful scene (and another and another) before our system can reach homeostasis, the arousal from the subsequent scenes builds upon whatever arousal remains from the earlier scenes, leading to what feels like even more and more suspense. This process is called **excitation transfer** (Zillmann, 1971; 1991). More often than not, when we are at this highly elevated state of arousal, the narrative outcome is shown: the chase scene ends, the explosions stop, the whistle blows, the lovers' eyes meet across the crowded room, etc. The outcome itself is also arousing and usually enjoyable; so, our arousal level builds even more. But our brains perceive that *all* of that built-up arousal is due to the final scene. As a result, highly suspenseful narratives that have a happy ending are felt and perceived as incredibly enjoyable because our bodies have been unable to return to homeostasis over the course of the film due to a continual barrage of suspenseful scenes, leading to a building up of physiological arousal that we attribute to the joyous outcome, once it is revealed.

Narrative Engagement

Viewers, readers, and players alike often share the common experience of becoming completely immersed inside a narrative world, losing track of time and of their material surroundings. This experience can broadly be described as narrative engagement. When media consumers experience a high degree of engagement, they feel as if they are actually present in the narrative world, with their emotional and cognitive capacities dedicated to experiencing the characters and events as if they were real. Several related constructs are involved in and associated with narrative engagement, including transportation (Green, Brock, & Kaufman, 2004), presence (Lombard & Ditton, 1997), and flow (Sherry, 2004). In their model of narrative comprehension and engagement, Busselle and Bilandzic (2008) argued that perceptions of realism are key for narrative engagement to occur. Consumers of entertainment, by default, accept that narratives are fictional and eagerly shift their sense of perspective from the real world to adopt that of the narrative world, leading to greater narrative engagement. However, engagement is interrupted when the audience perceives unexplained inconsistencies or implausibility between the narrative and the real world (external realism) or within the narrative itself (internal realism). Their model ultimately demonstrates how narrative engagement facilitates enjoyment.

Character Identification

Related to narrative engagement and to the affective dispositions discussed earlier, character identification is an imaginative process in which an audience member merges with and takes on the perspective of a character (Cohen, 2001). When media users highly identify with a character, they are able to understand and appreciate the character's motivations, emotions, thoughts, and actions while still maintaining their own sense of self. Character identification is a primary means through which audience members become engaged in a narrative world. At times, audiences also experience wishful identification, which is the desire to be like or act like a character (Hoffner 1996). Clearly, we do not always identify or wishfully identify with media characters, but when we do—assuming positive things happen to those characters—our enjoyment tends to increase.

Parasocial Interactions

Like identification, parasocial interactions (PSIs) take place between audience members and media characters. The term describes the imagined, one-way social interactions between the two (Horton & Wohl, 1956). Put another way, PSI describes the way audience members react to characters as friends or companions when watching a movie, TV show, YouTube channel, gaming stream, or even reading a book. PSIs are experienced like face-to-face interactions; for instance, we might speak to the screen, calling the character by name. Of course, PSIs occur without the expectation that the media character will speak back to us. Over time and multiple interactions, audiences can form parasocial relationships (PSRs) with media characters. For example, studies show that readers and viewers of the *Harry Potter* series routinely thought of and even talked about Harry, Hermione, and Ron as if they were friends. The experience of PSIs and PSRs further contribute to the enjoyment and other emotional reactions we experience with media content. In fact, parasocial processes can be so important to media enjoyment that when a character dies, gets written out of a series, or a show is unexpectedly cancelled, the end of that relationship—that is, the resulting parasocial breakup—can trigger the same negative emotions that arise when we end other friendships (Cohen, 2004).

Social Comparisons

As humans, we routinely compare ourselves to others as a natural part of our ongoing identity formation (Festinger, 1954). At times, we compare ourselves to people we perceive as having a characteristic we desire (upward assimilative comparisons); at other times, we judge ourselves against those we perceive as inferior to us on some dimension (downward contrastive comparisons). Media entertainment, with its wide cast of characters, offers a never-ending opportunity for both types of social comparisons. For instance, studies of reality television and daytime talk shows reveal that viewers often enjoy comparing themselves to other people whose lives seem worse off than their own. However, content can also trigger comparisons that make us feel bad about ourselves—for instance, perceiving that we are not as attractive or talented as someone on a show—which can lead to less enjoyment.

Reception Context

A final factor impacting enjoyment, which has received relatively less research attention, is the social context in which entertainment is encountered. As media technologies have become less expensive and more portable, the entertainment experience has become increasingly personalized and solitary. Nevertheless, entertainment is still routinely enjoyed with others in living rooms, minivans, cineplexes, sports bars, arcades, and online. In some situations, the social context is required for enjoyment. For example, massively multiplayer online role-playing games (MMORPGs) involve interacting with and against others in the game world, with the interactions themselves—at times without regard to success or failure in the game—playing a prominent role in enjoyment. In other situations, like posting real-time comments to Twitter during the airing of a much-anticipated television season premier, interactions with virtual others through a second screen may play a dynamic, supporting role in the enjoyment process compared to what is occurring on the "first screen."

In terms of the physical presence of others, shared emotional reactions can facilitate enjoyment. **Emotional contagion**, which is defined as the emotional convergence with another person through the mimicry of and synchronization with their emotional behaviors, routinely occurs while consuming entertainment with others. Of particular note is the influence of another person's laughter on one's own laugh response. In fact, the canned laughter or "laugh track" that often accompanies television sitcoms has been shown to enhance laughter and enjoyment in audiences. Another person's applause has been shown to have a similar sway on one's appreciation of, for instance, music.

Summary

One of the primary ways that media content and technologies contribute to our well-being and happiness is through the enjoyment and pleasure that they bring to our lives. Often that pleasure is experienced in relation to needs being satisfied. Some of those needs, like autonomy, competence, and relatedness, are foundational to everyone's psychological makeup. Other needs, such as mood, escape, and companionship, vary across situations, time, and people. Regardless, uses and gratifications and selective exposure research demonstrates how people choose media to meet various needs. Enjoyment of a particular media content results from several psychological processes that occur during reception, with great emphasis placed on emotional responses to characters. Affective disposition theory, identification, parasocial interactions and relationships, and social comparisons all explain ways that characters can impact enjoyment. Engagement with the story world and social contexts also contribute to media enjoyment. Additional factors further enhance or detract from enjoyment, but the processes discussed above are the ones most closely related to the use of media for enjoyment and pleasure, leading to subjective well-being.

References

Blumler, J. G., & Katz, E. (1974). *The uses of mass communications: Current perspectives on gratifications research*. Beverly Hills, CA: Sage.

Bryant, J., Comisky, P., & Zillmann, D. (1981). The appeal of rough-and-tumble play in televised professional football. *Communication Quarterly*, 29, 256–262. doi:10.1080/01463378109369413.

Busselle, R., & Bilandzic, H. (2008). Fictionality and perceived realism in experiencing stories: A model of narrative comprehension and engagement. *Communication Theory*, 18, 255–280. doi:10.1111/j.1468-2885.2008.00322.x.

Cohen, J. (2001). Defining identification: A theoretical look at the identification of audiences with media characters. *Mass Communication and Society*, 4, 245–264. doi:10.1207/S15327825MCS0403_01.

Cohen, J. (2004). Parasocial break-up from favorite television characters: The role of attachment styles and relationship intensity. *Journal of Social and Personal relationships*, 21, 187–202. doi:10.1177/0265407504041374.

Deci, E. L., & Ryan, R. M. (2000). The "what" and "why" of goal pursuits: Human needs and the self-determination of behavior. *Psychological Inquiry*, 11, 227–268. doi:10.1207/S15327965PLI1104_01.

Eden, A., Daalmans, S., van Ommen, M., & Weljers, A. (2017). Melfi's choice: Morally conflicted content leads to moral rumination in viewers. *Journal of Media Ethics*, 32, 142–153. doi:10.1080/23736992.2017.1329019.

Festinger, L. (1954). A theory of social comparison processes. *Human Relations*, 7, 117–140. doi:10.1177/001872675400700202.

Festinger, L. (1957). *A theory of cognitive dissonance*. Stanford, CA: Stanford University Press.

Green, M. C., Brock, T. C., & Kaufman, G. F. (2004). Understanding media enjoyment: The role of transportation into narrative worlds. *Communication Theory*, 14, 311–327. doi:10.1111/j.1468-2885.2004.tb00317.x.

Heider, F. (1958). *The psychology of interpersonal relations*. Hillsdale, NJ: Lawrence Erlbaum Associates.

Henning, B., & Vorderer, P. (2001). Psychological escapism: Predicting the amount of television viewing by need for cognition. *Journal of Communication*, 51, 100–120. doi:10.1111/j.1460-2466.2001.tb02874.x.

Hoffner, C. (1996). Children's wishful identification and parasocial interaction with favorite television characters. *Journal of Broadcasting & Electronic Media*, 40, 389–402. doi:10.1080/08838159609364360.

Horton, D., & Wohl, R. R. (1956). Mass communication and para-social interaction. *Psychiatry: Journal for the Study of Interpersonal Processes*, 19, 215–229. doi:10.1080/00332747.1956.11023049.

Katz, E., Haas, H., & Gurevitch, M. (1973). On the use of the mass media for important things. *American Sociological Review*, 38, 164–181. doi:10.2307/2094393.

Lombard, M., & Ditton, T. (1997). At the heart of it all: The concept of presence. *Journal of Computer-Mediated Communication*, 3(2). doi:10.1111/j.1083-6101.1997.tb00072.x.

Ryan, R. M., Rigby, C. S. & Przybylski, A. (2006). The motivational pull of video games: A self-determination theory approach. *Motivation and Emotion*, 30, 344–360. doi:10.1007/s11031-006-9051-8.

Sherry, J. L. (2004). Flow and media enjoyment. *Communication Theory*, 14, 328–347. doi:10.1111/j.1468-2885.2004.tb00318.x.

Sonnentag, S., & Zijlstra, F. R. (2006). Job characteristics and off-job activities as predictors of need for recovery, well-being, and fatigue. *Journal of Applied Psychology*, 91, 330–350. doi:10.1037/0021-9010.91.2.330.

Vorderer, P. (2001). It's all entertainment—sure. But what exactly is entertainment? Communication research, media psychology, and the explanation of entertainment experiences. *Poetics*, 29, 247–261. doi:10.1016/S0304-422X(01)00037-7.

Zillmann, D. (1971). Excitation transfer in communication-mediated aggressive behavior. *Journal of Experimental Social Psychology*, 7, 419–434. doi:10.1016/0022-1031(71)90075-8.

Zillmann, D. (1988). Mood management through communication choices. *American Behavioral Scientist*, 31, 327–340. doi:10.1177/000276488031003005.

Zillmann, D. (1991). The logic of suspense and mystery. In J. Bryant & D. Zillmann (Eds.), *Responding to the screen: Reception and reaction processes* (pp. 281–303). Hillsdale, NJ: Lawrence Erlbaum Associates.

Zillmann, D., & Bryant, J. (Eds.) (1985). *Selective exposure to communication*. Hillsdale, NJ: Lawrence Erlbaum Associates.

Zillmann, D., & Bryant, J. (1994). Entertainment as media effect. In J. Bryant & D. Zillmann (Eds.), *Media effects: Advances in theory and research* (pp. 437–461). Hillsdale, NJ: Lawrence Erlbaum Associates.

Zillmann, D., & Cantor, J. (1976). A disposition theory of humor and mirth. In A. J. Chapman & H. C. Foot (Eds.), *Humour and laughter: Theory, research and applications* (pp. 93–115). London, UK: John Wiley & Sons.

Additional Reading

Banjo, O. (2011). What are *you* laughing at? Examining White identity and enjoyment of Black entertainment. *Journal of Broadcasting & Electronic Media*, 55, 137–159. doi:10.1080/08838151.2011.570822.

Banjo, O. O., Appiah, O., Wang, Z., Brown, C., & Walther, W. O. (2015). Co-viewing effects of ethnic-oriented programming: An examination of in-group bias and racial comedy exposure. *Journalism & Mass Communication Quarterly*, 92, 662–680. doi:10.1177/1077699015581804.

Bryant, J., & Davies, J. (2006). Selective exposure processes. In J. Bryant & P. Vorderer (Eds.), *Psychology of entertainment* (pp. 19–33). Mahwah, NJ: Lawrence Erlbaum Associates.

Csikszentmihalyi, M. (1990). *Flow: The psychology of optimal experience*. New York, NY: Harper & Row.

Ferchaud, A., Grzeslo, J., Orme, S., & LaGroue, J. (2018). Parasocial attributes and YouTube personalities: Exploring content trends across the most subscribed YouTube channels. *Computers in Human Behavior*, 80, 88–96. doi:10.1016/j.chb.2017.10.041.

Goldstein, J. H. (Ed.). (1998). *Why we watch: The attractions of violent entertainment*. New York, NY: Oxford University Press.

Klimmt, C., Hartmann, T., & Schramm, H. (2006). Parasocial interactions and relationships. In J. Bryant & P. Vorderer (Eds.), *Psychology of entertainment* (pp. 291–313). Mahwah, NJ: Lawrence Erlbaum Associates.

Knobloch-Westerwick, S. (2015). *Choice and preference in media use: Advances in selective-exposure theory and research*. New York, NY: Routledge.

Lewis, R. J., Tamborini, R., & Weber, R. (2014). Testing a dual-process model of media enjoyment and appreciation. *Journal of Communication*, 64, 397–416. doi:10.1111/jcom.12101.

Raney, A. A. (2006). The psychology of disposition-based theories of media enjoyment. In J. Bryant & P. Vorderer (Eds.), *Psychology of entertainment* (pp. 137–150). Mahwah, NJ: Lawrence Erlbaum Associates.

Raney, A. A., & Ji, Q. (2017). Entertaining each other? Modeling the socially shared television viewing experience. *Human Communication Research*, 43, 424–435. doi:10.1111/hcre.12121.

Sanders, M. S. (2010). Making a good (bad) impression: Examining the cognitive processes of disposition theory to form a synthesized model of media character impression formation. *Communication Theory*, 20, 147–168. doi:10.1111/j.1468-2885.2010.01358.x.

Tamborini, R., Bowman, N. D., Eden, A., Grizzard, M., & Organ, A. (2010). Defining media enjoyment as the satisfaction of intrinsic needs. *Journal of Communication*, 60, 758–777. doi:10.1111/j.1460-2466.2010.01513.x.

Vorderer, P., Klimmt, C., & Ritterfeld, U. (2004). Enjoyment: At the heart of media entertainment. *Communication Theory*, 14, 388–408. doi:10.1111/j.1468-2885.2004.tb00321.x.

Vorderer, P., Wulff, H. J., & Friedrichsen, M. (Eds.) (1996). *Suspense: Conceptualizations, theoretical analyses, and empirical explorations*. Mahwah, NJ: Lawrence Erlbaum Associates.

Zillmann, D., Bryant, J., & Sapolsky, B. S. (1979). The enjoyment of watching sports contests. In J. H. Goldstein (Ed.), *Sports, games and play* (pp. 297–335). Hillsdale, NJ: Lawrence Erlbaum Associates.

5

MEANINGFUL ENTERTAINMENT

Source: Shutterstock 1520532782

Trevor, a 7th grader, takes the assignment of his social science teacher to change the world for the better seriously. He challenges himself and others to do a favor for three people, who then have to each "pay it forward" to three others. For his first favor, Trevor gives a homeless man a place to sleep, who in turn helps repair his mother's car and saves a suicidal woman's life. The ripple effects begin to be felt across whole city. For Trevor's second favor, he plays matchmaker for his single mother and his teacher, who both had persevered through many hardships in life and, therefore, share similar vulnerabilities. Tragically, while Trevor is conducting his third act of kindness, helping a bullied kid in school, he gets injured and dics. The whole neighborhood meets in front of Trevor's house to pay their condolences to the grieving new couple and show their gratitude for the change Trevor has brought to their lives. You might know this story: It is the plot of the movie *Pay It Forward* (2000). As audience members, when we encounter media content like this we often experience bittersweetness, poignancy, and contemplation. Positive media psychologists refer to movies and other content like this as **eudaimonic or meaningful entertainment**. Such content concerns the deeper aspects of humanity and can provide insight, meaning, and social connectedness for media users (Oliver & Bartsch, 2010; Oliver & Raney, 2011; Wirth, Hofer, & Schramm, 2012). In this chapter, we outline the specifics of eudaimonic entertainment experiences, their effects, and theories that explain their attraction.

Two-Factor Model of Entertainment

In the last chapter, we explored the various ways that people seek out media content to fulfill our basic hedonistic needs. From an historical perspective, this has been the focus of most entertainment studies by media psychologists over the past century. But by the beginning of the 21st century, it was clear that the entertainment models and theories that had emerged had difficulty in explaining the appeal, function, and enjoyment of sad and poignant entertainment. To address this shortcoming, scholars developed a two-factor model of entertainment (Oliver & Bartsch, 2010; Vorderer, 2011). The first factor is the one discussed in Chapter 4: entertainment consumed for purely hedonic and pleasurable reasons. The second factor is the focus of this chapter: entertainment consumed for eudaimonic (or meaningful) reasons, leading to more complex experiences involving mixed affect, feeling tender, moved, contemplation, reflection, and meaning-making.

The scholarly literature in the area states—and our own media experiences confirm—that people turn to entertainment for more than pleasure seeking and unpleasant mood repair. Routinely, individuals seek out entertainment that makes them feel sad and thoughtful, giving rise to the opportunity to cope with their own hardships or obtain a sense of meaning and purpose in life. Thus, even short-term negative feelings can contribute to emotional stability and well-being in the long term by strengthening a person's ability to deal and cope with the difficult aspects of life and satisfy basic intrinsic needs (per self-determination theory; see Chapter 3). In particular, research has shown that eudaimonic entertainment experiences can contribute to a sense of connection, care toward others, or feeling cared for by others (relatedness needs), perceptions of oneself as effective in manipulating the environment in a way that results in valued outcomes (competence needs), and having a sense of control, volition, or freedom when engaging in an activity (autonomy needs; see Tamborini, Bowman, Eden, Grizzard, & Organ, 2010). In addition to the satisfaction of innate needs, eudaimonic entertainment also involves specific media gratifications that are different from those experienced during hedonic entertainment use. Bartsch (2012) conceptualized various **eudaimonic media gratifications**, which include emotional engagement with the character, social sharing of emotions, contemplative emotional experiences, empathic sadness, vicarious release of emotions, and thrill.

Eudaimonic entertainment commonly involves stories that address difficult aspects of the human condition, such as life struggles, death and suffering, and portrayals of human virtue such as kindness, helpfulness, love, and connection (e.g., Oliver, Hartmann, & Woolley, 2012). Naturally, such content provides more opportunities to contemplate life's deeper meanings. Admittedly, eudaimonic films for example rarely generate the top box office revenues. However, they are more likely than hedonic fare to receive critical acclaim through award nominations and wins (e.g., Academy Awards) or audience ratings (e.g., Rotten Tomatoes) (Oliver, Ash, Woolley, Shade, & Kim, 2014).

This is not to suggest that box office hits—such as Marvel's *Avengers: End Game* or *Avatar*—are devoid of content that is meaningful; in fact, they often include storylines about more difficult aspects of the human condition, such as connectedness, kindness, suffering, justice, and sacrifice. But other films, like those nominated for the Academy Award for Best Picture (e.g., 2020: *Parasite, Little Women, Marriage Story*), tend to explore those storylines and themes more deeply. The larger point here is this: Virtually *all* forms of media may be meaningful to *some* audience members, though some forms and genres tend to be more likely to be so. In light of this, researchers tend to speak about **eudaimonic media experiences** more so than eudaimonic media per se, in acknowledgement of the idiosyncratic nature with which media content is perceived and interpreted by the audience and the reality of narrative formulas that often contain a multitude of themes and storylines.

Whereas research has shown that eudaimonic media experiences are more often elicited from drama, history, documentary, or art-film genres as compared to comedy (e.g., Oliver et al., 2012), even hedonically oriented, lighthearted fare (e.g., films like *Bridesmaids* and *Trainwreck*) can include meaningful content—such as depictions of overcoming hardship, suffering, or kindness—and therefore can elicit eudaimonic experiences as well. However, research indicates that some narratives are more likely to elicit eudaimonic experiences than others. Such experiences involve a specific set of affective and cognitive processes and responses that will be outlined now.

Affective Components of Eudaimonic Entertainment Experiences

Appreciation

Everyone has watched what you might call a "sad movie," one that makes you tear up, makes your heart feel heavy, leaves you feeling emotionally spent. Think about the saddest movie you have ever seen. Would you say that you *enjoyed* it? Maybe, but surely not in the same way you enjoyed your favorite comedy or action film. The two-factor model of entertainment attempts to distinguish the outcome (or the evaluation) of hedonic and eudaimonic entertainment experiences. With the former, the term *enjoyment* is used. With the latter, we rely on the term **appreciation**. Appreciation is "an experiential state that is characterized by the perception of deeper meaning, the feeling of being moved, and the motivation to elaborate on thoughts and feelings inspired by the experience" (Oliver & Bartsch, 2010, p. 76). Thus, much like enjoyment, appreciation is the outcome of entertainment. But enjoyment and appreciation are not mutually exclusive or two ends of a continuum. Enjoyment and appreciation can—and do—co-occur with entertainment; the outcomes are not bound to a specific content or situation. That is, an action movie, while primarily enjoyed, can elicit feelings of appreciation (albeit likely to a smaller degree); similarly, touching and tragic films, while generally appreciated, can generate enjoyment as well.

Broadly speaking, appreciation is often related to the perceived artistic quality of the media content, as well as to it having a lasting impression on the viewer (Oliver & Bartsch, 2010). Appreciation responses are characterized by self-reflection, self-acceptance, self-development, and personal growth (Bartsch, 2012; Wirth et al., 2012). For example, Knobloch-Westerwick, Gong, Hagner, and Kerbeykian (2013) found that watching a tragic film lead to self-, relationship, and happiness reflection, which ultimately lead to a positive evaluation of the film. Numerous studies have also established that cognitively challenging narratives, or those with more (morally) complex storylines, lead to greater appreciation than enjoyment (e.g., Lewis, Tamborini, & Weber, 2014; Oliver & Bartsch, 2010).

Mixed Affect

Another way that eudaimonic entertainment experiences differ from hedonic ones is the elicitation of more negative emotions, such as sadness, gloominess, depression, or melancholy. Negative affect, however, does not prevent the simultaneous experience of happiness, cheerfulness, and joy. This occurrence of positive and negative emotions at the same time has been labeled as **mixed affect**, bittersweetness, or poignancy (Bartsch, 2012; Oliver & Raney, 2011; Slater, Oliver, & Appel, 2019). Mixed affect, conceptualized as the co-occurrence of positive and negative affect, has been found to be associated with feelings of elevation, which can lead to an increased awareness about life's values (e.g., "mediated wisdom of experience," see Slater et al. 2019). The emergence of mixed affect is a common characteristic in eudaimonic media experiences.

Elevation

Elevation, often also conceptualized as meaningful affect, is another common eudaimonic entertainment experience. It involves feeling moved, touched, tender, inspired, and compassionate; it is elicited by portrayals of moral beauty such as kindness, generosity, loyalty, or other virtuous behaviors. Elevation is one of several moral or self-transcendent emotions (see Chapter 6), all of which "make people care about the state of the social world, and make them want to do something to improve it" (Haidt & Algoe, 2004, p. 330). That is, they make one focused on others more so than oneself, which is why they are also often referred to as outward-oriented emotions.

In addition to mixed affect, elevation is also often accompanied by specific physiological indicators including a warm feeling in the chest, opening of the chest, a lump in the throat, and chills or goosebumps. Research has shown that elevation is a common response in eudaimonic media experience that can be elicited by news stories depicting extraordinary kindness, inspiring television shows, films, or meaningful social media memes. Multiple research studies have found elevation to be a significant mediator between the relationship of eudaimonic entertainment and outcomes of connectedness to humanity, more favorable attitudes toward diverse others, and altruistic behaviors (see Chapter 6). As such, elevation shows great promise to explain some of the second-order (or downstream) effects from eudaimonic entertainment.

Cognitive Components of Eudaimonic Entertainment Experiences

Cognitive Elaboration

Another way to differentiate hedonic and eudaimonic entertainment experiences is in terms of the cognitive activity elicited. Eudaimonic forms of emotional involvement have been found to be processed systematically or deliberately, compared to hedonic forms of emotional involvement, which are processed heuristically (Lewis et al., 2014; see also the dual-process models of cognitive information processing in Chapter 3, Box 3.1). It is thought that narratives that elicit eudaimonic experiences often feature storylines dealing with difficult aspects of the human condition, resulting in a more complex narrative, which requires more systematic processing to understand. For example, Lewis and colleagues (2014) found that morally complex narratives were processed more slowly when they led to more appreciation than enjoyment. Also, Das, Nobbe, and Oliver (2017) showed that cognitive load impacted mixed affect for an emotionally moving narrative and consequently impacted related behavioral intentions; the research supports the assumption that eudaimonic narratives require elaboration to result in a fully satisfactory entertainment experience. The deliberate processing of narratives with more complex storylines has also been shown to encourage attitude change, issue interest, and information seeking about social and political issues.

Contemplation and Meaning Making

The systematic cognitive processing of entertainment content reflects not only engagement in the moment but also greater mental stimulation or contemplation afterwards. That is, in contrast to hedonic entertainment experiences that often promote escapism and diversion from thinking about troubling issues, eudaimonic experiences encourage just the opposite: contemplation, reflection, and pondering. In many ways, they challenge media consumers to contemplate life's struggles (Bartsch, 2012). Bartsch and her colleagues (2014) found that an emotionally moving narrative elicited more reflection than a less-moving narrative, which in turn predicted an overall positive response to the content. Moreover, they found that the resulting eudaimonic affective states (i.e., mixed affect, feeling moved, moderate arousal, negative valence) predicted reflective thoughts, indicating that contemplation is a direct response to the affective responses to the narrative. For example, feeling sad, moved, touched, and heartbroken after watching Chris Gardner, in *The Pursuit of Happyness*, play-pretending to be hiding from the attack of imaginary dinosaurs in a subway bathroom stall for his son to downplay the reality of their homelessness can force people to reflect and contemplate about the general hardships of life.

Films perceived by audiences to be meaningful have also been shown to elicit thoughts about human connection, love, caring for and maintaining interpersonal relationships, human virtues, the overcoming of struggles, life as fleeting, and an appreciation for the goodness and preciousness of life (Oliver & Hartmann, 2010). Being exposed to portrayals of human struggles, hardship, pain, and suffering challenges the viewer to make meaning out of the negative portrayals. **Meaning-making** is aroused by exposure to a violation of an individual's belief in a just world, where suffering and hardship don't happen to good and moral people (e.g., Chris Gardner in *The Pursuit of Happyness*). The cognitive dissonance from exposure to injustice can be resolved by either focusing on any *material benefit* that the suffering person gains in the end (e.g., in the film *50/50*, the main character suffering from cancer ends up with his romantic interest), or by focusing on *immaterial rewards*, such as greater insight, truth finding, and personal growth. Through contemplation the viewer derives meaning from learning deeper lessons, values, relationships, and purpose, even from the most tragic entertainment storylines. Thus, eudaimonic affective experiences, cognitive elaboration, and contemplation go hand in hand for audiences to derive deeper meaning through media.

Morally Complex Characters

Storylines that elicit eudaimonic experiences tend to be complex, often including morally opposing values. According to the **model of intuitive morality and exemplars** (MIME) (Tamborini, 2013), narrative complexity can result from moral dilemmas that are presented to the audiences, where a character upholds some moral principles (e.g., fairness) but violates others (e.g., respect for authority). The moral conflict elicits deliberative processing that is associated with appreciation of the narrative. One particular storytelling form that portrays characters who uphold some moral domains but violate others is the antihero narrative (e.g., Raney & Janicke, 2013), which typically feature **morally ambiguous characters** (MACs) (Krakowiak & Tsay-Vogel, 2013).

MACs are characters who often behave in morally questionable ways but do so for a positive outcome, often for the greater good. That is, they do the wrong things but for the right reason. Examples are protagonists such as Dexter Morgan in the TV show *Dexter*, who murders serial killers who have escaped the justice system; Walter White of the TV show *Breaking Bad*, who changes careers from high school teacher to crystal meth dealer after learning that he has terminal cancer; or Batman in the film *The Dark Knight*, who fights against terror using morally questionable means. MACs vary on a continuum of morality ranging from violating only a few moral domains (e.g., morally very good, more hero-like) to violating many moral domains (e.g., morally very bad, more villain-like). In many cases MACs are more relatable than "pure" heroes, because viewers often perceive themselves to be more similar to characters who are morally complex. That is, MACs seem to be particularly relatable because of their perceived realism, *because of*—not in spite of—their flaws and fallibility. They are multi-dimensional and therefore offer more opportunities for viewers to relate.

One process through which viewers relate to media characters is **identification**, which is defined as "an imaginative process through which an audience member assumes the identity, goals, and perspective of a character" (Cohen, 2001, p. 261; see also Chapter 4). Research indicates that for MACs specifically, **wishful identification**—the process by which viewers want to become like or live through the character—might play an important role in their appeal. This makes sense when we understand that MACs often engage in moral violations for the greater good. As argued by Raney and Janicke (2013), morally complex media characters consistently overcome oppression and bring justice, even to the most unlikely of justice-serving circumstances. Antihero narratives "can offer viewers the assurance that somewhere, somehow, someone is getting what (s)he deserves, and in doing so, may allow us to compensate for or satisfy certain needs that are limited to address in real life" (Raney & Janicke, 2013, p. 162). The existential need to believe in the possibility of a just world, then, can be vicariously satisfied by wishfully identifying with the MAC.

But how can viewers identify with a character who murders, deceives, and tortures others? Research has found that the more a media user identifies with a MAC, the more they seem to engage in **moral disengagement** processes to justify the immoral means through which MACs achieve the greater good (e.g., Krakowiak & Tsay-Vogel, 2013). The results of those processes are greater enjoyment and appreciation of the narrative. Moral disengagement is a cognitive process by which one's own moral standards are deactivated and morally questionable behavior is excused in order to avoid cognitive dissonance between one's moral beliefs and the observed behaviors (Bandura, 2002). Narratives do a good job of providing the viewer with moral disengagement cues (e.g., the backstory of Dexter's or Batman's troubled childhood) that allow audiences to overlook and excuse the violations of morality, focusing on the moral virtues instead that can lead to positive affective dispositions (see ADT, Chapter 4) toward the character, resulting in enjoyment and appreciation.

Moreover, narratives with MACs provide viewers the opportunity to compare their own moral standards to those of the character in a social comparison process. Meier and Neubaum (2019) found that identification with MACs predicted social comparison, which in turn predicted appreciation of narratives. These results provide support for the idea that antihero narratives provide a safe playground for viewers to grapple with their own morality, helping to reduce moral uncertainty in viewers as they compare their own moral decisions to those made by the MAC (Meier & Neubaum, 2019; Raney & Janicke, 2013). This social-comparative process provides viewers with meaning and a deeper understanding of their own (im)moral thoughts and behaviors, which results in an overall appreciation of the narrative. As such, antihero narratives can be seen as special forms of entertainment that lead to eudaimonic experiences specifically related to moral contemplation.

Theories of Eudaimonic Entertainment Experiences

Eudaimonic Experiences and Well-Being

The distinction between hedonic and eudaimonic media experiences conceptually overlaps with the distinction between different theories of well-being (see Chapter 3). Hedonic entertainment experiences are more associated with **subjective well-being**, which involves the maximization of pleasure and positive affect, the minimization of unpleasant states, and satisfaction with life. In contrast, eudaimonic entertainment experiences are more associated with **psychological well-being**, which involves actions that lead to personal growth, meaningfulness, environmental mastery, self-acceptance, and purpose in life. To empirically investigate these differences, Wirth and colleagues (2012) developed the **Eudaimonic Entertainment Experience Scale** based on psychological well-being theory to assess audience experiences in terms of how much the content helped them to accept themselves (self-acceptance), recognize their life as meaningful (purpose in life), make them feel like they are in charge of their own life (autonomy), feel challenged (personal growth/competence), feel empathy for the protagonist (relatedness), feel good because the protagonist acted in a responsible way (activation of central values), or simply feel entertained (hedonic entertainment). As one might imagine, the specific constellation of these factors varies widely across content and even within an audience member's own experiences. Nevertheless, when prototypical eudaimonic entertainment experiences are elicited (e.g., appreciation, mixed affect, contemplation, meaning finding), specific well-being effects are consistently observed. For example, exposure to film or online video clips that elicit eudaimonic experiences predict mood repair, mastery recovery experiences, and increased feelings of vitality (Rieger, Reinecke, Frischlich, & Bente, 2014). Additionally, elevation- and gratitude-eliciting videos can positively impact an employee's perception of their meaning at work, relatedness at work, and, again, vitality (Janicke-Bowles, Rieger, & Connor III, 2019).

Meaningful media can also motivate an audience member to be a better person, increase levels of spirituality, hope, mature cognitive thinking styles, universality orientation, and death acceptance (Janicke & Oliver, 2017; Oliver et al., 2012; also see Chapter 6), all of which are related to greater psychological well-being. Several other studies suggest an indirect effect of eudaimonic entertainment experiences on aspects of well-being. For example, Khoo and Graham-Engeland (2014) found that reflecting on a tragic film led to greater self-compassion and self-efficacy, which predicted reduced anxiety, depressive symptoms, and better perceived general health four weeks afterwards.

BOX 5.1 LONG-TERM EFFECTS OF EUDAIMONIC ENTERTAINMENT EXPERIENCES?

Knowing that eudaimonic well-being is a more stable and long-term emotional and cognitive state, we must ask: Are the positive benefits of eudaimonic entertainment experiences long-lasting? Or do they fade away as our bodies return to homeostasis and our minds wander to other concerns? It is still the early days of searching for answers to these questions. But initial studies suggest that the power of eudaimonic media experiences to lead to long-term well-being effects may depend on dosage, personality differences, media type, and context.

One long-term elevation study demonstrated no direct effects on flourishing or intended interaction with stereotyped groups after six-weeks exposure to three videos depicting human kindness per week (Neubaum, Krämer, & Alt, 2020). However, the researchers did find a mediating effect of condition (human kindness condition vs. violent content condition) on prosocial motivations and positive conceptions of humanity over time via elevation. The reason for the nonsignificant findings of repeated human kindness videos on the second-order outcome variables (flourishing, social interactions) may have been due to the involuntary exposure to the videos (i.e., participants did not choose which videos to watch). The authors identify other research that found self-selection of elevating video content moderates the effects on prosocial motivations (Ellithorpe, Oliver, & Ewoldsen, 2015). Thus, long-term effects may depend on whether you choose to expose yourself to media that makes you feel moved, contemplative, and provides you with meaning.

Another longitudinal study on repeated exposure of human kindness videos over seven, 10, or 12 days revealed increased prosocial motivations and decreased self-protective behaviors over time, specifically when the videos were spaced out over time (i.e., over the course of a month; Erickson et al., 2018). Thus, in addition to selective exposure, intentionally watching elevating videos only a couple a times a week might have specific beneficial long-term effects for consumers. Think about your own daily media consumption. What would happen if you chose to watch content that leaves you with meaning, purpose, reflection, and warm feelings in the heart three to four times during the week? Could it leave a lasting impression on you? Could it change your worldview? Perhaps you should try it to see for yourself.

Meta-Emotions

Another concept that helps explain the appeal and effects of repeated exposure to meaningful narratives is meta-emotions. Simply stated, meta-emotions are the thoughts and feelings we have about our emotions (Bartsch, Vorderer, Mangold, & Viehoff, 2008; Oliver, 1993). Meta-emotions arise when primary emotions are appraised. For instance, when watching a tragic film, we experience sadness (primary emotion), but that leads us to reflect (appraisal) on our capacity to empathize with others, which helps us to feel contented (meta-emotion). The **appraisal process** for primary and meta-emotions both involve the appraisal of a specific eliciting event, the affective reactions, and the resulting action tendencies (see Figure 5.1). The only difference in the appraisal processes is that, for the primary emotion, the appraising event is the environmental stimuli (e.g., tragic

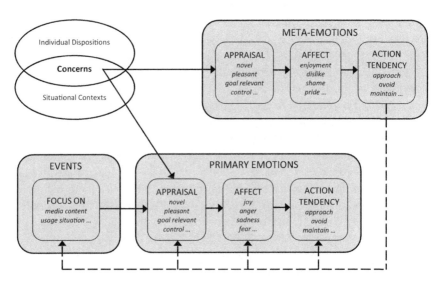

FIGURE 5.1 Extended Process Model of Emotion, Meta-Emotion, and Emotion Regulation in Media Use (Based on Bartsch et al., 2008)

film), whereas for the meta-emotions the appraising event is the primary emotion itself (e.g., sadness).

Reappraising one's primary emotional reactions to a narrative has been used to explain the appreciation of sad films (Oliver, 1993). Experiencing sadness or melancholy from the exposure to a sad film can be reappraised as the feeling of appreciation for the meaning and truth of the displayed human suffering. The motivation for this reappraisal can stem from individual dispositions and situational contexts. For sad media in particular, it has been argued that positive norms about the value of other-directed sadness and empathy influence the appraisal process in a positive way. That is, people know that showing compassion to others is regarded as a positive character quality, which leads them to feel good about their negative emotional experience at the end of a moving video or film and motivates them to seek out similar experiences in the future.

Other variables that impact the appraisal process include stimuli novelty, pleasantness, goal conduciveness, and controllability (Bartsch et al., 2008). For example, for goal conduciveness, you might be highly motivated to regulate your emotions in a way that would lead to a "worthwhile" experience given the emotional and cognitive investment (high personal concern), as well as the time, you devoted to the media product. That is, you spent 90 minutes on an emotional roller coaster ride watching the narrative; as a result, you feel that an overall positive evaluation of the experience is warranted in order to avoid the cognitive dissonance that would arise from feeling like you wasted your time. A positive appraisal of emotions during media use leads to repeated exposure to content of similar nature.

In contrast, a negative meta-emotion appraisal would motivate a suppression of the primary emotion and an avoidance of similar media formats in the future. For example, mediated joy, love, and inspiration (primary emotion) from a meaningful social media meme, for example, can be regarded as corny and cheesy (meta-emotion), leading to the rejection of the content in the future (e.g., unsubscribing from the social media channels where you encountered the content). For the same individual, if a primary emotional reaction of joy and love were elicited from the content, it could spark a social-comparison process through which they realize the lack of those emotions in the rest of their life, which could make it too painful for them to continue to experience them. Driven by the desire for pleasant experiences, the person reappraises the primary emotions as corny and cheesy, allowing them to devalue a positive emotional response to such content, which motivates them to avoid exposure to similar content in the future. Thus, the reappraisal becomes an emotional coping strategy of sorts.

The motives for meta-emotional appraisals to arise are vast. However, when the primary emotions are appraised to be relevant to personal concerns (based on context or personality), they can help us to explain how primary eudaimonic experiences—which can be ambivalent, cognitively challenging, and outright negative—still lead to an overall positive evaluation of the media content, motivating subsequent exposure to similar content.

Recovery

The theory of recovery also helps to explain specific benefits of eudaimonic entertainment experiences. The demands of life require individuals to replenish their depleted resources and recover from demanding activities in order to avoid long-term stress and negative health consequences. According to Sonnentag and Fritz (2007) four different types of **recovery experiences** are beneficial to replenish depleted resources: (1) *psychological detachment*, which includes a mental and physical distancing from work or other stress-inducing tasks or rumination, (2) *relaxation*, which refers to returning back to baseline level of psychophysiological activation after a stressful event, (3) *mastery experiences*, which consist of challenges or learning opportunities taken on during leisure time activities, resulting in replenishing of internal resources such as self-efficacy and positive moods, and (4) *control*, which refers to the freedom to choose activities voluntarily at one's discretion during leisure-time activities, in turn promoting feelings of autonomy and competence.

Research indicates that entertaining media can be an important activity that aids these recovery experiences. Although hedonically pleasing media content can specifically aid the psychological detachment and relaxation recovery experiences, eudaimonic experiences can predict mastery recovery experiences, as well as increased energetic arousal (Rieger et al., 2014). These results reinforce the understanding that eudaimonic entertainment experiences are challenging to process, but when done so, lead to a feeling of accomplishment or mastery, self-efficacy, and positive mood, which can have further benefits for well-being in the long term.

However, selecting challenging media fare when you come home after a long day at work with few cognitive resources remaining might be the last thing you want to do. In support of this, research has shown that ego-depleted (i.e., reduced self-control capacity) individuals are less likely to select challenging-to-process, eudaimonically oriented TV content (e.g., Reinecke, Hartmann, & Eden, 2014). Additionally, ego-depleted individuals are also more likely to appraise entertainment media in general as a form of procrastination, which when consumed can lead to guilt and reduced recovery experiences. Because of their ego-depletion, these individuals are more likely to choose undemanding and hedonically oriented content, which could increase their risk of feeling guilty about their media use. In turn, consuming media content that is appreciated and perceived as a meaningful and more valuable form of entertainment could reverse the detrimental effect of perceiving entertainment as a waste of time when willpower is depleted.

Thus, in order for you to receive recovery benefits from entertaining media, it is crucial to appraise the media content positively, especially when your willpower is exhausted (like after a long day at work). For someone who appraises media as procrastination, it might be easier to argue for the benefits of media content that is prone to elicit eudaimonic experiences than hedonically oriented fare. As such, eudaimonic entertainment experiences may be uniquely powerful to impact entertainment appraisal and recovery as a result.

Terror Management Theory

A final theory that helps explain the positive appeal and benefit of eudaimonic media experiences is **terror management theory** (TMT) (e.g., Pyszczynski, Greenberg, & Solomon, 1999). TMT helps explain what happens when we are reminded, for whatever reason, that our own life will someday end (i.e., **mortality salience**), which typically leads to increased anxiety. TMT assumes that people best manage their anxiety toward their own mortality by striving for "symbolic immortality" through leaving a meaningful contribution in the world. Eudaimonic content that deals with tragedy, suffering, and death can help audience members deal with their own mortality in a safe environment by providing them with an understanding of life's values and meaning overall, even after their own death. It can provide viewers with a coping mechanism to deal with the threats of mortality by providing opportunities to relate to the media characters and, through them, vicariously feel validated in one's cultural values, worldviews, or virtues beneficial for self-esteem.

As outlined earlier, self-acceptance, purpose in life, and autonomy are part of the eudaimonic entertainment experience and as such can serve as an **anxiety buffer** against self-threatening states such as when one's own death is made salient. For example, participants exposed to a eudaimonic media clip, after their mortality was made salient, not only appreciated the clip more but also were less likely to engage in self-enhancement as opposed to those who watched a pleasurable or informative clip (Rieger et al., 2015). This provides further evidence that eudaimonic media experiences (more so than other types) may serve as an anxiety buffer against mortality threats. Thus, the meaning that can be derived from media content that stimulates reflective thoughts can alleviate distress and anxiety in viewers suffering from self-threatening states such as being reminded of one's own mortality.

Summary

Feeling tender-hearted, moved to tears, contemplative, and searching for meaning are common entertainment experiences summarized under eudaimonic entertainment theories. Such experiences can help people grapple with the meaning of life, their stress-levels (e.g., recovery), and their own mortality (e.g., terror management). Narratives with (moral) complexity or featuring morally ambiguous characters can capture the deeper aspects of the human condition, leaving audiences with a lingering feeling that there is more than pleasure and light-heartedness to this human existence. Although eudaimonic entertainment experiences contain what are generally thought of as "more negative" aspects, they are often not perceived as such by audiences (e.g., meta-emotions), as they provide a safe space in which viewers can come to understand their own struggles or moral uncertainties. While not everyone is drawn to such narratives (see Chapter 12), they do make up a large part of our contemporary media landscape and cultural references. Future investigation of the long-term benefits of eudaimonic media experiences and their relationship to psychological well-being is a promising research avenue.

References

Bandura, A. (2002). Selective moral disengagement in the exercise of moral agency. *Journal of Moral Education*, 31, 101–119. doi:10.1080/0305724022014322.

Bartsch, A. (2012). Emotional gratification in entertainment experience: Why viewers of movies and television series find it rewarding to experience emotions. *Media Psychology*, 15, 267–302. doi:10.1080/15213269.2012.693811.

Bartsch, A., Kalch, A., & Oliver, M. B. (2014). Moved to think: The role of emotional media experiences in stimulating reflective thoughts. *Journal of Media Psychology*, 26, 125–140. doi:10.1027/1864-1105/a000118.

Bartsch, A., Vorderer, P., Mangold, R., & Viehoff, R. (2008). Appraisal of emotions in media use: Toward a process model of meta-emotion and emotion regulation. *Media Psychology*, 11, 7–27. doi:10.1080/15213260701813447.

Cohen, J. (2001). Defining identification: A theoretical look at the identification of audiences with media characters. *Mass Communication and Society*, 4, 245–264. doi:10.1207/S15327825MCS0403_01.

Das, E., Nobbe, T., & Oliver, M. B. (2017). Health communication| moved to act: Examining the role of mixed affect and cognitive elaboration in "accidental" narrative persuasion. *International Journal of Communication*, 11, 4907–4923. https://ijoc.org/index.php/ijoc/article/view/7213/2204.

Ellithorpe, M., Oliver, M. B., & Ewoldsen, D. (2015). Elevation (sometimes) increases altruism: Choice and number of outcomes in elevating media effects. *Psychology of Popular Media Culture*, 4, 236–250. doi:10.1037/ppm0000023.

Erickson, T. M., McGuire, A. P., Scarsella, G. M., Crouch, T. A., Lewis, J. A., Eisenlohr, A. P., & Muresan, T. J. (2018). Viral videos and virtue: Moral elevation inductions shift affect and interpersonal goals in daily life. *Journal of Positive Psychology*, 13, 643–654. doi:10.1080/17439760.2017.1365163.

Haidt, J., & Algoe, S. (2004). Moral amplification and the emotions that attach us to saints and demons. In J. Greenberg, S. L. Koole, & T. Pyszczynski (Eds.), *Handbook of experimental existential psychology* (pp. 322–335). New York, NY: Guilford Press.

Janicke, S. H., & Oliver, M. B. (2017). The relationship between elevation, connectedness and compassionate love in meaningful films. *Psychology of Popular Media Culture*, 6, 274–289. doi:10.1037/ppm0000105.

Janicke-Bowles, S. H., Rieger, D., & Connor III, W. (2019). Finding meaning at work: the role of inspiring and funny YouTube videos on work-related well-being. *Journal of Happiness Studies*, 20, 619–640. doi:10.1007/s10902-018-9959-1.

Khoo, G. S., & Graham-Engeland, J. E. (2014). The benefits of contemplating tragic drama on self-regulation and health. *Health Promotion International*, 31, 187–199. doi:10.1093/heapro/dau056.

Knobloch-Westerwick, S., Gong, Y., Hagner, H., & Kerbeykian, L. (2013). Tragedy viewers count their blessings: Feeling low on fiction leads to feeling high on life. *Communication Research*, 40, 747–766. doi:10.1177/0093650212437758.

Krakowiak, K. M., & Tsay-Vogel, M. (2013). What makes characters' bad behaviors acceptable? The effects of character motivation and outcome on perceptions, character liking, and moral disengagement. *Mass Communication and Society*, 16, 179–199. doi:10.1080/15205436.2012.690926.

Lewis, R. J., Tamborini, R., & Weber, R. (2014). Testing a dual-process model of media enjoyment and appreciation. *Journal of Communication*, 64, 397–416. doi:10.1111/jcom.12101.

Meier, Y., & Neubaum, G. (2019). Gratifying ambiguity: Psychological processes leading to enjoyment and appreciation of TV series with morally ambiguous characters. *Mass Communication and Society*, 22, 631–653. doi:10.1080/15205436.2019.1614195.

Neubaum, G., Krämer, N. C., & Alt, K. (2020). Psychological effects of repeated exposure to elevating entertainment: An experiment over the period of 6 weeks. *Psychology of Popular Media Culture*, 9, 194–207. doi:10.1037/ppm0000235.

Oliver, M. B. (1993). Exploring the paradox of the enjoyment of sad films. *Human Communication Research*, 19, 315–342. doi:10.1111/j.1468-2958.1993.tb00304.x.

Oliver, M. B., Ash, E., Woolley, J. K., Shade, D. D., & Kim, K. (2014). Entertainment we watch and entertainment we appreciate: Patterns of motion picture consumption and acclaim over three decades. *Mass Communication and Society*, 17, 853–873. doi:10.1080/15205436.2013.872277.

Oliver, M. B., & Bartsch, A. (2010). Appreciation as audience response: Exploring entertainment gratifications beyond hedonism. *Human Communication Research*, 36, 53–81. doi:10.1111/j.1468-2958.2009.01368.x.

Oliver, M. B., & Hartmann, T. (2010). Exploring the role of meaningful experiences in users' appreciation of good movies. *Projections*, 4, 128–150. doi:10.3167/proj.2010.040208.

Oliver, M. B., Hartmann, T., & Woolley, J. K. (2012). Elevation in response to entertainment portrayals of moral virtue. *Human Communication Research*, 38, 360–378. doi:10.1111/j.1468-2958.2012.01427.x.

Oliver, M. B., & Raney, A. A. (2011). Entertainment as pleasurable and meaningful: Identifying hedonic and eudaimonic motivations for entertainment consumption. *Journal of Communication*, 61, 984–1004. doi:10.1111/j.1460-2466.2011.01585.x.

Pyszczynski, T., Greenberg, J., & Solomon, S. (1999). A dual-process model of defense against conscious and unconscious death-related thoughts: An extension of terror management theory. *Psychological Review*, 106, 835–845. doi:10.1037/0033-295x.106.4.835.

Raney, A. A., & Janicke, S. H. (2013). How we enjoy and why we seek out morally complex characters in media entertainment. In R. Tamborini (Ed.), *Media and the moral mind* (pp. 152–169). London, UK: Routledge.

Reinecke, L., Hartmann, T., & Eden, A. (2014). The guilty couch potato: The role of ego depletion in reducing recovery through media use. *Journal of Communication*, 64, 569–589. doi:10.1111/jcom.12107.

Rieger, D., Frischlich, L., Högden, F., Kauf, R., Schramm, K., & Tappe, E. (2015). Appreciation in the face of death: Meaningful films buffer against death-related anxiety. *Journal of Communication*, 65, 351–372. doi:10.1111/jcom.12152.

Rieger, D., Reinecke, L., Frischlich, L., & Bente, G. (2014). Media entertainment and well-being: Linking hedonic and eudaimonic entertainment experience to media-induced recovery and vitality. *Journal of Communication*, 64, 456–478. doi:10.1111/jcom.12097.

Slater, M. D., Oliver, M. B., & Appel, M. (2019). Poignancy and mediated wisdom of experience: Narrative impacts on willingness to accept delayed rewards. *Communication Research*, 46, 333–354. doi:10.1177/0093650215623838.

Sonnentag, S., & Fritz, C. (2007). The Recovery Experience Questionnaire: Development and validation of a measure for assessing recuperation and unwinding from work. *Journal of Occupational Health Psychology*, 12, 204–221. doi:10.1037/1076-8998.12.3.204.

Tamborini, R. (2013). A model of intuitive morality and exemplars. In R. Tamborini (Ed.), *Media and the moral mind* (pp. 43–74). London, UK: Routledge.

Tamborini, R., Bowman, N. D., Eden, A., Grizzard, M., & Organ, A. (2010). Defining media enjoyment as the satisfaction of intrinsic needs. *Journal of Communication*, 60, 758–777. doi:10.1111/j.1460-2466.2010.01513.x.

Vorderer, P. (2011). What's next? Remarks on the current vitalization of entertainment theory. *Journal of Media Psychology*, 23, 60–63. doi:10.1027/1864-1105/a000034.

Wirth, W., Hofer, M., & Schramm, H. (2012). Beyond pleasure: Exploring the eudaimonic entertainment experience. *Human Communication Research*, 38, 406–428. doi:10.1111/j.1468-2958.2012.01434.x.

Additional Readings

Algoe, S. B., & Haidt, J. (2009). Witnessing excellence in action: The 'other-praising' emotions of elevation, gratitude, and admiration. *Journal of Positive Psychology*, 4, 105–127. doi:10.1080/17439760802650519.

Bartsch, A., & Hartmann, T. (2017). The role of cognitive and affective challenge in entertainment experience. *Communication Research*, 44, 29–53. doi:10.1177/0093650214565921.

Bartsch, A., & Schneider, F. M. (2014). Entertainment and politics revisited: How non-escapist forms of entertainment can stimulate political interest and information seeking. *Journal of Communication*, 64, 369–396. doi:10.1111/jcom.12095.

Eden, A. L., Grizzard, M., & Lewis, R. (2011). Disposition development in drama: The role of moral, immoral, and ambiguously moral characters. *International Journal of Arts and Technology*, 4, 33–47. doi:10.1504/IJART.2011.037768.

Eden, A., Johnson, B. K., & Hartmann, T. (2018). Entertainment as a creature comfort: Self-control and selection of challenging media. *Media Psychology*, 21, 352–376. doi:10.1080/15213269.2017.1345640.

Ersner-Hershfield, H., Mikels, J. A., Sullivan, S. J., & Carstensen, L. L. (2008). Poignancy: Mixed emotional experience in the face of meaningful endings. *Journal of Personality and Social Psychology*, 94, 158–167. doi:10.1037/0022-3514.94.1.158.

Krakowiak, K. M., & Tsay-Vogel, M. (2018). Are good characters better for us? The effect of morality salience on entertainment selection and recovery outcomes. *Mass Communication and Society*, 21, 320–344. doi:10.1080/15205436.2017.1407797.

Oliver, M. B., Raney, A. A., Slater, M., Appel, M., Hartmann, T., Bartsch, A., Schneider, F., Janicke-Bowles, S. H., Krämer, N., Mares, M. L., Vorderer, P., Rieger, D., Dale, K. R., & Das, H. H. J. (2018). Self- transcendent media experiences: Taking meaningful media to a higher level. *Journal of Communication*, 68, 380–389. doi:10.1093/joc/jqx020.

Rieger, D., & Hofer, M. (2017). How movies can ease the fear of death: The survival or death of the protagonists in meaningful movies. *Mass Communication and Society*, 20, 710–733. doi:10.1080/15205436.2017.1300666.

Sanders, M. S., & Tsay-Vogel, M. (2016). Beyond heroes and villains: Examining explanatory mechanisms underlying moral disengagement. *Mass Communication and Society*, 19, 230–252. doi:10.1080/15205436.2015.1096944.

Slater, M. D., Oliver, M. B., Appel, M., Tchernev, J. M., & Silver, N. A. (2018). Mediated wisdom of experience revisited: Delay discounting, acceptance of death, and closeness to future self. *Human Communication Research*, 44, 80–101. doi:10.1093/hcr/hqx004.

Wulf, T., Bonus, J. A., & Rieger, D. (2019). The inspired time traveler: Examining the implications of nostalgic entertainment experiences for two-factor models of entertainment. *Media Psychology*, 22, 795–817. doi:10.1080/15213269.2018.1532299.

6

TRANSCENDENT ENTERTAINMENT

Source: Shutterstock 1022645329

In 2018, social media influencer Jay Shetty gave an inspirational talk to a group of middle school students on rethinking their definition of success. "Before You Feel Pressure Watch This" was just one of more than 775 million posts on Facebook that year. But none garnered more user engagement than it did (Peters, 2019). Social media posts like Shetty's, films like *The Shawshank Redemption, Forrest Gump*, and *The Pursuit of Happyness*, and TV shows like *The Biggest Loser, The Voice*, and *This Is Us* leave many people feeling inspired, grateful, hopeful, and motivated to help others or change their own lives for the better. In fact, more than six out of ten U.S. adults (63.5%) say they feel inspired at least a few times a week by something they see in the media (Janicke-Bowles et al., 2019). But what makes media inspiring? Is it different from media that elicits eudaimonic experiences in consumers? What are the specific effects of such inspirational media on an individual's well-being, their outlook on the world, and interaction with others? These questions and more will be discussed in this chapter.

What Is Transcendent Entertainment?

As we discussed in Chapter 5, eudaimonic entertainment experiences are multidimensional, including cognitive and emotional elements that can impact well-being in the short- and (potentially) long-term by fostering a sense of meaning, connectedness, and understanding about life or humanity as a whole. But media psychologist Mary Beth Oliver and colleagues (2018) noted that these experiences are often quite different from one another, evoking a wide range of emotions and thought patterns. The researchers suggested that these differences in eudaimonic entertainment experiences could be represented on a continuum, with those fostering self-focused insight on one end and outward-focused, self-transcendent experience on the other. More self-focused entertainment experiences manifest in prototypical eudaimonic entertainment ways: mixed affect, contemplation, and basic need satisfaction. In contrast, **self-transcendent media experiences** take the audience member beyond personal benefits to a greater understanding of their interconnectedness with others or with a higher nature. Increased appreciation for and understanding of shared humanity and values of moral beauty, hope, courage, and humility are at the heart of self-transcendent media experiences. After experiencing self-transcendence with media, audiences are oriented outwardly toward the needs of others, nature, or powers beyond themselves. This definition parallels others found in positive psychology for (non-mediated) self-transcendent experiences, which are thought to include two key components: (1) the dissolution of a sense of self (i.e., seeing oneself as small compared to other beings or objects; annihilation component), and (2) the feelings of relatedness (i.e., relational component) (see Yaden, Haidt, Hood, Vago, & Newberg, 2017). Thus, transcendent entertainment is a special type of eudaimonic entertainment involving self-transcendent experiences.

Self-Transcendent Emotions

One aspect that characterizes both mediated and non-mediated self-transcendent experiences is the emotions involved. **Self-transcendent emotions** differ from hedonic positive emotions—those solely related to pleasure and joy—in that they do not primarily concern the self or the goals of the self. Instead, self-transcendent emotions promote a loss of ego and an openness to others. Scholars somewhat disagree on what emotions actually meet this criterion, but most contend that the prototypical self-transcendent emotions are a subset of moral emotions and include awe, elevation, gratitude, admiration, hope, and love (e.g., Algoe & Haidt, 2009). But, again, what is not in dispute is that self-transcendent emotions are "other oriented," drawing people out of their usual state of ego-centric self-consciousness, motivating them to better the self or humanity. In fact, self-transcendent emotions predict a variety of outward-oriented outcomes including interconnectedness (e.g., Janicke & Oliver, 2017; Krämer et al., 2017), prosociality (e.g., Freeman, Aquino, & McFerran, 2009; Schnall, Roper, & Fessler, 2010), and spirituality (Van Cappellen, Saroglou, Iweins, Piovesana, & Fredrickson, 2013).

Additionally, these emotions can develop our core human virtue of transcendence (Peterson & Seligman, 2004; see also Chapter 3), which is the disposition to strive for and connect with purpose and meaning greater than ourselves. Transcendence as a virtue is expressed in character strengths reflected in particular patterns of thought, emotion, and behavior. The five character strengths associated with transcendence are an appreciation for (moral) beauty and excellence, gratitude, spirituality, hope, and humor. Thus, when we acknowledge an appreciation for the moral beauty in another person's kindness, or when we participate in a meaningful discussion on spiritual matters, we are enacting, experiencing, and further developing the virtue transcendence. Furthermore, seeing others (including media characters) portraying transcendent character strengths—for instance, expressing gratitude to a benefactor by saying "thank you"—can elicit self-transcendent emotions (in this case, likely gratitude) in the witness. Further, the emotional experience can trigger **inspiration**, which is a motivational state that includes transcendence (Thrash & Elliot, 2004). Self-transcendent emotions and inspiration, in turn, contribute positively to well-being, especially promoting durable, authentic happiness.

BOX 6.1 *INSPIRATIONAL* MEDIA EXPERIENCES

Positive media psychologists use the term *self-transcendent* to describe some media experiences as a way to connect the study of positive media to existing work in emotion psychology on self-transcendent emotions. But many people—media users, content providers, and scholars—refer to the same content as *inspirational*. We think this is a perfectly fine term as well.

Fundamentally, inspiration is a complex psychological state with three core characteristics (Thrash & Elliot, 2004). First, inspiration involves **transcendence**, an awareness of something that is beyond our ordinary concerns. Second, inspiration involves an **evocation** by something outside of ourselves. It is not self-generated; we do not inspire ourselves. Finally, inspiration involves the **motivation** to act on our new insight. Inspiration is experienced as an episode that unfolds across time, involving two component processes: being inspired *by* and being inspired *to*. Being inspired by encompasses the realization and perception that the evocative object is to be appreciated in its own right, without regard to our own personal concern. Being inspired to involves the motivation to make manifest the perceived intrinsic values and qualities in the evocative object.

So, it is perfectly reasonable to say that you were *inspired by* a video *to* donate money to charity. That would definitely be an inspirational media experience ... and a self-transcendent one, too.

Of the various emotions designated as self-transcendent by psychologists, six have been the greatest focus of study in positive media psychology.

Elevation

Elevation is the emotion experienced when we encounter moral beauty and humanity's better nature, such as altruism, charity, loyalty, generosity, collectivism, and universal values. It is associated with a desire to be less selfish and to emulate acts of virtue, a motivation to engage in prosocial actions, and a will to become a better person. The experience of elevation is characterized by a particular set of physiological indicators, including feeling warmth and an expansion in the chest, goosebumps or chills, and feeling choked up or teary eyed. When people talk about the experience of elevation, they often describe it as feeling moved, touched, tender, compassionate, and inspired.

Admiration

Admiration as a self-transcendent emotion is quite similar to elevation. It is elicited by *non-moral* excellence, extraordinary skill, talent, or achievement; it inspires and energizes one to emulate the eliciting role model, work toward success (such as cultivating a skill or talent), and praise others. The physiological indicators of admiration are also like elevation: warm feeling in the chest, tears in the eyes, chills or goosebumps. However, some research indicates that those responses are even more pronounced with admiration, which is also accompanied by perceptions of high energy and increased heart rate (Algoe & Haidt, 2009).

Gratitude

Gratitude is a feeling of thankfulness and appreciation toward someone or something other than the self. It is often expressed as an acknowledgement of and appreciation for the situation, benefactor, or the good things in life in general. Gratitude is elicited by others doing good deeds for the self or observing others doing good deeds for a third party. Gratitude can also be elicited from nonhuman benefactors (e.g., God, life force), and it can manifest as thankfulness for simply waking up in the morning or feeling the warm sun shining on one's face. From an evolutionary perspective, gratitude is beneficial for the sharing of resources by coordinating reciprocity to another person's altruism. It fosters a tit-for-tat strategy that can extend toward other people. According to Algoe and Haidt (2009), gratitude does not have distinct physiological sensations like elevation or admiration. The immediate effects of gratitude involve a motivation to repay the benefactor or praise the benefactor publicly and a desire for a closer relationship with the benefactor. Beyond repaying the direct benefactor, gratitude also fosters altruism toward strangers, a feeling of greater connection to others, prosocial behaviors, and greater life meaning and life satisfaction (Bartlett & DeSteno, 2006; McCullough, Kilpatrick, Emmons, & Larson, 2001). People who regularly express gratitude also report experiencing more positive emotions, feeling more alive, sleeping better, and having better physical health (Emmons & McCullough, 2003; Jackowska, Brown, Ronaldson, & Steptoe, 2016).

Hope

Hope involves the feeling of yearning for an outcome, typically one that is unlikely to happen (Prestin, 2013). Hope can be elicited from circumstances that are dire or uncertain and from seeing others successfully overcome obstacles, show perseverance, remain optimistic about the future, and express encouragement (Dale, Raney, Janicke, Sanders, & Oliverjanicke, 2017b; Prestin, 2013). Hope provides emotional fuel for people to persevere themselves, even in the presence of obstacles. It is a self-motivating emotion, in contrast to optimism which entails the belief that somehow, with or without one's own doing, one's favorable and wished-for outcome will manifest (Alarcon, Bowling, & Khazon, 2013). Hope involves having both the will to achieve a goal (agency thinking) and the ideas about how to accomplish that goal (pathways thinking; Snyder et al., 1991).

Awe

Awe is defined by feeling small and insignificant in the presence of something vast, requiring the need to adjust one's mental structures to accommodate the experience. The experience of awe is often accompanied by amazement and wonder, as well as fear. It includes physical responses of wide eyes, raised eyebrows, slightly drop-jawed mouth, and deep inhalation (Shiota, Keltner, & Mossman, 2007). Awe is generally elicited by novel, complex, or vast stimuli, such as certain forms of natural beauty, ability, perfection, or supernatural causality. For example, watching the sun set over the ocean, feeling small in the presence of a life-size T-Rex skeleton, or observing Earth from outer space are prototypical examples that induce awe. Research has shown great benefits from the experience of awe, including feeling more connected to others, feeling humble, increased skepticism to persuasive messages, greater prosocial behavior and generosity, greater life satisfaction, increased spirituality, and better physical health (e.g, Piff, Dietz, Feinberg, Stancato, & Keltner, 2015).

Love (Kama Muta)

A new emotional concept that helps capture experiences previously identified as elevation is kama muta, or feeling moved by love. In fact, some scholars argue that kama muta may be a better concept than elevation to capture the effect of feeling moved, touched, and inspired (Janicke-Bowles, Schubert, & Blomster, in press). It is experienced as the response to the appraisal of distinct stimuli, namely moral beauty and non-moral sudden increases of interpersonal connectedness. **Relational models theory** (RMT) (Fiske, 2004) explains that a *sudden intensification of communal sharing* between two people or a person and non-human agent (e.g., mountain, God, weather) elicits kama muta and motivates the person to commit more strongly to the relationship or act generally kindly and with compassion toward others. Reunions, engagements, weddings, childbirth, connecting with nature or the divine, and sacrificing for others are examples where communal relationships suddenly intensify and from which kama muta may emerge. The physiological indicators of kama muta are moist eyes, chills, warm feeling in the chest, and motivations including affective devotion and prosociality. Several cross-cultural studies have supported the validity of kama muta as an emotional experience, its elicitation from real-world stimuli, and its distinction from sadness, awe, amusement, and mixed affect (e.g., Zickfeld et al., 2019).

Elicitors of Self-Transcendent Emotions in Media Content

As was discussed in Chapter 2, emotions emerge as reactions to and evaluations of a relevant stimulus in our environment. Part of the work of emotion researchers is to identify the stimuli that tend to consistently elicit specific discrete emotions. Many of the real-world elicitors of elevation, gratitude, admiration, hope, awe, and kama muta are listed above. But the questions remain: How often do events and situations known to elicit self-transcendent emotions in the material world actually appear in media content? And, if they do appear often, can they elicit the same emotion in audiences? A small (but growing) set of laboratory experiments has begun to explore the latter question. But first we must address the former. In doing so, of particular note is work by media psychologist Katherine Dale and her colleagues (2017b), in which a codebook was developed to analyze media content based on the appearance of 20 direct and modeled (i.e., displayed or experienced by a character) elicitors of self-transcendent emotions that map onto the VIA framework for the character strengths related to trait transcendence (Peterson & Seligman, 2004; see also Chapter 3). The coding scheme included depictions such as beautiful artwork or nature, extraordinary skills, kindness, thankfulness, perseverance, the overcoming of obstacles, and religious symbols. Research employing this coding scheme has revealed that many self-transcendent elicitors are indeed frequently portrayed across the media landscape, particularly in content identified as inspiring by audiences and content providers. We highlight some of those findings now.

Films

Compared to other forms of mass media, film has received the greatest attention by researchers studying eudaimonic entertainment experiences in general. The longer narrative form provides greater possibilities for character development and fleshing out of complex issues of humanity, which are main aspects of eudaimonic entertainment. Similarly, films provide a great platform on which self-transcendent experiences can be encountered. In fact, 86.9% of U.S. adults report having been inspired, touched, and moved by a film (Raney et al., 2018), and, in one study, 31% indicated to have felt so within the past week (Janicke-Bowles et al., 2019).

It is not surprising then that, in a content analysis of 50 films identified by audiences and critics as "most inspiring," Dale and colleagues (2017a) found a large number of self-transcendent emotional elicitors. Many were representations of events or stimuli that are known to trigger those emotions in the real-world (i.e., **direct elicitors**). The most common portrayals were scenes including nature (appearing in 28.2% of the 2,023 scenes analyzed) and kindness (13.2%), which can elicit awe and elevation respectively. Other elicitors were displayed through the actions of characters, who were shown behaving in ways consistent with trait transcendence (i.e., **modeled elicitors**). The most prominent modeled elicitors were characters overcoming obstacles and showing perseverance (25.0%; potentially triggering hope), followed by characters saying "thank you" or showing kindness (20.2%; potentially triggering gratitude). In the study, the films with the highest number of self-transcendent elicitors were *The Shawshank Redemption, Forrest Gump*, and *Rudy*.

Television

Similar to film, television can provide a great opportunity for viewers to identify with characters and learn from and be inspired by their behaviors and surroundings. Especially with streaming services, binge watching—viewing at least five episodes in one sitting—can make exposure particularly impactful. Thus, it is not surprising that 80.2% of U.S. adults report having been inspired by television before, in particular from dramas and documentaries (Raney et al., 2018), with 42% having felt inspired by a television show within the past week (Janicke-Bowles et al., 2019). The inspiration experienced by television viewers seems to stem from the depiction of specific self-transcendent elicitors. Applying the same codebook as applied to film, Dale and colleagues (2017a) investigated 75 episodes of 25 TV shows (three episodes of each show from the two most recently completed seasons) identified by audiences as inspirational. The researchers found, similar to films, that character strengths of hope (appearing in 35.4% of the 2,213 scenes analyzed) and gratitude (27.2%) were most common, followed by direct elicitors of nature (17.7%) and kindness (16.8%). The television shows with the most transcendent elicitors were episodes from *The Voice* and *American Idol*.

Social Media and Online Videos

With 72% of U.S. adults using at least one platform (Pew Research Center, 2019), it seems reasonable to assume that, given the vastness of content curated, they might encounter transcendence via social media, at least sometimes. Indeed, more than half (53.0%) of U.S. adults said they have at one time experienced self-transcendent experiences via social media, with the proportion even greater (67.3%) for people under 30 years of age (Raney et al., 2018).

A content analysis of posts gathered across an entire year from 50 publicly available, inspirational Facebook pages showed that images of or references to nature (e.g., beaches, forests, mountains, stars) were the most prevalent elicitors of self-transcendent emotions (43.9% of all posts). Encouragement (36.3%), which can trigger hope was also quite prevalent, including posts that stated things such as "Just keep believing," "Keep smiling," and "The temptation to quit is huge. Don't." Art, which can trigger awe and admiration, was present in 18.1% of the posts (Dale et al., 2019). Additionally, the researchers found that the more self-transcendent elicitors present in a post strongly predicted the likelihood of a post going viral (as measured by the number of likes and reactions a post received). Another content analysis showed that elicitors of appreciation of beauty and excellence, as well as hope, were most often depicted in 4,000 Facebook posts in response to Mark Zuckerberg's pledge to donate 99% of his Facebook shares to charity in 2015 (Zhao & Dale, 2019).

Of course, a key element of social media is online videos, which can also inspire users. For example, 62.7% of U.S. adults indicate having been inspired by an online video (Raney et al., 2018). A content analysis of inspiring YouTube videos (Dale et al., 2017b) found that character portrayals of overcoming obstacles were most prevalent (49.7%), followed by those associated with an appreciation of beauty and excellence (14.8%). Similarly, portrayals of appreciation of beauty and excellence and hope accounted for the vast majority of the direct elicitors in the videos. Also, inspiring YouTube videos with hope appear to be more likely to go viral than videos primarily containing other elicitors.

Effects of Mediated Self-Transcendent Emotions

Beyond verifying the presence of self-transcendent emotional elicitors in content spanning the media landscape, researchers have consistently found that exposure to that content is associated with transcendent–related outcomes. For one, to answer the earlier question: Yes, mediated elicitors of self-transcendent emotions can trigger those emotions in audiences. Participants in numerous studies (cited below) report elicitor-related emotional responses to specific representations in content. Additionally, researchers have evidenced changes in several physiologically indices in direct response to self-transcendent elicitors present in a video (Clayton et al., 2019). Further, self-transcendent emotions appear to mediate the relationship between media exposure and other transcendent outcomes (e.g., stereotype reduction; see Bartsch, Oliver, Nitsch, & Scherr, 2018; Krämer et al., 2017). Because self-transcendent emotions all share the feature of transcendence or other orientation, the observed outcomes are similar despite the presence of differing self-transcendent emotions (e.g., prosociality resulting from elevation and awe; Piff et al., 2015; Schnall et al., 2010). Nevertheless, the mechanism through which such outcomes occur appears to differ between the self-transcendent emotions. Therefore, we discuss the effects of the six self-transcendent emotions most examined by positive media psychologists separately below.

Elevation

As an experience resulting from encountering moral beauty and humanity's better nature, elevation has been examined more than any other self-transcendent emotion. Two primary outcomes are associated with mediated elevation: prosocial intentions and behavior and greater connectedness to others. Schnall, Roper, and Fessler (2010) found that watching clips from *The Oprah Winfrey Show* elicited elevation leading to greater motivation to be kind toward other people and actual helping behavior (e.g., donating money to a charity, helping another researcher complete a survey), compared to watching a neutral or happiness-inducing video. Similarly, Freeman and colleagues (2009) observed participants donating money—even to a charity affiliated with an outgroup—following elevation elicited by media. Beyond exposure to elevating content, similar prosocial effects have been found by simply allowing participants to recall a film they found meaningful (Janicke & Oliver, 2017). Tsay-Vogel and Krakowiak (2016) extended the research on elevating media to the reality TV format and showed that lifestyle-transforming reality TV shows (e.g., *Supernanny, Undercover Boss*) could also elicit intense elevation and altruistic motivations.

In terms of connectedness to others, Janicke and Oliver (2017) found that participants who recalled a meaningful film experienced more elevation than participants who recalled a funny film, which in turn predicted feelings of connectedness toward close others, their family, and a higher power. Oliver, along with a set of other colleagues (2017), also found that participants who took mobile-phone pictures of love, kindness, and beautiful nature across a one-week period experienced heightened positive affect and elevation, resulting in greater feelings of connectedness to others, increased perception of the good of humanity, and altruistic motivations. Similarly, Waddell and Bailey (2017) found that reading positive comments about an elevating news article increased feelings of connectedness to all humankind.

Elevation can also increase connectedness toward stereotyped groups. For example, Lai, Haidt, and Nosek (2013) found that elevation elicited from short videos highlighting inspirational and sacrificial acts from the real world reduced explicit and implicit prejudices toward gay men. Additional studies have verified these findings, showing that videos that elicit elevation predict intentions to interact with various stereotyped groups (e.g., LGBTQ individuals, African Americans, Jews; Krämer et al., 2017) and a destigmatization effect for persons with disabilities (Bartsch et al., 2018).

In sum, elevation seems to be a powerful self-transcendent emotion that is elicited via moral beauty portrayals and promotes audiences to emulate such virtuous depictions. It has been found across multiple media platforms and even from simply recalling meaningful media.

Admiration

Elevation and admiration are quite similar in that they are both triggered by moral and non-moral human excellence, respectively. Thus, it is not surprising that both may be triggered within the same content. For example, in her former television program and magazine, Oprah Winfrey modeled moral beauty by showcasing her contribution to worthy causes while at the same time showcasing her accomplishments. Thus, elicitors for both elevation and admiration can be present at the same time. Research by Schnall and colleagues (2010) supports this notion by demonstrating that audience members experienced not only elevation but also admiration when watching *The Oprah Winfrey Show*, leading to greater motivation to be kind toward other people, increased donation behavior, and greater willingness to help others. In another context, Van Cappellen and colleagues (2013) found that elevation and admiration as elicited from short videos increased perception of the importance of spirituality, especially for nonreligious individuals.

Given that most of the studies on elevation reported above did not assess admiration as well, it is unclear which of the two self-transcendent emotions might be more responsible for motivating transcendence-related outcomes. Algoe and Haidt (2009) outline that admiration is an energizing emotion, more in line with the motivational state of inspiration, whereas elevation is a calming, stress-reducing emotion motivating openness and warmth toward others. Given the inspirational nature of social media, it can be speculated that admiration plays a specifically important role in the context of social media use. In a semantic-network analysis of social media posts with the hashtags #inspiration and #meaningful, Rieger and Klimmt (2019) found that posts with the hashtag #inspiration were more closely associated with motivational topics (e.g., work and fitness goals), whereas posts with the hashtag #meaningful were more closely related to artistic and natural beauty and depth. Thus, it is reasonable to speculate that admiration plays a particular role in the context of inspirational social media, (maybe) even more so than elevation.

Gratitude

Even though gratitude activities are the most prominent in happiness interventions, when it comes to experiencing gratitude via media, only limited research exists. One study by Janicke, Rieger, Reinecke, and Connor III (2018) found that videos that elicit gratitude and elevation impacted employee's perception of their meaning, relatedness, and vitality in the workplace. Another experimental study reported increased connectedness to humanity and altruistic values immediately after exposure to a gratitude-themed film (i.e., *Pursuit of Happyness, Radio, The Blindside,* or *Rudy*; Janicke, Hendry, & Dale, 2018).

Within the social media context, research on body dissatisfaction in women showed that a short gratitude intervention lowered women's body dissatisfaction after seeing slides of thin women, compared to a control group that listed their daily hassles before seeing the images (Homan, Sedlak, & Boyd, 2014). Thus, it seems like if you find something to be grateful for before scrolling through Instagram or Snapchat stories, some of the negative feelings in response to some of the portrayals may be dampened (for more on this, see Chapters 7 and 13).

BOX 6.2 THE POWER OF GRATITUDE IN TECHNOLOGY

Several apps for smartphones, tablets, and other digital devices are available now that focus specifically on the practice of gratitude. For example, *Happier* provides options for users to track three good things that happen to them each week and share those things with others; the app *Grateful* allows users to start a gratitude journal. The app *Happify*, which has closely worked with insurance companies as part of their business model to improve mental health, provides a variety of tools to practice gratitude in one's daily life.

A randomized controlled trial (RCT) study that evaluated an app specifically designed to track expressions of gratitude to other users throughout the day found that mood, psychological well-being, and expressions of gratitude increased for app users over a five-week period. Expressions of gratitude were most commonly observed after social interactions, location changes, or physical activities (Ghandeharioun, Azaria, Taylor, & Picard, 2016). It can be assumed that the arousal and positive emotions that are elicited from such circumstances are internal triggers for sending gratitude to someone.

Today's digital technologies offer promising tools to elicit gratitude and increase well-being as they allow for personalized interventions that are accessible to wide range of groups. Maybe you would like to try a gratitude app yourself?

Hope

Hope can be elicited from circumstances that are dire or uncertain, as well as from portrayals of characters successfully overcoming obstacles, showing perseverance, being optimistic about the future, and expressing encouragement (Dale et al., 2017b; Prestin, 2013). The most prototypical media depiction to elicit hope is the "underdog" character who overcomes challenges against all odds. Examples include Harry Potter defeating Lord Voldemort, or the Avengers defeating Thanos in the Marvel epic *Avengers: Endgame*. Even in the context of news and advertisement, stories of underdog characters are common. The story of Lual Mayen, once a refugee from South Sudan who is now CEO of his own video game company Junub Games, designing video games that promote peace, provides an example of an underdog character, eliciting inspiration in news. Also, sports-related advertisements often make use of hope elicitors by portraying underdog characters who persevere through hard training to achieve their goals (e.g., Nike's *Find Your Greatness* campaign).

The experience of hope motivates people to act, change things, pursue and orient toward future goals, and generally do better. It has been shown to predict well-being (Ciarrochi, Parker, Kashdan, Heaven, & Barkus, 2015), particularly in the health context (Brazeau & Davis 2018). Prestin (2013) showed that exposure to an underdog video for five days increased feelings of hope and motivation to pursue one's own goals in the future. Moreover, levels of hope persisted up to three days after the daily video exposure ended. Although this is only one initial study on hope in the media, given the high proliferation of hope elicitors in different media contexts, ample grounds are given for future studies about the effects of hope.

Awe

Because awe challenges existing mental structures and leads to greater connectedness to humanity, researchers have explored the effects of awe on social aggression. For example, one study found that awe, compared to amusement or neutral affect, reduced aggressive behaviors in a shooting game and, in turn, increased prosociality (Yang, Yang, Bao, Liu, & Passmore, 2016). Furthermore, awe seems to play a particularly important role in the media context of music. In fact, music may be the most inspiring medium of all: 90.5% of U.S. adults indicated having been inspired by music at some point in their lives, with 56.0% having been inspired by music within the last week (Janicke-Bowles et al. 2019; Raney et al., 2018). It can be expected that inspiring music might also have beneficial consequences for the listener. Indeed, initial research indicates that awe-inspiring music can affect well-being outcomes such as meaning in life, moral motivations, and universality orientation via the motivational state of inspiration (Ji, Janicke-Bowles, De Leeuw, & Oliver, 2019).

With regard to stereotype reduction, however, Dale and colleagues (2020) found that awe-inspiring videos did not attenuate stereotypes of African Americans that were elicited in a subsequent video; in fact, on the contrary, an increase in bias was observed. Their study indicates the impact that self-transcendent emotions (or awe specifically) may have on subsequent negative emotional responses to media content, which demands future research.

Love (Kama Muta)

Kama muta has been reliably elicited from videos and films that depict an increase in communal sharing relationships (e.g., *A Beautiful Day in the Neighborhood* [2019]). In fact, research on kama muta can possibly explain our "obsession" with videos of cute kittens or other animals that we encounter on social media platforms. Steinnes, Blomster, Seibt, Zickfeld, and Fiske (2019) presented participants videos of cute animals that were either interacting or not interacting and found that the animals that played with each other elicited more kama muta and were perceived as more human. Thus, even the portrayal of non-moral interaction seems to elicit experiences that have previously been labeled as moral elevation (e.g., feeling moved, touched, lump in throat, warm chest). Similar to elevation, experiences of kama muta have also been shown to predict prosocial tendencies, greater openness, and connectedness toward others, even members of an outgroup. For example, exposure to kama muta-eliciting political advertisements from the 2016 U.S. presidential campaign between Hillary Clinton and Donald Trump increased voting intention for one's preferred candidate, as you might expect. However, if an advertisement from the opponent also triggered kama muta, then viewers reported greater voting intention for the opponent as well (Seibt, Schubert, Zickfeld, & Fiske, 2019). Similarly, kama muta-eliciting videos have also been shown to predict warmth, social closeness, and trust toward an outgroup, even without the portrayal of the outgroup in the kama muta event. In sum, the concept of kama muta is relatively new in positive media psychology studies. However, conceptually it might encompass the experience of many of the self-transcendent emotions that media elicits; further, it could possibly reflect a superordinate emotional state that includes many of the self-transcendent effects previously observed from entertainment.

Summary

Transcendent media experiences are a particular type of eudaimonic experiences that are focused on others more so than the self. Self-transcendent emotions—elevation, admiration, gratitude, awe, hope, and kama muta—have been shown to be reliably elicited from transcendent portrayals across a wide range of media contexts. Specifically, portrayals of nature, beauty and art, kindness, encouragement, perseverance, and the overcoming of obstacles are most often found in media that viewers describe as "moving, touching, or inspiring." Many promising effects of media that elicit self-transcendent emotions for an individual's well-being and health have been reported, specifically in relation to prosociality and human connectedness. Different media contexts may provide unique opportunities for different groups of people to experience self-transcendence, whereas music seems to be the number one inspiring media regardless of demographics. Future research on transcendent media experiences, compared to more general eudaimonic ones, are necessary to further tease out their unique effects.

References

Alarcon, G. M., Bowling, N. A., & Khazon, S. (2013). Great expectations: A meta-analytic examination of optimism and hope. *Personality and Individual Differences*, 54, 821–827. doi:10.1016/j.paid.2012.12.004.

Algoe, S. B., & Haidt, J. (2009). Witnessing excellence in action: The 'other-praising' emotions of elevation, gratitude, and admiration. *Journal of Positive Psychology*, 4, 105–127. doi:10.1080/17439760802650519.

Bartlett, M.Y., & DeSteno, D. (2006). Gratitude and prosocial behavior: Helping when it costs you. *Psychological Science*, 17, 319–325. doi:10.1111/j.1467-9280.2006.01705.x.

Bartsch, A., Oliver, M. B., Nitsch, C., & Scherr, S. (2018). Inspired by the Paralympics: Effects of empathy on audience interest in para-sports and on the destigmatization of persons with disabilities. *Communication Research*, 45, 525–553. doi:10.1177/0093650215626984.

Brazeau, H., & Davis, C. G. (2018). Hope and psychological health and well-being following spinal cord injury. *Rehabilitation Psychology*, 63, 258–266. doi:10.1037/rep0000209.

Ciarrochi, J., Parker, P., Kashdan, T. B., Heaven, P. C., & Barkus, E. (2015). Hope and emotional well-being: A six-year study to distinguish antecedents, correlates, and consequences. *The Journal of Positive Psychology*, 10, 520–532. doi:10.1080/17439760.2015.1015154.

Clayton, R. B., Raney, A. A., Oliver, M. B., Neumann, D., Janicke-Bowles, S. H., & Dale, K. R. (2019). Feeling transcendent? Measuring psychophysiological responses to self-transcendent media content. *Media Psychology*. Advanced online publication. doi:10.1080/15213269.2019.1700135.

Dale, K. R., Janicke-Bowles, S. H., Raney, A. A., Oliver, M. B., Huse, L. K., Lopez, J., Reed, A., Seibert, J. C., & Zhao, D. (2020). Awe and stereotypes: Examining awe as an intervention against stereotypical media portrayals of African Americans. *Communication Studies*. Advanced online publication. doi:10.1080/10510974.2020.1754264.

Dale, K. R., Raney, A. A., Janicke, S. H., Baldwin, J., Rowlett, J., Wang, C., & Zhao, D. (2017a, November). *Narratives and self-transcendent emotions: A content analysis of inspirational movies and television shows*. Presented at the annual meeting of the National Communication Association, Dallas, TX.

Dale, K. R., Raney, A. A., Janicke, S. H., Sanders, M. S., & Oliver, M. B. (2017b). YouTube for good: A content analysis and examination of elicitors of self-transcendent media. *Journal of Communication*, 67, 897–919. doi:10.1111/jcom.12333.

Dale, K. R., Raney, A. A., Ji, Q., Janicke-Bowles, S. H., Baldwin, J., Rowlett, J., Wang, C., & Oliver, M.B. (2019). Self-transcendent emotions and social media: Exploring the content and consumers of inspirational Facebook posts. *New Media & Society*, 22, 507–527. doi:10.1177/1461444819865720.

Emmons, R. A., & McCullough, M. E. (2003). Counting blessings versus burdens: An experimental investigation of gratitude and subjective well-being in daily life. *Journal of Personality and Social Psychology*, 84, 377–389. doi:10.1037/0022-3514.84.2.377.

Fiske, A. P. (2004). Relational models theory 2.0. In N. Haslam (Ed.), *Relational models theory: A contemporary overview* (pp. 3–25). Mahwah, NJ: Lawrence Erlbaum Associates.

Freeman, D., Aquino, K., & McFerran, B. (2009). Overcoming beneficiary race as an impediment to charitable donation: Social dominance orientation, the experience of moral elevation, and donation behavior. *Personality and Social Psychology Bulletin*, 35, 72–84. doi:10.1177/0146167208325415.

Ghandeharioun, A., Azaria, A., Taylor, S., & Picard, R. W. (2016). "Kind and grateful": A context-sensitive smartphone app utilizing inspirational content to promote gratitude. *Psychology of Well-Being*, 6(9). doi:10.1186/s13612-016-0046-2.

Homan, K. J., Sedlak, B. L., & Boyd, E. A. (2014). Gratitude buffers the adverse effect of viewing the thin ideal on body dissatisfaction. *Body Image*, 11, 245–250. doi:10.1016/j.bodyim.2014.03.005.

Jackowska, M., Brown, J., Ronaldson, A., & Steptoe, A. (2016). The impact of a brief gratitude intervention on subjective well-being, biology and sleep. *Journal of Health Psychology*, 21, 2207–2217. doi:10.1177/1359105315572455.

Janicke, S. H., Hendry, A., & Dale, K. R., (2018, May). *Gratitude in the context of film and its effects on well-being.* Presented at annual meeting of the International Communication Association Conference, Prague, CZ.

Janicke, S. H. & Oliver, M. B. (2017). The relationship between elevation, connectedness and compassionate love in meaningful films. *Psychology of Popular Media Culture*, 6, 274–289. doi:10.1037/ppm0000105.

Janicke, S. H. Rieger, D., Reinecke, L., & ConnorIII, W. (2018). Watching online videos at work: The role of positive and meaningful affect for recovery experiences and well-being at the workplace. *Mass Communication & Society*, 21, 345–367. doi:10.1080/15205436.2017.1381264.

Janicke-Bowles, S. H., Raney, A. A., Oliver, M. B., Dale, K. R., Jones, R. P., & Cox, D. (2019). Exploring the spirit in U.S. audiences: The role of the virtue of transcendence in inspiring media consumption. *Journalism & Mass Communication Quarterly*. Advanced online publication. doi:10.1177/1077699019894927.

Janicke-Bowles, S. H., Schubert, T., & Blomster, J. K. (in press). Feeling moved by mediated love: Kama muta as an eudaimonic entertainment experience. To be published in P. Vorderer & C. Klimmt (Eds.), *The Oxford handbook of entertainment theory*. New York, NY: Oxford University Press.

Ji, Q., Janicke-Bowles, S. H., De Leeuw, R. N. H., & Oliver, M. B. (2019). The melody to inspiration: The effects of awe-eliciting music on approach motivation and positive well-being. *Media Psychology*. Advanced online publication. doi:10.1080/15213269.2019.1693402.

Krämer, N., Eimler, S. C., Neubaum, G., Winter, S., Rösner, L., & Oliver, M. B. (2017). Broadcasting one world: How watching online videos can elicit elevation and reduce stereotypes. *New Media & Society*, 19, 1349–1368. doi:10.1177/1461444816639963.

Lai, C. K., Haidt, J., & Nosek, B. A. (2013). Moral elevation reduces prejudice against gay men. *Cognition & Emotion*, 28, 781–794. doi:10.1080/02699931.2013.861342.

McCullough, M. E., Kilpatrick, S. D., Emmons, R. A., & Larson, D. B. (2001). Is gratitude a moral affect? *Psychological Bulletin*, 127, 249–266. doi:10.1037/0033-2909.127.2.249.

Oliver, M. B., Ferchaud, A., Huang, Y., Janicke, S. H., Yang, C., & Bailey, E. (2017, November). *Seeing the world through a rose-colored lens: Examining mobile phone photography as meaningful media.* Presented at the annual meeting of the National Communication, Dallas, TX.

Oliver, M. B., Raney, A. A., Slater, M., Appel, M., Hartmann, T., Bartsch, A., Schneider, F., Janicke-Bowles, S. H., Krämer, N., Mares, M. L., Vorderer, P., Rieger, D., Dale, K. R., & Das, H. H. J. (2018). Self- transcendent media experiences: Taking meaningful media to a higher level. *Journal of Communication,* 68, 380–389. doi:10.1093/joc/jqx020.

Peters, B. (2019, January 10). What 777,367,063 Facebook posts tell us about successful content in 2019: New research. Buffer. https://buffer.com/resources/facebook-market ing-2019/.

Peterson, C., & Seligman, M. E. P. (2004). *Character strengths and virtues: A classification and handbook.* Washington, DC: American Psychological Association.

Pew Research Center. (2019, June 12). Social Media Fact Sheet. Pew Research Center: Internet & Technology. https://www.pewresearch.org/internet/fact-sheet/social-m edia/.

Piff, P. K., Dietz, P., Feinberg, M., Stancato, D. M., & Keltner, D. (2015). Awe, the small self, and prosocial behavior. *Journal of Personality and Social Psychology,* 108, 883–899. doi:10.1037/pspi0000018.

Prestin, A. (2013). The pursuit of hopefulness: Operationalizing hope in entertainment media narratives. *Media Psychology,* 16, 318–346. doi:10.1080/15213269.2013.773494.

Raney, A. A., Janicke, S. H., Oliver, M. B., Dale, K. R., Jones, R. P., & Cox, D. (2018). Profiling the sources of and audiences for inspiring media content: A national survey. *Mass Communication & Society,* 21, 296–319. doi:10.1080/15205436.2017.1413195.

Rieger, D., & Klimmt, C. (2019). The daily dose of digital inspiration: A multi-method exploration of meaningful communication in social media. *New Media & Society,* 21, 97–118. doi:10.1177/1461444818788323.

Schnall, S., Roper, J., & Fessler, D. M. T. (2010). Elevation leads to altruistic behavior. *Psychological Science,* 21, 315–320. doi:10.1177/0956797609359882.

Seibt, B., Schubert, T. W., Zickfeld, J. H., & Fiske, A. P. (2019). Touching the base: heart-warming ads from the 2016 US election moved viewers to partisan tears. *Cognition & Emotion,* 33, 197–212. doi:10.1080/02699931.2018.1441128.

Shiota, M. N., Keltner, D., & Mossman, A. (2007). The nature of awe: Elicitors, appraisals, and effects on self-concept. *Cognition and Emotion,* 21, 944–963. doi:10.1080/02699930600923668.

Snyder, C. R., Harris, C., Anderson, J. R., Holleran, S. A., Irving, L. M., Sigmon, S. T., Yoshinobu, L., Gibb, J., Langelle, C., & Harney, P. (1991). The will and the ways: Development and validation of an individual-difference measure of hope. *Journal of Personality and Social Psychology,* 60, 570–585. doi:10.1037//0022-3514.60.4.570.

Steinnes, K. K., Blomster, J. K., Seibt, B., Zickfeld, J. H., & Fiske, A. P. (2019). Too cute for words: Cuteness evokes the heartwarming emotion of kama muta. *Frontiers in Psychology,* 10, 1–17. doi:10.3389/fpsyg.2019.00387.

Thrash, T. M., & Elliot, A. J. (2004). Inspiration: Core characteristics, component processes, antecedents, and function. *Journal of Personality and Social Psychology,* 87, 957–973. doi:10.1037/0022-3514.87.6.957.

Tsay-Vogel, M., & Krakowiak, K. M. (2016). Inspirational reality TV: The prosocial effects of lifestyle transforming reality programs on elevation and altruism. *Journal of Broadcasting & Electronic Media,* 60, 567–586. doi:10.1080/08838151.2016.1234474.

Van Cappellen, P., Saroglou, V., Iweins, C., Piovesana, M., & Fredrickson, B. L. (2013). Self-transcendent positive emotions increase spirituality through basic world assumptions. *Cognition and Emotion*, 27, 1378–1394. doi:10.1080/02699931.2013.787395.

Waddell, T. F., & Bailey, A. (2017). Inspired by the crowd: The effect of online comments on elevation and universal orientation. *Communication Monographs*, 84, 534–550. doi:10.1080/03637751.2017.1369137.

Yaden, D. B., Haidt, J., Hood, R. W., Vago, D. R., & Newberg, A. B. (2017). The varieties of self-transcendent experience. *Review of General Psychology*, 21, 143–160. doi:10.1037/gpr0000102.

Yang, Y., Yang, Z., Bao, T., Liu, Y., & Passmore, H.-A. (2016.). Elicited awe decreases aggression. *Journal of Pacific Rim Psychology*, 10, 11e. doi:10.1017/prp.2016.8.

Zhao, D., & Dale, K. R. (2019). Pro-social messages and transcendence: A content analysis of Facebook reactions to Mark Zuckerberg's donation pledge. *Computers in Human Behavior*, 91, 236–243. doi:10.1016/j.chb.2018.09.042.

Zickfeld, J. H., Schubert, T. W., Seibt, B., Blomster, J. K., Arriaga, P., Basabe, N., ... Fiske, A. P. (2019). Kama muta: Conceptualizing and measuring the experience often labelled being moved across 19 nations and 15 languages. *Emotion*, 19, 402–424. doi:10.31234/osf.io/sr7e9.

Additional Readings

Haidt, J. (2003). The moral emotions. In R. J. Davidson, K. R. Scherer, & H. H. Goldsmith (Eds.), *Handbook of affective sciences* (pp. 852–870). Oxford, UK: Oxford University Press.

Nelson-Coffey, S. K., Ruberton, P. M., Chancellor, J., Cornick, J. E., Blascovich, J., & Lyubomirsky, S. (2019). The proximal experience of awe. *PloS One*, 14(5), e0216780. doi:10.1371/journal.pone.0216780.

Wood, A. M., Froh, J. J., & Geraghty, A. W. A. (2010). Gratitude and well-being: A review and theoretical integration. *Clinical Psychology Review*, 30, 890–905. doi:10.1016/j.cpr.2010.03.005.

7

SOCIAL MEDIA

Source: Shutterstock 763552732

Social media platforms have a mixed reputation in popular culture, but the dominant narrative has typically centered on their potential negative impact on users and society as a whole. This is significant because, according to the Pew Research Center, 81% of Americans own a smartphone (2019a) and 72% use some form of social media (2019b). With so many people using social media, it is vital that we understand the ways that use can affect individuals. However, as was the case when other new media technologies were widely adopted, a bias toward exploring the potential negative effects of social media was first to emerge. For instance, researchers have examined the connection between social media use and negative body image (for an overview of current body image research, see

Fardouly & Vartanian, 2016), but the results are complicated. Some studies show a correlation between social media use and negative body image; some experiments have shown mixed results. Researchers have also examined cyberbullying and hate speech on social media sites and found that both occur on a variety of sites, suggesting that social media platforms may have the potential to be used to spread negative messages.

Just as social media sites can be used in negative ways resulting in negative effects, they can also be used in positive ways leading to positive effects. This chapter will focus on the positive uses and effects of social media and provide an overview of the ways users can benefit from engaging with social media.

Defining Social Media

We often think of social media as a relatively recent phenomenon, but social media sites have been around for decades. In fact, the platform Six Degrees, which is widely credited as the first social media platform, was started in 1997. From there, Friendster and Myspace became popular sites, followed by the creation of Facebook, Twitter, Instagram, Snapchat, TikTok, and many others.

The fact that so many platforms with so many features exist can make it difficult to define exactly what social media is. You may have somewhat of an inherent cultural understanding of why Facebook is a social media platform but Amazon is not. However, it becomes a little more difficult to articulate why Twitter is considered a social media platform while *The New York Times* website, which allows users to comment on articles from personal accounts, is not.

The discussion as to *what social media is* is vital to our exploration of the positive effects the various platforms can have on users. One way to work toward a definition of social media would be to list all of the different social media platforms. However, by the time a textbook or journal article is published, many of those platforms may no longer exist (see Vine, Google+, Myspace, or any number of other now defunct platforms). Rather than deciding which platforms and sites "count" as social media, it is often more helpful to define social media according to the affordances each site offers. **Affordances** are the features or characteristics that the platform design allows users to use. An affordance perspective helps us to narrow the definition of social media.

For our purposes, to be considered social media, a site must afford users the ability to **personalize** content (e.g., create a personal homepage, select a username or handle). For instance, Facebook allows individuals and groups to create profiles featuring photos, lists of interests, and other original content. Instagram and Twitter likewise allow individuals to create a profile and upload original content. Further, these platforms allow users to curate and personalize the content to which they are exposed.

The second distinguishing affordance is that users must be able to **interact** with other people on the site (or at least have the perception of interaction, as in the case of artificial intelligence systems). Commenting, exchanging messages, liking content, and sharing posts are all forms of interaction. On TikTok, for instance, users can like videos, follow accounts, comment on videos, and create new content based on existing content (e.g., using existing audio, dueting with an existing video).

The third distinguishing affordance is that users must be able to **create and post content that is visible to others**. On Instagram, users can take, edit, and post photos. On Twitter, users can create and share tweets. This content can be created elsewhere and then uploaded to the site (e.g., taking a photo on your camera and then uploading it to Facebook), but the social media site must allow for (1) the creation of content and (2) the public or semi-public sharing of that content. Although users may choose restrictive privacy settings allowing only a small number of close friends or family to access content, the affordances on a social media site still *allow* for the sharing of content.

Together, these three affordances provide objective criteria for determining which sites should and should not be considered social media. Facebook, for instance, would qualify as social media using these criteria: it allows users to create a personalized profile, create and share content with their friends, and interact with others within the site by commenting, reacting to, and sharing posts. A trickier example is Snapchat, which is often used by individuals to send personal messages to their friends. If this was the only feature of the platform, we might consider it more akin to text messaging than social media. However, Snapchat allows users to create personal accounts and broadcast stories to those who follow them. Users can also see content from friends, strangers, and brands on the Discover page. But does Snapchat afford interactions? Users can certainly interact by sending messages, but without likes or comments, determining whether the platform truly fits the interaction requirement is a challenge. However, users can share public snaps created by others with their friends. If we consider sharing the content of others as interaction, then Snapchat can be classified as a social media site. On the other hand, the earlier example of *The New York Times* website would not meet the criteria because the primary content (i.e., news articles) is created by the administrators of the site itself. Although users can create personal accounts and interact with the news articles by leaving comments, they cannot create news articles themselves.

Thus, for the purposes of this chapter, we define social media based on affordances offered by each site. Social media are web-based platforms or sites that allow users to create personalized accounts, create and share content, and interact with other users. This definition is fairly broad, but it provides flexibility to assess new platforms as they arise, while also limiting the scope of social media to include only those platforms that include specific, objective characteristics.

Sites that fit this definition can still differ from each other in terms of privacy, anonymity, and synchronicity (among other ways). **Privacy** refers to the extent to which the content created and shared by users is accessible by others. Many social media platforms allow users to control their privacy settings and determine which content will be entirely private (i.e., visible only to the user), shared with a small group of predetermined people (e.g., friends list) or shared publicly, such that anyone with internet access can see it. In some cases, privacy settings are given other names, such as "protected tweets" on Twitter, but the function of "protecting" tweets is similar to other privacy options available on a variety of social media platforms. Ultimately, different platforms offer different privacy options, along with different levels of security regarding those privacy options.

Social media platforms also differ regarding **anonymity**, or the extent to which users and content can remain anonymous. The official Facebook policy is that all users must create accounts using their "real" names (i.e., the names they go by in everyday life), though the site has a mixed record of enforcing this policy. Other platforms like TikTok allow anonymous access to content but require accounts for users to create or interact with content. On the other end of the spectrum, some platforms require verification of identity. For instance, during the early years of Cyworld, a Korean social media platform similar to Myspace or Facebook, users were required to use their real name and their resident registration number (similar to a social security number in the U.S.) to create an account. The extent to which users are able to remain anonymous can influence the experience had with sites.

A third way in which social media platforms differ is **synchronicity**, or the extent to which users can interact with and share content in real time. On some sites, like Twitter, users must first post content before replies can be posted. Although others may interact with and comment on posts in something close to real time, Twitter is technically considered an asynchronous site. Facebook Live would be considered synchronous because users can post live video feeds in real time, which users can comment on and interact with during a live broadcast. The live video is also saved on the creator's page and available for viewing after it is finished, thus enabling asynchronous interactions as well.

Although social media platforms may differ in many ways, their similarities based upon the affordances they offer allow us to examine the technologies as a whole. Our ultimate goal is to understand how people use the platforms and what positive effects may result from doing so.

Positive Social Media Use

Reducing Loneliness and Maintaining Relationships

One of the most important characteristics of social media is that they allow connections with others. After all, they are called "social" media for a reason. The technologies provide a unique way to stay in touch with people whom we see frequently, as well as those who are physically distant from us. Although other communication technologies (e.g., written word, telephone) have allowed people to keep in touch with friends and family in a relatively simple and convenient way for many centuries, social media platforms have expanded and altered this possibility in stunning ways. We can now see photos and updates from our childhood friends, relatives around the world, celebrities we likely do not know in real life, and a host of other people in (near) real time. In many ways, social media are designed for connection. These connections with others are an important component of eudaimonic well-being (see Chapter 3 and Ryff, 1989), and social media provide a unique way to build and nourish positive relationships.

Despite this, some researchers have found a connection between social media use and loneliness. However, much of this research is correlational in nature (see Chapter 1), which means we cannot be certain that social media use *causes* loneliness. In one experimental study, Hunt, Marx, Lipson, and Young (2018) found that individuals who limited social media use to ten minutes per platform per day experienced less loneliness and depression compared to individuals who did not limit their use. Although it may be tempting to conclude from this study that social media use causes loneliness and depression whereas limiting its use can increase well-being, what the study really shows is that *how* we use social media matters.

BOX 7.1 WHY DO STUDIES FIND (SEEMINGLY) CONTRADICTORY RESULTS?

When it comes to social media research, studies have shown mixed results. For instance, some studies show that social media use is associated with *increased* loneliness (e.g., Song et al. 2014), and others report that it is associated with *decreased* loneliness (e.g., Deters & Mehl, 2016). Still others have found no relationship between social media use and loneliness (e.g., Brusilovskiy, Townley, Snethen, & Salzer, 2016). Similarly, social media use can be associated with *higher* and *lower* levels of well-being (e.g., positive effects on mental well-being among LGBTQ users, Chong, Zhang, Mak, and Pang [2015]; negative effects on happiness, Brooks [2015]). At first glance, it may seem like these studies contradict each other, but that is not necessarily the case. Why do studies find seemingly opposing results?

One reason that studies find different results is that the researchers may be examining different populations. As mentioned in the chapter, a great deal of social media research has examined undergraduate students at research universities in the U.S. and Europe. However, scholars are increasingly studying the effects of social media use on other populations as well. One reason for differing results may be that social media use affects different populations differently. For instance, it might be that undergraduate students who are typically considered **digital natives** (i.e., they grew up with social media technology) have a different experience when using these platforms than older generations who came to the technology later in life. Or, it may be that certain cultural values and experiences affect the way we use social media, which then influences the effects that it has on us. Our mental health status can also influence the effects of social media, as seen in the study by Brusilovskiy and colleagues (2016) mentioned earlier. The study examined individuals with serious mental illnesses, suggesting that the lack of relationship between social media and loneliness may be unique to a specific population.

A second reason why results may differ is that researchers might be examining different platforms. In the study by Pittman and Reich (2016) mentioned in the chapter, the researchers directly compared photo-based (Instagram and Snapchat) and text-based (Twitter and YikYak) platforms to examine effects. However, many studies examine only one or two social media platforms per study. These studies then get generalized as "social media" studies, when in reality, they primarily reflect user experiences with and effects of a specific platform. Given what we know about the differences in affordances between platforms, it makes sense that different platforms likely have different effects.

So, what do we do with all of this information? How can we know what the "real" effects of social media are? Truth be told, there is no one set of "real" effects. Each of the studies that seem to contradict each other is likely correct given the specific situation examined. For instance, Song and colleagues (2014) conducted a meta-analysis (see Chapter 1) in which they examined previous research on the effects of social media and found that social media use was associated with loneliness. However, the researchers examined the results from the previous studies more closely and determined that it is not the case that social media use causes loneliness, but rather that lonely people tend to use social media more often. This study is a great example of why we need to look at who was studied, which platform was examined, the specific effect that was measured, and the direction of causality between variables when discussing social media effects. This will help us to piece together the effects of social media use on specific populations in specific instances. It is unlikely that effects are identical across populations and platforms; thus, it is unsurprising that some studies lead to different conclusions.

Further supporting the idea that how we use social media matters, Yang (2016) found that the specific acts of browsing Instagram and interacting with posts were associated with less loneliness. The author argued that this may be because seeing posts from a variety of friends may remind a user about how large their number of connections is, making them feel like they have a lot of connections with others. However, Yang also noted that this association with loneliness was less for those who were inclined to compare themselves with others. That is, individuals who compared themselves with other people featured in the content they observed or with which they interacted did not benefit as much as those who were less likely to compare themselves with others. This may be because of **upward social comparisons** (see social judgment theory; Festinger, 1954). When we engage in upward social comparisons, we compare ourselves with others who we think are better or in a better situation than us. For instance, when we see photos on Instagram of people who we think are more attractive, richer, happier, or possess more of any other positive attribute than we do, we are inclined to feel worse about ourselves as a result. Yang (2016) found that those who compared themselves with others in the Instagram post did not experience the same reduction in loneliness as those who were not inclined to do so, suggesting that personality traits and personal inclinations may influence the way social media affect us. These results also suggest that, in order to reap the most benefits from social media use, we should avoid engaging in upward social comparisons, though that is easier said than done (see also Chapter 13).

Which sites we use also influences the effects of social media. Pittman and Reich (2016) found that using image-based social media sites such as Instagram was associated with less loneliness, more happiness, and more satisfaction with life. In this study, the researchers conducted a survey of undergraduate students that asked about their use of Instagram, Snapchat, Twitter, and YikYak (a now defunct, anonymous social media site). They found that the use of image-based social media platforms was associated with increased happiness and satisfaction with life and decreased loneliness. The researchers argued that this may be because image-based platforms make users feel like they are communicating and interacting with a real person rather than just text. The extent to which it seems like you are really communicating with someone is called **social presence** (see Biocca, Harms, & Burgoon, 2003; Short, Williams, & Christie, 1976). The basic idea is that seeing a photo or video of a real person makes your brain think that the person is physically with you. In order to truly mimic real-life conversations, the social media platforms would need to allow for synchronicity and intimacy. Many do allow for very quick responses, though as discussed earlier, they may technically be asynchronous. The intimacy aspect is more difficult to replicate, but photos can help achieve a version of this feeling in a way that may not be as satisfactory as text. Thus, Pittman and Reich (2016) demonstrated that different social media sites may influence feelings of loneliness in different ways.

Social media can also serve as a tool for monitoring what is happening in your personal social circle and the world around you. Additionally, it can serve as a way for individuals to maintain relationships. These relationships may be ones that you nurture daily through online and face-to-face channels, or they may be ones that are more difficult to maintain due to physical distance. Social media provide a tool for relationship maintenance that is unique from other technologies, thus providing valuable avenues for building the meaningful connections that can improve eudaimonic well-being. Due to the sharing and privacy affordances, users can post updates and share content about their lives with many people at once or with a few select individuals. This can help individuals stay up-to-date about major life events, everyday occurrences, and many things in-between. Vitak (2014) found that those who use social media to maintain physically distant friendships benefit the most from the technologies. She argued that social media permit users to keep in touch with friends without even having contact information (e.g., phone number, email address). All that is needed is an online connection: to "friend" them, follow them, or otherwise connect through a platform. This makes maintaining physically distant relationships easier. Maintaining personal relationships can have a positive effect on well-being, and social media make it easier than ever to stay in touch with those we care about.

The results of these studies suggest that using social media can help reduce loneliness and help us maintain relationships, so long as we follow several guidelines. You'll likely notice this theme in many of the following sections: if we use social media according to "best practices" found in research, we may experience more benefits. For instance, photo-based platforms may be better suited than text-based platforms when it comes to reducing loneliness, but only if we can avoid upward social comparisons. And the relationships that are most likely to benefit from social media use are those where we are physically distant from the friend.

Connecting with Similar Others

As much as new technologies allow us to connect with friends and family regardless of physical proximity, many also allow us to connect with strangers over shared interests or experiences in an unprecedented way. Facebook groups, for instance, facilitate communication with strangers who share our love of gardening, our political views, or our preferred method of exercise, among other topics. We can get tips for our hobbies, connect with others who share our viewpoints, and get and give support from people we never would have been able to interact with in real life. Researchers have examined peer support in a wide range of communities including those designed for parents and breastfeeding mothers, weight management communities, communities for helping college students adjust to college life, and health-related communities like those for individuals with diabetes. Peer-to-peer support provided on social media can be beneficial for all kinds of communities, and they can help users create and maintain positive relationships with these communities. Furthermore, they may contribute to feelings of environmental mastery, another key component of eudaimonic well-being.

For instance, DeAndrea, Ellison, LaRose, Steinfield, and Fiore (2012) examined how social media use before arriving at college affected adjustment to college life among first-semester students. For many students, going to college can be both exciting and anxiety-producing; for many, it is a new town with new living arrangements, new people, and new professors. Some of the anxiety first-year students experience may be due to uncertainty about what to expect at college. One way that students can gain information about what college life might be like is by interacting with other students via social media. DeAndrea and colleagues (2012) examined a student-only, school-specific social media site that allowed incoming students to interact with each other and residence hall mentors. They found that use of the site predicted student feelings of **self-efficacy** regarding their ability to connect with and get help from a variety of individuals including faculty and peers. On the site, students asked questions and used the opportunity to help each other find resources and information, building connections in the process.

Stress Management

Stress is something that people typically try to avoid, though it is inevitable for most of us. Increased stress levels are associated with negative physical and mental health outcomes and lower levels of subjective well-being; so, most people try to minimize, or at least mitigate, stress levels through various behaviors. People generally cope with stress in one of two ways: by focusing on the emotion or on the problem. Emotion-focused strategies attempt to address the feelings of or emotions related to stress. For instance, if you are experiencing stress as a result of an upcoming exam, you might distract yourself by scrolling through social media or by talking to a friend. Problem-focused strategies attempt to address the cause of the stress itself. For exam-related stress, this might include studying more than usual and making sure you are prepared. Both emotion- and problem-focused strategies provide ways to address stress, and both are valuable in different circumstances. Although emotion-focused coping may seem like avoiding the problem, it can be incredibly important in circumstances that are outside of your immediate control.

Social media provide opportunities for both emotion- and problem-focused coping, and social media use can help to mitigate stress. In a study of general smartphone use, Karsay, Schmuck, Matthes, and Stevic (2019) found that self-disclosure plays an important role in the effects on stress and loneliness. In this case, **self-disclosure** included sharing personal information about one's problems and feelings, including through social media platforms. In the study, for those who used their smartphones for self-disclosure, smartphone use was associated with reduced loneliness and decreased stress. Regarding loneliness, this is perhaps unsurprising considering the earlier discussion of social media and loneliness; meaningful connections with others are an important aspect of well-being. The findings regarding stress may be more surprising though. In a more specific examination of the effects of social media on stress levels, Zhang (2017) found similar results: Sharing personal information about stresses with others through social media was associated with reduced stress levels. Thus, research suggests that sharing your problems with someone via technology can lead you to feel relief from your stress, and it may lead to you receiving support.

In fact, Nabi, Prestin, and So (2013) found further support that feelings of social support were associated with reduced stress levels. Feelings of social support increased with the number of Facebook friends a person had, supporting the earlier argument that online connections can make an individual feel supported in real life. Specifically, the study found that having more Facebook friends was associated with greater feelings of social support, which was associated with less stress. Taking this a step further, the authors found that reduced stress was associated with both a higher level of general well-being and a lower level of physical illness.

Social Media and Advocacy

In many ways, social media has revolutionized how we keep in touch and connect with people. It has also changed the way we learn about major news stories, events, and causes. For many people, social media sites are often the first place they hear about breaking news. They have also become forums for advocacy, from posting requests for donations to encouraging people to protest and take direct action. The #MeToo and #BlackLivesMatter movements, although stemming primarily from offline injustices, gained widespread attention through social media as they encouraged real-world action. Yet scholars disagree as to the extent to which social media has fundamentally changed activism.

In order to explore the ways that social media has altered advocacy and activism, we must first consider the reasons why people engage in these activities in the first place. For instance, why would someone protest at a #BLM rally or advocate for stricter sexual harassment rules in the workplace? For someone to decide to take action for a cause, four requirements must be met. First, they have to care about the issue. This might be because they have a personal connection to the issue (e.g., they have experienced police brutality or sexual harassment) or because someone they care about has been affected by the issue. It may even be that they simply feel empathy for others who are affected by the issue, even though they do not personally know anyone affected. The second requirement for action is that they must know that an event or action is occurring. A person cannot attend a protest that they do not know is happening. The third requirement is that they have to want to participate. This is different than simply caring about the issue and requires that the person actually desires and is motivated to engage in the action or activity. And the final requirement is that they have to be able to participate. They must have the personal resources (e.g., time off from work, physical ability, financial ability) to engage in action. Someone might want to attend a protest, but they are unable to physically make it to the rally. Someone else might want to advocate for changes in the workplace, but they do not feel secure enough in their employment to challenge authority. The question then becomes: Has social media fundamentally changed these requirements for action?

Three major viewpoints have emerged regarding this question. The first is that social media platforms have substantially and meaningfully changed the way social movements form and take action. From this viewpoint, it is argued that social media sites have changed the way people get information about movements and activism in remarkable ways. Platforms have increased access to stories of people facing injustices around the world, perhaps increasing the likelihood that others will empathize with and care about the situation. Information about events and actions is more easily accessed and widely distributed with social media. A friend might post about a call to action or a protest, and we encounter the information without ever seeking it out ourselves. Social media also allow people to take part in demonstrations of solidarity, like sharing stories using hashtags, promoting donations to causes, and connecting with others who share similar interests. In many ways, social media have changed the way we advocate for change.

However, a second view is that social media has *not* fundamentally changed the requirements for action. Although it might be easier to get information about social movements and action, those who support this viewpoint argue that this has not changed the actual requirements for action. We might have access to more information, but does that information actually make us care more about the cause and want to take action? Does it make us any more capable of taking action? An individual might want to attend a protest they learned about online, but if they are still unable to take time off from work, then they are still unable to participate.

A third viewpoint falls in the middle between these two extremes, and scholars who support this view argue that it is not so much a matter of fundamental change but rather a change in degree. As Earl, Kimport, Prieto, Rush, and Reynoso (2010) explain, social media have "super-sized" our ability to advocate for change. Although the requirements for change remain the same, social media platforms make it easier to advocate for change and encourage action on a much larger scale than what was possible before the platforms were available. In this way, the requirements for action are not fundamentally different, but the ways we can satisfy the requirements are much easier and more accessible to the general population. With perseverance, intention, and a little luck, anyone can begin an online movement. Social media makes powerful tools for change available to anyone with internet access, which can lead to positive social change.

Entertaining, Meaningful, and Transcendent Content Online

Another positive effect of social media use is entertainment. More specifically, through the consumption of, participation in, and production of social media content, users find pleasure (i.e., enjoyment) and meaning (i.e., appreciation) by satisfying foundational human needs such as belonging, social interaction, self-presentation, identity management, self efficacy, and self-affirmation, in support of subjective and eudaimonic well-being (e.g., Toma & Hancock, 2013;

Valkenburg, Peter, & Schouten, 2006). From the perspective of self-determination theory (see Chapter 3), Reinecke, Vorderer, and Knop (2014) found that enjoyment of Facebook use was significantly associated with the satisfaction of the basic need for autonomy and competence, similar to what has been found with video game play (e.g., Ryan, Rigby, & Przybylski, 2006). Interestingly, the researchers found that external pressure from friends and family to use social media (i.e., extrinsic motivation) may also positively contribute to enjoyment through the satisfaction of competence needs.

Additionally, social media content can promote meaningful and transcendent media experiences. In a series of studies examining inspirational social media content, researchers found that elicitors of self-transcendent emotions (see Chapter 6) were commonly found in Facebook posts (Dale et al., 2020) and YouTube videos (Dale, Raney, Janicke, Sanders, & Oliver, 2017). Elicitors of self-transcendent emotions include people (and their behavior), places, or things that can cause you to feel a specific emotion. For instance, seeing the Grand Canyon may elicit feelings of awe, or watching someone overcome a difficult obstacle may elicit feelings of hope. These are examples of direct elicitors, which include depictions of things known to elicit self-transcendent emotions in real life (e.g. nature, perseverance). Online content can also contain modeled elicitors, which involve someone enacting a self-transcendent emotion. This terminology has its roots in social cognitive theory (Chapter 2) and is based on the idea that media users can experience emotions that are displayed by characters. For instance, seeing someone who is grateful for the kindness they have received may also make us feel grateful in response.

In these studies, Dale and colleagues found that social media content contains many examples of self-transcendent emotions and their elicitors. They also found that these depictions actually lead to increased feelings of inspiration among viewers (Dale et al., 2017). In this particular study, the researchers had participants watch a series of YouTube videos and indicate their feelings of inspiration using a device that measured second-by-second reactions. Using the resulting fine-grained data, the researchers found that participants turned their dials up (indicating higher levels of inspiration) when elicitors of self-transcendent emotions appeared onscreen. This work was the first to directly connect specific types of social media content to feelings of inspiration.

Meaningful and inspirational content is also common in internet memes. For instance, Rieger and Klimmt (2019) showed that Tumblr users regularly encounter what they call "small doses" of eudaimonic content online. These regular encounters can be beneficial to social media users in many ways. In fact, Janicke and colleagues (2018) found that watching meaningful YouTube videos at work improved employees' workplace well-being. Specifically, employees watched four meaningful or funny YouTube videos while at work. Both types of content resulted in positive, but different, responses: those who watched funny videos felt more relaxed and more satisfied with their work, and those who watched meaningful videos felt higher levels of mastery and energy. Although few bosses would likely encourage their employees to surf social media while at work, this study showed that viewing both funny and meaningful content can be beneficial and that meaningful content may play a unique role in helping employees recover from work-related stress.

However, the *way* we use social media again plays an important role in the effects on well-being. Janicke-Bowles and colleagues (2020) explored the extent to which sharing different kinds of content affected subjective and eudaimonic well-being. In the study, participants were asked to either use Facebook actively or passively for ten days. Those who were asked to use social media actively were further divided into two groups: one set of participants posted funny content and the other posted inspirational content. Those who were asked to use social media passively were told to simply scroll through their Facebook feeds without posting any content. The researchers found that actively posting inspirational content was associated with increased life satisfaction. Furthermore, although levels of positive affect were not affected over time, levels of negative affect (associated with subjective well-being) decreased for these users. Conversely, participants who posted funny content reported *decreased* eudaimonic well-being over time. Surprisingly, passive use affected neither subjective nor eudaimonic well-being.

BOX 7.2 WHAT ABOUT DIGITAL WELL-BEING APPS?

Increasingly, the market is being flooded with smartphone apps aimed at self-improvement, many with the purported goal of increasing your well-being. Not all of these apps meet our criteria for social media, but some do. Certain meditation and productivity apps fall into this category. Perhaps you have an app like that on your smartphone right now.

Interestingly though, most self-improvement and health apps are not developed based on theories of psychology or health behavior; furthermore, most have not been evaluated using scientific methods. Therefore, the effectiveness of such applications remains questionable (which you may be able attest to from your own experience). Diefenbach (2018) outlines several design features that seem to be specifically beneficial for habit-change apps. Self-improvement apps seem to be most effective when (1) their design provides a clear demand to change the behavior (e.g., concrete action or steps), while also (2) providing the user autonomy in executing the behavior (e.g., freedom to choose when and how to engage in the behavior). Effective apps also (3) encourage feedback and reward (e.g., social support from other users, motivational quotes). When these three affordances are provided, apps may indeed contribute to digital well-being and flourishing. The next time you download a new app, see if the app provides these three aspects for you.

Limitations of Positive Social Media Research

As with all research, the scholarship on social media effects has some limitations that need to be considered. The way that research is conducted, the people studied, and the technology examined can all affect the results of studies. We must recognize each of these limitations when we discuss research so that we can accurately understand the implications of the findings.

One limitation of some social media research is that it is often correlational in design. That is, the study used surveys to gain information. This means that the researchers send out questionnaires to participants that ask about their social media use and any other variables the researchers are interested in (e.g., well-being, life satisfaction). This kind of data can provide valuable insight into relationships between various factors, but it cannot establish a causal relationship between those factors (see Chapter 1). It is impossible to determine whether social media causes a variable of interest (e.g., loneliness, stress) from this type of research.

A second limitation is that social media research is often conducted using a sample of undergraduate students. This makes sense for many reasons, as young adults are some of the primary users of social media and are usually available for academic studies. However, it makes it difficult to generalize the results of studies to older or other populations. We cannot be sure that social media affect young, educated people in the same way as middle-aged or elderly individuals. As a result, researchers are starting to expand their study populations to see how these generations might differ.

A third limitation of social media research is that technology changes much faster than articles and textbooks can be written. It often takes months or even years to design and publish studies in academic outlets. During that time, it is possible that a social media platform could change many times or be no longer active. For instance, a study about Facebook privacy settings could become irrelevant before it is even published if Facebook changes the way their privacy settings work. This makes it difficult for researchers to keep up-to-date with the effects of current technology. Despite these limitations social media research can provide valuable insight into the way individuals use and are affected by social media platforms.

Summary

The term *social media* can be applied to a wide variety of online platforms. Because of the diverse platforms categorized under this umbrella, we define social media in terms of the affordances offered by the platforms. Instead of asking if social media are good or bad, we might benefit more from exploring the circumstances under which social media use can improve well-being. Research has shown that social media and mobile technologies can be used in a variety of helpful ways. These platforms and technologies can help to reduce loneliness among users by allowing them to connect with others, thus helping us to maintain positive meaningful relationships and receive social support. Social media can also be used as a tool for stress management and a way for individuals to advocate for social change in their communities. By adopting research-based use strategies, we can all reap the benefits of positive social media use.

References

Biocca, F., Harms, C., & Burgoon, J. K. (2003). Toward a more robust theory and measure of social presence: Review and suggested criteria. *Presence: Teleoperators & Virtual Environments*, 12, 456–480. doi:10.1162/105474603322761270.

Brooks, S. (2015). Does personal social media usage affect efficiency and well-being? *Computers in Human Behavior*, 46, 26–37. doi:10.1016/j.chb.2014.12.053.

Brusilovskiy, E., Townley, G., Snethen, G., & Salzer, M. S. (2016). Social media use, community participation and psychological well-being among individuals with serious mental illnesses. *Computers in Human Behavior*, 65, 232–240. doi:10.1016/j.chb.2016.08.036.

Chong, E. S., Zhang, Y., Mak, W. W., & Pang, I. H. (2015). Social media as social capital of LGB individuals in Hong Kong: Its relations with group membership, stigma, and mental well-being. *American Journal of Community Psychology*, 55, 228–238. doi:10.1007/s10464-014-9699-2.

Dale, K. R., Raney, A. A., Janicke, S. H., Sanders, M. S., & Oliver, M. B. (2017). YouTube for good: A content analysis and examination of elicitors of self-transcendent media. *Journal of Communication*, 67, 897–919. doi:10.1111/jcom.12333.

Dale, K. R., Raney, A. A., Ji, Q., Janicke-Bowles, S. H., Baldwin, J., Rowlett, J. T., Wang, C., & Oliver, M. B. (2020). Self-transcendent emotions and social media: Exploring the content and consumers of inspirational Facebook posts. *New Media & Society*, 22(3), 507–527. doi:10.1177/1461444819865720.

DeAndrea, D. C., Ellison, N. B., LaRose, R., Steinfield, C., & Fiore, A. (2012). Serious social media: On the use of social media for improving students' adjustment to college. *The Internet and Higher Education*, 15, 15–23. doi:10.1016/j.iheduc.2011.05.009.

Deters, F. G., & Mehl, M. R. (2016). Does posting Facebook status updates increase or decrease loneliness? An online social networking experiment. *Social Psychological and Personality Science*, 4, 579–586. doi:10.1177/1948550612469233.

Diefenbach, S. (2018). The potential and challenges of digital well-being interventions: Positive technology research and design in light of the bitter-sweet ambivalence of change. *Frontiers in Psychology*, 9, e331. doi:10.3389/fpsyg.2018.00331.

Earl, J., Kimport, K., Prieto, G., Rush, C., & Reynoso, K. (2010). Changing the world one webpage at a time: Conceptualizing and explaining Internet activism. *Mobilization: An International Quarterly*, 15, 425–446. doi:10.17813/maiq.15.4.w03123213lh37042.

Fardouly, J., & Vartanian, L. R. (2016). Social media and body image concerns: Current research and future directions. *Current Opinion in Psychology*, 9, 1–5. doi:10.1016/j.copsyc.2015.09.005.

Festinger, L. (1954). A theory of social comparison processes. *Human Relations*, 7, 117–140. doi:10.1177/001872675400700202.

Hunt, M. G., Marx, R., Lipson, C., & Young, J. (2018). No more FOMO: Limiting social media decreases loneliness and depression. *Journal of Social and Clinical Psychology*, 37,

751–768. doi:10.1521/jscp.2018.37.10.751. Janicke, S. H., Rieger, D., Reinecke, L., & Connor, W. (2018). Watching online videos at work: The role of positive and meaningful affect for recovery experiences and well-being at the workplace. *Mass Communication and Society*, 21, 345–367. doi:10.1080/15205436.2017.1381264.

Janicke-Bowles, S. H., Raney, A. A., Oliver, M. B., Dale, K. R., Zhao, D., Neumann, D., Clayton, R., & Hendry, A. (2020, May). *Content matters: Effects of inspiring Facebook posts on subjective and eudaimonic well-being*. Paper presented virtually at the annual meeting of the International Communication Association, Gold Coast, AU.

Karsay, K., Schmuck, D., Matthes, J., & Stevic, A. (2019). Longitudinal effects of excessive smartphone use on stress and loneliness: the moderating role of self-disclosure. *Cyberpsychology, Behavior, and Social Networking*, 22, 706–713. doi:10.1089/cyber.2019.0255.

Nabi, R. L., Prestin, A., & So, J. (2013). Facebook friends with (health) benefits? Exploring social network site use and perceptions of social support, stress, and well-being. *Cyberpsychology, Behavior, and Social Networking*, 16, 721–727. doi:10.1089/cyber.2012.0521.

Pew Research Center. (2019a, June 12). Mobile Fact Sheet. Pew Research Center: Internet & Technology. https://www.pewresearch.org/internet/fact-sheet/mobile/.

Pew Research Center. (2019b, June 12). *Social Media Fact Sheet*. Pew Research Center: Internet & Technology. https://www.pewresearch.org/internet/fact-sheet/social-media/.

Pittman, M., & Reich, B. (2016). Social media and loneliness: Why an Instagram picture may be worth more than a thousand Twitter words. *Computers in Human Behavior*, 62, 155–167. doi:10.1016/j.chb.2016.03.084.

Reinecke, L., Vorderer, P., & Knop, K. (2014). Entertainment 2.0? The role of intrinsic and extrinsic need satisfaction for the enjoyment of Facebook use. *Journal of Communication*, 64, 417–438. doi:10.1111/jcom.12099.

Rieger, D., & Klimmt, C. (2019). The daily dose of digital inspiration: A multi-method exploration of meaningful communication in social media. *New Media & Society*, 21, 97–118. doi:10.1177/1461444818788323. Ryan, R. M., Rigby, C. S., & Przybylski, A. (2006). The motivational pull of video games: A self-determination theory approach. *Motivation & Emotion*, 30, 347–363. doi:10.1007/s11031-006-9051-8.

Ryff, C. D. (1989). Happiness is everything, or is it? Explorations on the meaning of psychological well-being. *Journal of Personality and Social Psychology*, 57, 1069–1081. doi:10.1037/0022-3514.57.6.1069.

Short, J., Williams, E., & Christie, B. (1976). *The social psychology of telecommunications*. London, UK: John Wiley & Sons.

Song, H., Zmyslinski-Seelig, A., Kim, J., Drent, A., Victor, A., Omori, K., & Allen, M. (2014). Does Facebook make you lonely? A meta analysis. *Computers in Human Behavior*, 36, 446–452. doi:10.1016/j.chb.2014.04.011.

Toma, C. L., & Hancock, J. T. (2013). Self-affirmation underlies Facebook use. *Personality and Social Psychology Bulletin*, 39, 321–331. doi:10.1177/0146167212474694.

Valkenburg, P. M., Peter, J., & Schouten, A. P. (2006). Friend networking sites and their relationship to adolescents' well-being and social self-esteem. *Cyberpsychology & Behavior*, 9, 584–590. doi:10.1089/cpb.2006.9.584.

Vitak, J. (2014, February). Facebook makes the heart grow fonder: Relationship maintenance strategies among geographically dispersed and communication-restricted connections. In *Proceedings of the 17th ACM Conference on Computer Supported Cooperative Work & Social Computing* (pp. 842–853). New York, NY: Association for Computing Machinery.

Yang, C. C. (2016). Instagram use, loneliness, and social comparison orientation: Interact and browse on social media, but don't compare. *Cyberpsychology, Behavior, and Social Networking*, 19, 703–708. doi:10.1089/cyber.2016.0201.

Zhang, R. (2017). The stress-buffering effect of self-disclosure on Facebook: An examination of stressful life events, social support, and mental health among college students. *Computers in Human Behavior*, 75, 527–537. doi:10.1016/j.chb.2017.05.043.

Additional Reading

Campbell, S. W., & Ling, R. (2020). Effects of mobile communication. Revolutions in an evolving field. In M. B. Oliver, A. A. Raney, & J. Bryant (Eds.), *Media effects: Advances in research and theory* (4th ed., pp. 389–403). New York, NY: Routledge.

Fox, J., & Holt, L. F. (2018). Fear of isolation and perceived affordances: The spiral of silence on social networking sites regarding police discrimination. *Mass Communication and Society*, 21(5), 533–554. doi:10.1080/15205436.2018.1442480.

Fox, J., & McEwan, B. (2020). Social media. In M. B. Oliver, A. A. Raney, & J. Bryant (Eds.), *Media effects: Advances in research and theory* (4th ed., pp. 373–388). New York, NY: Routledge. Rieger, D., & Klimmt, C. (2019). The daily dose of digital inspiration 2: Themes and affective user responses to meaningful memes in social media. *New Media & Society*, 21(10), 2201–2221. doi:10.1177/1461444819842875.

8

DIGITAL GAMES AND VIRTUAL REALITY

Source: Shutterstock 1275745447

As the world locked down in response to the outbreak of COVID-19 in early 2020, many online media platforms reported record numbers of users. Netflix and Zoom use skyrocketed as people everywhere sheltered in place to work and learn online. Twitch—the Amazon-owned, live streaming service that predominantly features video game play—also witnessed huge increases in viewership, including up to 50% gains in some European countries most affected by the virus (Bellanger, 2020). To compete, Facebook rushed the release of Facebook Gaming as a stand-alone platform available on Android devices while most of the world was still living in isolation. Both cases reflect the growing importance of digital gaming on the media landscape in general. In this chapter, we explore some of the reasons why that might be the case from a psychological perspective, highlighting the ways that media technologies that leverage interactivity and immersive virtual environments can positively affect users.

The technologies and media formats discussed below all have one important feature in common: They engage the user with some form of computer-generated reality. In some cases, this takes the form of **augmented reality** (AR), which generally involves the superimposing of digital information into a user's physical space. For example, *Pokémon GO* uses AR to make it appear that the game creatures exist in the player's real-world environment. But more often than not, the technologies create and display **virtual environments** (VEs), computer-generated worlds to be entered and explored by the user. One of the most familiar types of VE is the game world.

Technically speaking, games are rule-based activities involving a challenge to reach a goal, typically with feedback provided on one's progress toward reaching that goal. Throughout this chapter, we adopt the term **digital games** to refer to all games delivered by a console, computer, smartphone, or tablet, as well as through software, stand-alone streaming platforms, or integrated into websites or other outlets. Regardless of format or delivery method, the rules, challenges, and goals differ across game titles. Some games require players to complete specific tasks or missions in a particular order, whereas others ("sandbox games") provide open worlds to be encountered at the player's pace and whim.

Additionally, the virtual environments in which games are set vary widely in terms of their faithfulness to the real-world (e.g., aesthetics, time period, physical capabilities, tasks to complete, etc.), as well as the extent to which the user feels present or immersed in the game world. **Virtual reality** (VR) is the term associated with technologies that deliver the most immersive computer-generated experiences (see Kalyanaraman & Bailenson, 2020). Through head-mounted displays, headphones, hand controllers, and tracking sensors, VR technologies completely envelop the user's senses—particularly, sight, sound, and touch, but increasingly smell and even taste—in a VE, in which the user's physical movements are mirrored by an avatar or a virtual manifestation of the user. As will be discussed below, VR technologies support a host of games but are also used in many non-game contexts.

Understanding Digital Games as Media

Games have played a vital role in the history of computing, both in terms of technological development and public adoption. In the 1950s and 1960s, computer scientists developed games as a way to explore and demonstrate the computational and graphical display capabilities of early computers. In the late 1970s and early 1980s, consumers more readily embraced first-generation home computers like the Apple II and the Commodore 64 because of their positive experiences with Atari's classic arcade game *Pong* and early video game consoles like the Magnavox Odyssey. In-home consoles also set the stage for the converged media of today, as the living room television could seamlessly double as a video arcade. In the early 1990s, hand-held devices like Nintendo Game Boy made digital gaming a mobile activity, paving the way for *Angry Birds, Fruit Ninja,* and *Minecraft.* In truth, for most of us, playing some sort of digital game was likely our first direct experience with any sort of computing device.

Because of the intertwined histories of games, computers, and other communication technologies, it seems natural to think of digital games as a form of media. At the same time, though, games display several characteristics that fundamentally differentiate them from other media content such as television programs and films. These differences are important for our overall discussion because they lead to and influence specific processes associated with the positive effects of the content.

Interactivity

The terms *interactive* and *interactivity* apply to several aspects of digital games and game play. First, the terms can describe the features (or affordances) of the games or the systems upon which they are played (Vorderer, 2000). For example, although on-demand streaming of television content is now widespread, allowing the viewer to select a particular episode of a series, viewers cannot change the shirt color of the lead character or the city in which the show is set. Digital games, however, typically offer the user a degree of *selection* that is far greater than is offered with other media content: at which level to play, what avatar to embody, which mission to attempt, which music to accompany, and so forth. Digital games also offer users the ability to *manipulate* and *modify* the content. The player's keystrokes, joystick movements, button pushes, and in-game choices all alter the game experience itself, as the supporting software responds to the limitless inputs with myriad outputs and potential outcomes. As a result, games are uncertain; a player's progress or success is not predetermined. Contrast this with other forms of content—except for sports and other competitions—that have fixed and unalterable endings. Similarly, most media narratives are linear in nature, moving chronologically or thematically along a specific storyline, always the same for each viewer or reader. Many digital games, however, are *nonlinear.* When your avatar comes to a crossroads, you can literally choose any of the paths to take with differing results. In some games, if you just want to wander around you can do so, accomplishing nothing more than passing time and checking out the scenery. And with games played in virtual reality, what one encounters in those environments leads to greater *sensory activation* than most other forms of media content. For instance, using the hand-held controllers in some VR systems, users can lift, rotate, and even throw virtual objects using the same arm movements and muscles as they would with the same object in the material world.

Second, the terms interactive and interactivity can refer to the user's perceptions of the experience of engaging with those features: how immersed, in control, present, connected. Other factors influencing perceived interactivity include the responsiveness of the system and nature of the system's communication capabilities (McMillan & Hwang, 2002). Third and finally, the terms can also describe the nature of the communication process that results from the use of those features. Such a description can be applied to the way that users interact with the technology or the content (user-to-system interactivity), as well as how users interact with one another while using the technology (user-to-user interactivity; e.g., multiple players communicating in an online game).

All of these notions of interactivity make gaming different from most other forms of media, with important implications on the effects processes.

Immersion and Presence

Imagine getting into an elevator. Eighty stories later the doors open, not into a lobby but into the open air. You see skyscrapers and blue sky before you, tiny cars, and a distant sidewalk below. A six-foot plank stretches out beneath your feet. No rope. No handrail. Just a plank. Would you step out and walk the plank? What if you knew it wasn't real? *Richie's Plank Experience* is a VR application that terrifies even the bravest among us. Why? Because it feels *so real*. VR as a technology is designed to make users feel immersed—like they are actually "there"—in the virtual environment. To some degree, all digital games strive for the same result. **Immersion** is a multifaceted psychological process occurring between a user and media content, involving attention, cognitive and emotional engagement, time, effort, investment, mastery, and control (Brown & Cairns, 2004), with the pinnacle of the process being presence.

Presence is the psychological experience of "being there." It involves a user "forgetting" that what they are experiencing is mediated, or as Lee (2004, p. 32) put it, "a psychological state in which the virtuality of experience is unnoticed." Although presence is possible with all forms of media, many digital games and virtual environments strive for complete immersion (and thus, presence), inviting the user to accept the experience as real. Presence is a multidimensional experience and can involve spatial and physical, self-referential, and social aspects.

One of the manifestations of social presence is **identification**, in which users experience "being" a character (Klimmt, Hefner, & Vorderer, 2009). As noted in Chapter 4, character identification is also possible with other forms of media. But games and virtual environments offer qualitatively different opportunities for identification to occur, as users themselves typically control the actions, movement, and decisions of characters, who are often customized avatars that even physically resemble the players. As will be discussed below, this reality affords players unique opportunities to temporarily shift their self-perceptions to those of the character. Moreover, strong evidence for the **Proteus effect** exists, which describes how shifts in self-perception and self-representation that occur while playing games can actually influence the way that we act and interact with others in our daily lives (Yee & Bailenson, 2007).

Social Interactions

Finally, like few other media experiences today, digital gaming invites social interaction. The motivations for the interactions are varied, including competition, collaboration, criticism, instruction, and companionship. Further, as noted above, some gaming-related social interactions can be characterized as user-to-system, which includes interactions between players and computer-directed characters (e.g., parasocial interaction, paracommunication; see Hartmann, 2008). Others are user-to-user interactions, which may be mediated or not, synchronous or asynchronous, and game- or nongame-related. As a result, attempts to understand the breadth of the potential effects of digital gaming must not only rely on theoretical perspectives from media psychology but social psychology and interpersonal communication as well.

Positive Effects of Digital Games

As media entertainment, digital games can lead to many of the same effects discussed in earlier chapters. A rich research tradition offers vast evidence for this claim (for a recent review, we recommend Klimmt & Possler, 2020). Below we highlight this work while placing the biggest focus on effects that are uniquely dependent upon the characteristics discussed above.

Digital Games as Hedonic Entertainment

As hedonically motivated creatures, humans seek out pleasurable experiences. One of the primary reasons people play digital games is pleasure, and study after study—and likely your own lived experience—confirm that games are indeed pleasurable. Specifically, game play can lead to positive emotions, which support life satisfaction and well-being. Gaming has also been associated with other outcomes typically thought of as pleasurable, such as decreased stress, emotion and mood regulation, relaxation, recovery from work-related fatigue, and overcoming loneliness (e.g., Reinecke, 2009; Russoniello, O'Brien, & Parks, 2009).

Many of the sources of enjoyment from digital game play are the same as those found with other forms of media. For instance, genre and narrative storylines are important factors in digital game enjoyment, with difference found across genders, ages, and personality types (e.g., Fang & Zhao, 2010; Schneider, Lang, Shin, & Bradley, 2004). In terms of content characteristics and reception processes, presence and avatar identification are both strongly associated with game enjoyment. As previously found with films and televised sports, enjoyment of game play is also strongly predicted by the level of suspense (e.g., Klimmt, Rizzo, Vorderer,

Koch, & Fischer, 2009) and *physiological arousal* (Poels, Hoogen, Ijsselsteijn, & de Kort, 2012) experienced. In other words, people enjoy digital game play for many of the same reasons they find other forms of media entertaining.

Additionally, the interactive nature of gaming provides users with a level of control—in terms of selection, modification, manipulation, nonlinearity, etc.—of the narrative and the entertainment experience that is simply not available with other forms of media. For instance, the simple act of interacting with a game world through exploration can be enjoyable in and of itself (Wirth, Ryffel, Von Pape, & Karnowski, 2013); this exploration can be motivated both by sensory and cognitive curiosity. Similarly, just exerting control—causing and affecting changes in the game world ("effectance")—can also be highly pleasurable (Klimmt, Hartmann, & Frey, 2007). The same is true for engaging in fantasy: encountering worlds not bound by the limitations and properties of our everyday experiences (Malone, 1981).

Moreover, exercising autonomy over specific aspects of the game situation and environment, and then experiencing the consequences of those actions, can likewise be enjoyable. For instance, as noted above, avatar identification can lead to greater enjoyment of game play. This is particularly the case for role-playing games (RPGs), which often rely heavily upon character development and character-centric storylines. In fact, such games can promote **character attachment**, a particularly enjoyable phenomenon beyond mere identification in which the minds of the player and character meld into one (e.g., Bowman, Schultheiss, & Schumann, 2012). Strong evidence exists that avatar identification and attachment is higher when players customize the physical appearance or capabilities of an avatar, with subsequent impacts on enjoyment, presence, and arousal (e.g., Kim et al., 2015). Moreover, customizing an avatar to appear physically similar to players themselves can lead to even greater identification and enjoyment. However, these relationships may not be true of all types of games. For instance, in competitive games, where one's success or failure may have an impact on self-esteem and self-concept, playing with an avatar that looks like you could be a detriment to enjoyment (Trepte & Reinecke, 2010).

Another aspect of interactivity that can impact enjoyment is the manner in which control is exerted in the game world. Mapping describes how a player's actions correspond to changes in the game, typically via some sort of controller. Many gaming platforms leverage a form of natural mapping, in which the controller itself or the actions performed with the controller parallel the same action in the real-world (e.g., steering wheel in a racing game). Generally speaking, games that utilize naturally mapped controllers result in greater perceptions of reality, presence, and enjoyment (e.g., Skalski, Tamborini, Shelton, Buncher, & Lindmark, 2011). The leading explanation for this is that more naturally mapped gaming controllers facilitate a player's quick access to cognitive representations (or "mental models") of the corresponding real-world behavior, leading to greater accuracy and enjoyment. Greater accuracy should furthermore lead to greater success, which is also pleasurable. But research finds that in-game success alone is not always the most important factor for enjoyment (e.g., Shafer, 2012). Ultimately, it seems that mastering a challenge—defeating a superior player, winning in a close match—may be particularly joyful (e.g., Abuhamdeh & Csikszentmihalyi, 2012).

This desire to "master the challenge" is one that appears throughout the literature on the uses and gratifications of digital game play, often listed as the most common reason people say they play. The concept of **flow** (first introduced in Chapter 3; Csikszentmihalyi & Csikszentmihalyi, 1988) helps explain how the process of mastery is pleasurable. Broadly speaking, flow describes the pleasure that comes from being completely immersed in a task. Common examples of activities potentially leading to flow tend to be creative in nature, like painting or playing a musical instrument, but in reality, a flow state can be achieved with just about any task, as long as it sufficiently challenges one's skills but can still be mastered. In a state of flow, you are completely engrossed in the task, intensely focusing on the present moment only. Your actions seem to come effortlessly. You lose track of time. You lose your own self-awareness. And you keep doing the task largely because the "doing it" is so pleasurable; often the outcome or the end results are of secondary importance (Nakamura & Csikszentmihalyi, 2002). The results of flow include enjoyment, pleasure and other positive emotions, and subjective well-being. Heavy gamers who are reading this probably immediately see how digital game play can lead to a state of flow. It is little wonder that research supports that gaming can indeed promote flow (e.g., Sherry, 2004; Vella, Johnson, & Hides, 2013). Without a doubt: Flow is not guaranteed with gaming. Games that are too easy can bore, whereas those that are too difficult can frustrate. The key to potentially experiencing flow with gaming is a balance between game (or in-game task) difficulty and the player's skills (although the overall process is quite complex). Because of this, the possibility of achieving flow while playing a digital game is theoretically available to everyone.

Another theoretical perspective that explains the hedonic enjoyment that people receive from digital game play is **self-determination theory** (SDT) (Ryan & Deci, 2000a). As you may recall from Chapter 4, we are all intrinsically motivated to pursue goals and activities that help us to satisfy three basic needs: autonomy, competence, and relatedness. These needs are essential for growth, well-being, and happiness. Tamborini and colleagues (2010) conceptually aligned SDT with entertainment theory, suggesting that the satisfaction of the three basic needs represented an explicit and theoretically grounded definition of hedonic enjoyment. Evidence in support of this claim came from digital game play, with various game factors predicting autonomy, competence, and relatedness need satisfaction, which all strongly predicted enjoyment score. Other studies have further demonstrated how game play can meet the needs identified by SDT, leading to happiness and well-being (e.g., Ryan, Rigby, & Przybylski, 2006).

Digital Games as Meaningful Entertainment

Somewhat by definition, games are supposed to be fun, non-serious, distracting, and enjoyable. And without a doubt most are. But it is also undeniable that some games serve a function beyond (or in addition to) fun; they engage, impact, inspire, anger, and move us. In doing so, they can help users address eudaimonic concerns and needs, further develop psychological well-being, and pursue human flourishing (see Kowert, 2020). A good example of how this may be the case can be found by examining games from the perspective of the PERMA theory of well-being (see Box 8.1).

BOX 8.1 GAMES AND PERMA

You might remember from Chapter 5 that positive psychologists have developed several theories of eudaimonic well-being. One of the better known perspectives is PERMA theory (Seligman, 2011). The various gaming dimensions and outcomes discussed earlier in the chapter actually track nicely upon PERMA theory (see Kelly, 2020; Jones, Scholes, Johnson, Katsikitis, & Carras, 2014), suggesting how games can possibly lead to eudaimonic well-being.

- (P)ositive emotions come with enjoyment,
- (E)ngagement can come through immersion,
- Positive (R)elationships can be experienced with character identification and social interactions, and,
- (A)ccomplishment comes through mastering the challenge.

Furthermore, Ryan and Deci (2000b) argued that (M)eaningfulness is a byproduct of autonomy-, competence-, and relatedness-need fulfillment (which is a primary reason they align SDT with eudaimonic rather than subjective well-being). More specifically, the quest for meaning, in terms of essential truths and experiences, comes through reflection upon life in terms of basic need fulfillment.

Oliver and colleagues (2016) offered support for these ideas in relation to digital game play. The researchers examined perceptions of meaningful (vs. fun) games from the perspective of SDT and the two-factor model of entertainment (enjoyment and appreciation; see Chapter 5). Appreciation was strongly related to meaningful games. Furthermore, enjoyment was closely related to autonomy and competence need satisfaction, whereas appreciation was more strongly related to relatedness needs, as well as to insight, an additional need factor that emerged in the study. Both relatedness and insight were strongly predicted by the perceived quality of the narrative portrayed in the story.

Thus, from a PERMA perspective, games hold the potential to fulfill the essential elements for psychological well-being.

Although examinations of meaningful gaming experiences have only recently begun to appear, several studies have demonstrated their potential to yield positive effects. For example, as forms of entertainment, games—especially narrative-driven ones—can facilitate eudaimonic appreciation as a response (e.g., Possler, Kümpel, & Unkel, 2019), particularly for those who identify with the characters (Bowman et al., 2016). Games may also promote sad, moving, and other forms of mixed affect, empathy toward characters and other players, cognitive and affective challenges, contemplation and reflection, meaningful social connections, and moral deliberation (e.g, Bopp, Mekler, & Opwis, 2016; Daneels, Vandebosch, & Walrave, 2020; Kümpel & Unkel, 2017). Recalling past gaming experiences can trigger nostalgia, optimism, and increased feeling of social connectedness (Wulf, Bowman, Velez, & Breuer, 2020). Similarly, playing games from one's earlier life ("retro gaming") can promote reflection upon happy memories and the development of resilience (Bonus, Peebles, Mares, & Sarmiento, 2018).

Digital Games as Transcendent Entertainment

Although several scholars have theorized how digital games might promote transcendence, religion, and spirituality (e.g., Hayse, 2014; Scholtz, 2005), relatively few empirical studies have explicitly explored these topics. However, one transcendence-related construct has received some attention by game researchers: awe.

As discussed in Chapter 6, awe is an emotional response elicited by something in our environment that (1) is so vast that it exceeds our ordinary frame of reference, and (2) that does not fit into our existing mental structures, thus requiring an alteration to those structures ("accommodation"; Keltner & Haidt, 2003). The experience of awe typically includes physiological (e.g., goose bumps) and other expressive reactions (e.g., saying "Wow!"). As an emotion, awe is predominantly a positive experience, giving rise to other positive emotions such as joy; it is also accompanied by a diminished sense of self (i.e., "small self"). Based on these characteristics, it is reasonable to think that feeling awe while playing video games could add to hedonic enjoyment, through the co-activation of positive emotions and diminished self-concern leading to escapism.

But awe, as a self-transcendent emotional response, also triggers a shifting of one's focus outward, motivation for sense-making, and connectedness with something greater than the self (for an overview of awe, see Allen, 2018). It can also activate spiritual thoughts and spirituality. As a result, a few researchers have started examining how awe while playing digital games can possibly lead to transcendence-related outcomes (e.g., Possler, Klimmt, & Raney, 2018).

From the perspective of the component process model (see Chapter 2) and related appraisal theories (e.g., Scherer, Schorr, & Johnstone, 2001), all emotions occur as a response to a stimulus, with the type and intensity dependent upon a person's subjective evaluation (or appraisal) of the stimulus. With gaming, a player can subjectively evaluate the experience of play across several layers of perception

(Wirth & Schramm, 2007), including the fictional content, the artistic quality of game, the playing situation and setting, performance, and triggered memories from previous play. It is conceivable that awe could be elicited by a number of stimuli across these various layers: encountering vast and beautiful scenery and vistas, hearing compelling and touching music, completing an incredibly original and innovative mission, competing against an incredibly powerful opponent, seeing a teammate dominate an episode, or performing as never before ("playing out of your mind"). In one of the first studies of awe and gaming, Possler, Scheper, and colleagues (2019) found that, indeed, factors such as these can lead to feelings of awe in the player. Furthermore, awe was found to contribute uniquely to the experience of appreciation, even beyond its contribution through other meaningful aspects of play (e.g., narrative, social interaction, exploration). Whether the experience of awe with video games can lead to other transcendent-related outcomes such as prosociality and altruism remains to be tested.

Serious Games

To this point, the discussion has centered on games that are designed primarily for entertainment. But some games—**serious games**—are developed with the intention of being more than entertainment (Ritterfeld, Cody, & Vorderer, 2009; see also "persuasive computing"). Serious games are those that are *only advantageous* to the player, leading to benefits such as learning, insight, and growth (i.e., no potential for negative content effects; Ratan & Ritterfeld, 2009). James Paul Gee (2003; 2009), a leading scholar in the fields of linguistics and education, explained across several works how digital games are ideal vehicles for deep learning. For instance, games create worlds with rules that are willfully and enthusiastically adopted and accepted by players, facilitating personal and emotional investment in the outcomes. Furthermore, games permit players to control the game world, often on a micro-level, which promotes feelings of autonomy and competence, but also character identification and attachment since the control is generally exerted through an avatar. This microcontrol encourages players to explore, engage with, and move between the abstract and the concrete elements of the game world, resulting in the opportunity to continually and experientially learn from countless situations. Thus, games as personal, emotional, cognitively engaging, social, multidimensional, multisensory, experiential, open, *and* pleasurable activities are fertile fields in which learning and meaning can blossom. We now turn our attention to three specific areas where that learning and meaning have been examined. The theories and mechanisms thought to explain these effects are discussed in detail in Chapters 10 and 11.

Games for Learning

For centuries, teachers and parents have used games and other fun activities to convey information, particularly to children. Games are thought to be exceptionally effective for educational purposes because they (ideally) engage different cognitive capacities in learners as compared to lectures, memorization, and practice drills, leading to deeper learning and more interconnected knowledge structures. Further, as the self-determination theory literature states, game play can be an intrinsically motivated activity; thus, if information is intertwined with play, then learning becomes a byproduct of something done simply because it is enjoyable and personally gratifying. Therefore, from the earliest days of personal computing, it was only natural for game designers to develop digital games for education, with seemingly limitless content: games teaching colors, shapes, and numbers to toddlers; basic reading and early math skills to preschoolers; basic subjects, plus problem solving and other flexible thinking skills, for primary school students; advanced subjects, specialized training, and college prep for secondary students; art history, ancient architecture, second languages, and myriad other topics for life-long learners.

As the availability of educational titles and their adoption by school systems increased, questions about their effectiveness also grew. Mayer (2011) identified different types of research in the area, including media-comparison (e.g., how games compare to nongame approaches) and value-added (e.g., how different game features promote learning) studies. As with most highly complex phenomena examined across age ranges, socio-economic strata, abilities, and cultures (among other differences), the results from one study to the next can be somewhat conflicting. However, thanks in large part to several high-quality meta-analyses on the subject (e.g., Clark, Tanner-Smith, & Killingsworth, 2016; Vogel et al. 2006; Wouters, van Nimwegen, van Oostendorp, H. & van der Spek, 2013), a general sense of their effectiveness has emerged.

With regard to media-comparison research, learning via digital games is generally more effective than through traditional instruction methods, in terms of information acquisition, retention, motivation, and improved attitudes toward learning. These results tend to hold true across biological sex and age. Games played across multiple sessions (rather than a single session) tend to lead to more learning, as do situations in which the learner has unlimited access to the game. However, with regard to supplemental instruction, some meta-analyses conclude that related nongame instruction significantly supports learning, whereas others do not find those benefits.

In terms of value-added studies, meta-analyses also draw different conclusions with regard to individual- versus group-play situations. Some observe greater learning when the game is played individually, others find learning improves when gaming is a group activity, and still others show no difference between individual and group play. In these cases, the competitive or collaborative nature of the game seems to matter, with consensus being that competitive games played individually are the least effective. Games with more and more varied ways of interacting with the game appear to be quite beneficial. The presence of a narrative in the game does not seem to improve learning, though deep and complex storylines can diminish it. The visual realism of the graphics also tends to have little effect on learning.

Games for Health

Another type of serious game that has received a great deal of scholarly and popular attention deals with health-related topics and issues. In fact, one academic journal—the aptly titled *Games for Health Journal*—is entirely devoted to studies in the area. Although we include physical health and wellness under the broader positive media psychology banner, summarizing this far-ranging area in a few paragraphs would be impossible. Suffice it to say that games have been developed and utilized to support the diagnosis, treatment, and rehabilitation of a wide array of conditions, including cancer, diabetes, cardiovascular disease, and cystic fibrosis, just to name a few. Games have also been used for clinical and administrative training (see Lieberman, 2015). One of the most widely available and popular health game formats is the **exergame** (or active video game), such as *Dance Dance Revolution* and Nintendo's *Wii Fit*. As the name implies, exergames are digital games that double as a form of exercise, with most relying on technology that tracks the player's body movements and reactions. Playing such games can lead to energy expenditures equivalent to light-to-moderate exercise, but their ultimate effectiveness may actually come as tools for therapy and recovery (see Peng & Day, 2017).

One area of recent growth and promise has been games for mental health. Like other health interventions, games have been developed specifically for the diagnosis and treatment of various mental health conditions, such as depression, attention deficit hyperactivity disorder (ADHD), post-traumatic stress disorder (PTSD), anxiety disorder, and bipolar disorder. Additionally, numerous games focus on mental health literacy for players. For example, playing the game *Stigma-Stop* resulted in significant decreases in negative stereotyping related to schizophrenia among teenagers (Cangas et al., 2017). Some mass-released games feature characters living with and managing mental health conditions (e.g., *Hellblade: Senua's Sacrifice*), providing additional literacy and stigma reduction opportunities for players (e.g., decreased desire for social distance; Ferchaud, Seibert, Sellers, & Salazar, 2020).

Games for Social Change

Firmly established as a genre within the larger gaming community, games for social change are digital games designed to—as the term implies—change the player's beliefs, attitudes, or behaviors around a specific cause or issue. The subjects for such games are limitless: climate change, energy conservation, inequality, cyberbullying, poverty, genocide and war, racial prejudice, neurodiversity understanding, mental health support, drug and alcohol dependency, social justice, peace, just to name a few. Since 2004, the nonprofit organization Games for Change (G4C) has been encouraging game developers and social movements to coordinate to develop games and immersive environments intended to raise awareness and effect social change; their website hosts a list of more than 175 games for change, including former nominees and winners from their annual awards festival.

Perhaps because the titles and topics are so varied, academic research into the impacts of games for change has been slow to come. Single studies of game effectiveness and effects, as well as content analyses of existing games, are available, typically within journals specific to the academic discipline reflected in the issue on which the game is based. One work of particular note from the field of media psychology is Peng, Lee, and Heeter's (2010) seminal examination of *Darfur is Dying*, a game designed to raise awareness about the humanitarian crisis in Darfur resulting from an ongoing war during the first decade of the 21st century. Players selected one of several possible Darfurian refugee avatars with the task of finding water in the desert while avoiding militia members. When players failed the mission, they were presented with facts about what would happen to an actual man, woman, girl, or boy in the same situation. As expected, playing the game led to greater role-taking and willingness to help than reading the same text or watching someone else play the game. A subsequent study (Cohen, 2014) using the same game found that players experienced both positive and negative emotions during game play, with the latter better predicting the sharing of the game with others afterwards.

In general, empathy activation routinely emerges as an effect of playing games for change, which facilitates subsequent attitudinal change (e.g., especially about issues removed from the player; e.g., Kampf & Cuhadar, 2015), behavioral intentions (e.g., learning more about the issue; Bachen, Hernández-Ramos, Raphael, & Waldron, 2016), and actual behaviors (Steinemann, Mekler, & Opwis, 2015). As expected, presence and character identification also promote the effects of the games. Much more systematic research on games for change would be beneficial.

Positive Effects of Virtual Reality

Because of the greater perceptions of immersion and presence that are afforded with virtual reality technology, as well as the possibility for more natural mapping of controls, one might expect that VR games hold the potential for even greater positive effects than those discussed above. And generally speaking this is true. For instance, Possler, Klimmt, and colleagues (2019) found that playing a VR version of *The Elder Scrolls V: Skyrim* (vs. playing on a television display) generated more feelings of presence, which increased experiences of awe, leading to greater eudaimonic appreciation.

But the immersive environments created in VR are utilized for much more than games. VR's ability to make the user truly feel present in the environment—spatially, sensorially, socially, self-referentially—opens the door to even greater positive effects. For instance, the power of presence in VR has been harnessed in various clinical contexts, including the treatment of anxiety disorder, PTSD, pain, eating disorders, and numerous phobias, to name just a few (see Rivera, Arbona, García-Palacios, Castellano, & López, 2015). Even just spending time in virtual nature can help a person to relax and reduce stress (e.g., Anderson et al., 2017).

Moreover, the ability to simulate actual behaviors—or better yet, to perform actual behaviors within a simulated environment—promotes the development of self-efficacy, emotional memories, and new cognitive structures, leading to pro-social outcomes. For example, chopping down a virtual tree led to 20% less paper use in a subsequent task, with the effects lasting at least one week (Ahn, Bailenson, & Park, 2014). The potential effects even appear to extend to symbolically related situations, as individuals who experienced the simulated superpower of flying more quickly helped a person in need—like a fictional superhero would—than individuals who took a simulated helicopter ride (Rosenberg, Baughman, & Bailenson, 2013).

In some VR simulations, a user can encounter a version of their "virtual self," interacting face-to-face with the self as the "other." Like standing before a magic mirror, users can see their virtual selves/themselves become older, leaner, balder, another skin color, etc. Such interactions can have direct behavioral impacts on the user by, for instance, motivating them to go work out at the gym after seeing their "healthier self" (Fox & Bailenson, 2009), or putting more money in savings after interacting with their "older self" (Hershfield et al., 2011). The capacity of VR to simulate a variety of future events and scenarios has been utilized to promote other positive outcomes, including increased concern for the environment and other people (e.g., homeless individuals; Herrera, Bailenson, Weisz, Ogle, & Zaki, 2018).

Further, some VR environments allow the user to interact as another person altogether, embodying "someone else's skin." Seeing the world from another person's perspective in VR can have great impact on a user's empathy. Studies employing this technique have shown to decrease racial bias in White participants after embodying a Black avatar (Peck, Seinfeld, Aglioti, & Slater, 2013), increase tolerance toward people suffering from a mental illness after embodying an avatar with schizophrenia (Kalyanaraman, Penn, Ivory, & Judge, 2010), and increase connectedness to nature after embodying an animal avatar (Ahn et al., 2016).

Summary

Digital games and virtual environments offer unique opportunities for users to experience positive effects. These technologies deliver experiences that are more interactive, immersive, and socially connected than their "traditional" media siblings. As a result, users encounter novel but also familiar content features that support hedonic enjoyment, eudaimonic appreciation, and self-transcendence. By exploring the game world, being immersed and present, identifying with characters, and mastering challenges, users can enter flow states and gratify basic psychological needs, leading to happiness and well-being. Serious games for learning, health, and social change can facilitate caring, helping, healing, and additional forms of personal growth. And the emerging worlds created through virtual reality may teach us to empathize and mobilize in ways that transform our material world.

References

Abuhamdeh, S., & Csikszentmihalyi, M. (2012). The importance of challenge for the enjoyment of intrinsically motivated, goal-directed activities. *Personality and Social Psychology Bulletin*, 38, 317–330. doi:10.1177/0146167211427147.

Ahn, S. J. G., Bailenson, J. N., & Park, D. (2014). Short-and long-term effects of embodied experiences in immersive virtual environments on environmental locus of control and behavior. *Computers in Human Behavior*, 39, 235–245. doi:10.1016/j.chb.2014.07.025.

Ahn, S. J., Bostick, J., Ogle, E., Nowak, K. L., McGillicuddy, K. T., & Bailenson, J. N. (2016). Experiencing nature: Embodying animals in immersive virtual environments increases inclusion of nature in self and involvement with nature. *Journal of Computer-Mediated Communication*, 21, 399–419. doi:10.1111/jcc4.12173.

Allen, S. (2018). The science of awe. Greater Good Science Center. https://ggsc.berkeley.edu/images/uploads/GGSC-JTF_White_Paper-Awe_FINAL.pdf.

Anderson, A. P., Mayer, M. D., Fellows, A. M., Cowan, D. R., Hegel, M. T., & Buckey, J. C. (2017). Relaxation with immersive natural scenes presented using virtual reality. *Aerospace Medicine and Human Performance*, 88, 520–526. doi:10.3357/AMHP.4747.2017.

Bachen, C. M., Hernández-Ramos, P., Raphael, C., & Waldron, A. (2016). How do presence, flow, and character identification affect players' empathy and interest in learning from a serious computer game? *Computers in Human Behavior*, 64, 77–87. doi:10.1016/j.chb.2016.06.043.

Bellanger, C. (2020, March 30). New study from Upfluence finds COVID-19 lockdown restrictions resulted in a 24% viewership increase on live-streaming platform Twitch. Upfluence. https://www.upfluence.com/press-release/new-study-from-upfluence-finds-covid-19-lockdown-restrictions-resulted-in-a-24-viewership-increase-on-live-streaming-platform-twitch.

Bonus, J. A., Peebles, A., Mares, M. L., & Sarmiento, I. G. (2018). Look on the bright side (of media effects): Pokémon Go as a catalyst for positive life experiences. *Media Psychology*, 21, 263–287. doi:10.1080/15213269.2017.1305280.

Bopp, J. A., Mekler, E. D., & Opwis, K. (2016, May). Negative emotion, positive experience? Emotionally moving moments in digital games. In *Proceedings of the 2016 CHI Conference on Human Factors in Computing Systems* (pp. 2996–3006). New York, NY: Association for Computing Machinery.

Bowman, N., Oliver, M., Rogers, R., Sherrick, B., Woolley, J., & Chung, M.-Y. (2016). In control or in their shoes? How character attachment differentially influences video game enjoyment and appreciation. *Journal of Gaming & Virtual Worlds*, 8, 83–99. doi:10.1386/jgvw.8.1.83_1.

Bowman, N. D., Schultheiss, D., & Schumann, C. (2012). "I'm attached, and I'm a good guy/gal!": How character attachment influences pro-and anti-social motivations to play massively multiplayer online role-playing games. *Cyberpsychology, Behavior, and Social Networking*, 15, 169–174. doi:10.1089/cyber.2011.0311.

Brown, E., & Cairns, P. (2004, April). A grounded investigation of game immersion. In *CHI 2004 Extended Abstracts on Human Factors in Computing Systems* (pp. 1297–1300). New York, NY: Association for Computing Machinery.

Cangas, A. J., Navarro, N., Parra, J., Ojeda, J. J., Cangas, D., Piedra, J. A., & Gallego, J. (2017). Stigma-Stop: A serious game against the stigma toward mental health in educational settings. *Frontiers in Psychology*, 8, e1385. doi:10.3389/fpsyg.2017.01385.

Clark, D. B., Tanner-Smith, E. E., & Killingsworth, S. S. (2016). Digital games, design, and learning: A systematic review and meta-analysis. *Review of Educational Research*, 86, 79–122. doi:10.3102/0034654315582065.

Cohen, E. L. (2014). What makes good games go viral? The role of technology use, efficacy, emotion and enjoyment in players' decision to share a prosocial digital game. *Computers in Human Behavior*, 33, 321–329. doi:10.1016/j.chb.2013.07.013.

Csikszentmihalyi, M., & Csikszentmihalyi, I. S. (1988). *Optimal experience: Psychological studies of flow in consciousness*. New York: Cambridge University Press.

Daneels, R., Vandebosch, H., & Walrave, M. (2020). "Just for fun?": An exploration of digital games' potential for eudaimonic media experiences among Flemish adolescents. *Journal of Children and Media*. Advanced online publication. doi:10.1080/17482798.2020.1727934.

Fang, X., & Zhao, F. (2010). Personality and enjoyment of computer game play. *Computers in Industry*, 61, 342–349. doi:10.1016/j.compind.2009.12.005.

Ferchaud, A., Seibert, J. C., Sellers, N., Salazar, N. E. (2020). *Reducing mental health stigma through video game characters with mental illness*. *Frontiers in Psychology*, 11, 2240. doi:10.3389/fpsyg.2020.02240.

Fox, J., & Bailenson, J. N. (2009). Virtual self-modeling: The effects of vicarious reinforcement and identification on exercise behaviors. *Media Psychology*, 12, 1–25. doi:10.1080/15213260802669474.

Gee, J. P. (2003). *What video games have to teach us about learning and literacy*. New York, NY: Palgrave Macmillan.

Gee, J. P. (2009). Deep learning properties of good digital games: How far can they go? In U. Ritterfeld, M. Cody, & P. Vorderer (Eds), *Serious games: Mechanisms and effects* (pp. 65–80). New York, NY: Routledge.

Hartmann, T. (2008). Parasocial interactions and paracommunication with new media characters. In E. A. Konijn, S. Utz, M. Tanis, & S. B. Barnes (Eds.), *Mediated interpersonal communication* (pp. 177–199). New York, NY: Routledge.

Hayse, M. (2014). Transcendence. In M. J. P. Wofl & B. Perron (Eds.), *The Routledge companion to video game studies* (pp. 493–501). New York, NY: Routledge.

Herrera, F., Bailenson, J., Weisz, E., Ogle, E., & Zaki, J. (2018). Building long-term empathy: A large-scale comparison of traditional and virtual reality perspective-taking. *PLoS ONE*, 13(10), e0204494. doi:10.1371/journal.pone.0204494.

Hershfield, H. E., Goldstein, D. G., Sharpe, W. F., Fox, J., Yeykelis, L., Carstensen, L. L., & Bailenson, J. N. (2011). Increasing saving behavior through age-progressed renderings of the future self. *Journal of Marketing Research*, 48, S23–S37. doi:10.1509/jmkr.48.SPL.S23.

Jones, C., Scholes, L., Johnson, D., Katsikitis, M., & Carras, M. C. (2014). Gaming well: Links between videogames and flourishing mental health. *Frontiers in Psychology*, 5, 260. doi:10.3389/fpsyg.2014.00260.

Kalyanaraman, S., & Bailenson, J. (2020). Virtual reality in media effects. In M. B. Oliver, A. A. Raney, & J. Bryant (Eds.), *Media effects: Advances in research and theory* (4th ed., pp. 404–418). New York, NY: Routledge.

Kalyanaraman, S., Penn, D. L., Ivory, J. D., & Judge, A. (2010). The virtual doppelganger: Effects of a virtual reality simulator on perceptions of schizophrenia. *The Journal of Nervous and Mental Disease*, 198, 437–443. doi:10.1097/NMD.0b013e3181e07d66.

Kampf, R., & Cuhadar, E. (2015). Do computer games enhance learning about conflicts? A cross-national inquiry into proximate and distant scenarios in Global Conflicts. *Computers in Human Behavior*, 52, 541–549. doi:10.1016/j.chb.2014.08.008.

Kelly, R. (2020). Positive psychology and gaming: Strength and resilience +1. In R. Kowert (Ed.), *Video games and well-being: Press start* (pp. 77–96). Cham, CH: Palgrave Pivot.

Keltner, D., & Haidt, J. (2003). Approaching awe, a moral, spiritual, and aesthetic emotion. *Cognition and Emotion*, 17, 297–314. doi:10.1080/02699930302297.

Kim, K., Schmierbach, M. G., Bellur, S., Chung, M. Y., Fraustino, J. D., Dardis, F., & Ahern, L. (2015). Is it a sense of autonomy, control, or attachment? Exploring the effects of in-game customization on game enjoyment. *Computers in Human Behavior*, 48, 695–705. doi:10.1016/j.chb.2015.02.011.

Klimmt, C., Hartmann, T., & Frey, A. (2007). Effectance and control as determinants of video game enjoyment. *CyberPsychology & Behavior*, 10, 845–848. doi:10.1089/cpb.2007.9942.

Klimmt, C., Hefner, D., & Vorderer, P. (2009). The video game experience as "true" identification: A theory of enjoyable alterations of players' self-perception. *Communication Theory*, 19, 351–373. doi:10.1111/j.1468-2885.2009.01347.x.

Klimmt, C., & Possler, D. (2020). Video games. In M. B. Oliver, A. A. Raney, & J. Bryant (Eds.), *Media effects: Advances in research and theory* (4th ed., pp. 342–356). New York, NY: Routledge.

Klimmt, C., Rizzo, A., Vorderer, P., Koch, J., & Fischer, T. (2009). Experimental evidence for suspense as determinant of video game enjoyment. *CyberPsychology & Behavior*, 12, 29–31. doi:10.1089/cpb.2008.0060..

Kowert, R. (Ed.) (2020). *Video games and well-being: Press start*. Cham, CH: Palgrave Pivot.

Kümpel, A. S., & Unkel, J. (2017). The effects of digital games on hedonic, eudaimonic and telic entertainment experiences. *Journal of Gaming & Virtual Worlds*, 9, 21–37. doi:10.1386/jgvw.9.1.21_1.

Lee, K. M. (2004). Presence, explicated. *Communication Theory*, 14, 27–50. doi:10.1111/j.1468-2885.2004.tb00302.x.

Lieberman, D. A. (2015). Using digital games to promote health behavior change. In S. S. Sundar (Ed.), *The handbook of the psychology of communication technology* (pp. 507–527). West Sussex, UK: John Wiley & Sons.

Malone, T. W. (1981). Toward a theory of intrinsically motivating instruction. *Cognitive Science*, 4, 333–369. doi:10.1016/S0364-0213(81)80017-1.

Mayer, R. E. (2011). Multimedia learning and games. In S. Tobias & J. D. Fletcher (Eds.), *Computer games and instruction* (pp. 281–305). Charlotte, NC: Information Age Publishing.

McMillan, S. J., & Hwang, J. S. (2002). Measures of perceived interactivity: An exploration of the role of direction of communication, user control, and time in shaping perceptions of interactivity. *Journal of Advertising*, 31, 29–42. doi:10.1080/00913367.2002.10673674.

Nakamura, J., & Csikszentmihalyi, M. (2002). The concept of flow. In S. J. Lopez & C. R. Snyder (Eds.), *Handbook of positive psychology* (pp. 89–105). London, UK: Oxford University Press.

Oliver, M. B., Bowman, N. D., Woolley, J. K., Rogers, R., Sherrick, B. I., & Chung, M.-Y. (2016). Video games as meaningful entertainment experiences. *Psychology of Popular Media Culture*, 5, 390–405. doi:10.1037/ppm0000066.

Peck, T. C., Seinfeld, S., Aglioti, S. M., & Slater, M. (2013). Putting yourself in the skin of a black avatar reduces implicit racial bias. *Consciousness and Cognition*, 22, 779–787. doi:10.1016/j.concog.2013.04.016.

Peng, W., & Day, T. (2017). Media use and physical fitness: From time displacement to exergaming. In L. Reinecke & M. B. Oliver (Eds.), *The Routledge handbook of media use and well-being* (pp. 329–340). New York, NY: Routledge.

Peng, W., Lee, M., & Heeter, C. (2010). The effects of a serious game on role-taking and willingness to help. *Journal of Communication*, 60, 723–742. doi:10.1111/j.1460-2466.2010.01511.x.

Poels, K., Hoogen, W. V. D., Ijsselsteijn, W., & de Kort, Y. (2012). Pleasure to play, arousal to stay: The effect of player emotions on digital game preferences and playing time. *Cyberpsychology, Behavior, and Social Networking*, 15, 1–6. doi:10.1089/cyber.2010.0040.

Possler, D., Klimmt, C., & Raney, A. A. (2018). Gaming is awesome! A theoretical model on cognitive demands and the elicitation of awe during video game play. In N. D. Bowman (Ed.), *Video games: A medium that demands our attention* (pp. 74–91). New York, NY: Routledge.

Possler, D., Klimmt, C., Raney, A. A., Steger, F., Landmann, L., & Seibert, J. C. (2019, May). *The "wow!"-effect: Introducing awe as novel element of the (VR) video game experience.* Paper presented at the annual meeting of International Communication Association, Washington, DC.

Possler, D., Kümpel, A. S., & Unkel, J. (2019). Entertainment motivations and gaming-specific gratifications as antecedents of digital game enjoyment and appreciation. *Psychology of Popular Media Culture*. Advanced online publication. doi:10.1037/ppm0000248.

Possler, D., Scheper, J., Kreissl, J., Raney, A. A., Kuempel, A. S., & Unkel, J. (2019, May). *Awe-inspirational gaming: Exploring the formation and entertaining effects of awe in video games.* Paper presented at the annual meeting of International Communication Association, Washington, DC.

Ratan, R., & Ritterfeld, U. (2009). Classifying serious games. In U. Ritterfeld, M. Cody, & P. Vorderer (Eds.), *Serious games: Mechanisms and effects* (pp. 10–24). New York, NY: Routledge.

Reinecke, L. (2009). Games and recovery: The use of video and computer games to recuperate from stress and strain. *Journal of Media Psychology*, 21, 126–142. doi:10.1027/1864-1105.21.3.126.

Ritterfeld, U., Cody, M., & Vorderer, P. (Eds.) (2009). *Serious games: Mechanisms and effects*. New York, NY: Routledge.

Rivera, R. M. B., Arbona, C. B., García-Palacios, A., Castellano, S. Q., & López, J. B. (2015). Treating emotional problems with virtual and augmented reality. In S. S. Sundar (Eds.), *The handbook of the psychology of communication technology*, 32, 548–566. West Sussex, UK: John Wiley & Sons.

Rosenberg, R. S., Baughman, S. L., & Bailenson, J. N. (2013). Virtual superheroes: Using superpowers in virtual reality to encourage prosocial behavior. *PloS One*, 8(1), e55003. doi:10.1371/journal.pone.0055003.

Russoniello, C. V., O'Brien, K., & Parks, J. M. (2009). The effectiveness of casual video games in improving mood and decreasing stress. *Journal of CyberTherapy & Rehabilitation*, 2, 53–66. Gale Document Number: GALE|A225437126

Ryan, R. M., & Deci, E. L. (2000a). Self-determination theory and the facilitation of intrinsic motivation, social development, and well-being. *American Psychologist*, 55, 68–78. doi:10.1037/0003-066X.55.1.68.

Ryan, R. M., & Deci, E. L. (2000b). The darker and brighter sides of human existence: Basic psychological needs as a unifying concept. *Psychological Inquiry*, 11, 319–338. doi:10.1207/S15327965PLI1104_03.

Ryan, R. M., Rigby, C. S. & Przybylski, A. (2006). The motivational pull of video games: A self-determination theory approach. *Motivation and Emotion*, 30, 344–360. doi:10.1007/s11031-006-9051-8.

Scherer, K. R., Schorr, A., & Johnstone, T. (Eds.). (2001). *Appraisal processes in emotion: Theory, methods, research*. New York, NY: Oxford University Press.

Schneider, E. F., Lang, A., Shin, M., & Bradley, S. D. (2004). Death with a story: How story impacts emotional, motivational, and physiological responses to first-person shooter video games. *Human Communication Research*, 30, 361–375. doi:10.1111/j.1468-2958.2004.tb00736.x.

Scholtz, C. P. (2005). Fascinating technology: Computer games as an issue for religious education. *British Journal of Religious Education*, 27(2), 173–184. doi:10.1080/0141620042000336657.

Seligman, M. E. (2011). *Flourish: A visionary new understanding of happiness and well-being*. New York, NY: Free Press.

Shafer, D. M. (2012). Causes of state hostility and enjoyment in player versus player and player versus environment video games. *Journal of Communication*, 62, 719–737. doi:10.1111/j.1460-2466.2012.01654.x.

Sherry, J. L. (2004). Flow and media enjoyment. *Communication Theory*, 14, 328–347. doi:10.1111/j.1468-2885.2004.tb00318.x.

Skalski, P., Tamborini, R., Shelton, A., Buncher, M., & Lindmark, P. (2011). Mapping the road to fun: Natural video game controllers, presence, and game enjoyment. *New Media & Society*, 13, 224–242. doi:10.1177/1461444810370949.

Steinemann, S. T., Mekler, E. D., & Opwis, K. (2015, October). Increasing donating behavior through a game for change: The role of interactivity and appreciation. In *Proceedings of the 2015 Annual Symposium on Computer-Human Interaction in Play* (pp. 319–329). New York, NY: Association for Computing Machinery.

Tamborini, R., Bowman, N. D., Eden, A. L., Grizzard, M., & Organ, A. (2010). Defining media enjoyment as the satisfaction of intrinsic needs. *Journal of Communication*, 60, 758–777. doi:10.1111/j.1460-2466.2010.01513.x.

Trepte, S., & Reinecke, L. (2010). Avatar creation and video game enjoyment: Effects of life-satisfaction, game competitiveness, and identification with the avatar. *Journal of Media Psychology*, 22, 171–184. doi:10.1027/1864-1105/a000022.

Vella, K., Johnson, D., & Hides, L. (2013, October). Positively playful: When videogames lead to player wellbeing. In *Proceedings of the First International Conference on Gameful Design, Research, and Applications* (pp. 99–102). doi:10.1145/2583008.2583024.

Vogel, J. J., Vogel, D. S., Cannon-Bowers, J., Bowers, C. A., Muse, K., Wright, M. (2006). Computer gaming and interactive simulations for learning: A meta-analysis. *Journal of Educational Computing Research*, 34, 229–243. doi:10.2190/FLHV-K4WA-WPVQ-H0YM.

Vorderer, P. (2000). Interactive entertainment and beyond. In D. Zillmann & P. Vorderer (Eds.), *Media entertainment: The psychology of its appeal* (pp. 21–36). Mahwah, NJ: Lawrence Erlbaum Associates.

Wirth, W., Ryffel, F., Von Pape, T., & Karnowski, V. (2013). The development of video game enjoyment in a role playing game. *Cyberpsychology, Behavior, and Social Networking*, 16, 260–264. doi:10.1089/cyber.2012.0159.

Wirth, W., and Schramm, H. (2007). Emotionen, metaemotionen und regulationsstrategien bei der medienrezeption: Ein integratives modell. [Emotions, meta-emotions and emotion regulation during media consumption. An integrative model.] In W. Wirth, H.-J. Stiehler, and C. Wuensch (Eds.), *Dynamisch-transaktional denken: Theorie und Empirie in der Kommunikationswissenschaft* [*Thinking in a dynamic-transactional way: Theory and empirical research in communication science.*] (pp. 153–184). Cologne, DE: Halem.

Wouters, P., van Nimwegen, C., van Oostendorp, H., van der Spek, E. D. (2013). A meta-analysis of the cognitive and motivational effects of serious games. *Journal of Educational Psychology*, 105, 249–265. doi:10.1037/a0031311.

Wulf, T., Bowman, N. D., Velez, J. A., & Breuer, J. (2020). Once upon a game: Exploring video game nostalgia and its impact on well-being. *Psychology of Popular Media*, 9, 83–95. doi:10.1037/ppm0000208.

Yee, N., & Bailenson, J. (2007). The Proteus effect: The effect of transformed self-representation on behavior. *Human Communication Research*, 33, 271–290. doi:10.1111/j.1468-2958.2007.00299.x.

Additional Readings

Bailenson, J. N. (2018). *Experience on demand: What virtual reality is, how it works, and what it can do*. New York, NY: W.W. Norton.

Ferchaud, A., & Sanders, M. S. (2018). Seeing through the avatar's eyes: Effects of point-of-view and gender match on identification and enjoyment. *Imagination, Cognition and Personality*, 38, 82–105. doi:10.1177/0276236618761372.

Lombard, M., & Ditton, T. (1997). At the heart of it all: The concept of presence. *Journal of Computer-Mediated Communication*, 3. doi:10.1111/j.1083-6101.1997.tb00072.x.

9

POSITIVE NEWS AND NONFICTION

Source: Shutterstock 1059533777

When thinking of news content, it seems likely that many people think of messages that are troubling or disturbing. The commonly used phrase "if it bleeds, it leads" refers to the idea that news coverage often prioritizes information that is violent, dramatic, sensational, and emotionally distressing. Stories about crime, war, gun violence, and suffering are indeed common. As a result, numerous studies have examined the deleterious effects of news consumption on attitudes and beliefs. At the same time, news can also depict stories of human resilience, hope, and kindness. Further, because news is generally perceived to depict "real" people and "real" issues, these positive types of news stories may be particularly influential. In this chapter, we first overview some of the foundational theories of news, and we then turn to the emerging research on positive news and how it may provide a pathway forward.

Foundational Theories of News

Numerous theories of media influence have examined the effects of news on audiences, perhaps because news is considered essential to democratic societies, not only in terms of informing its citizens, but also in terms of its function as the "fourth estate," a metaphorical phrase referring to a free press that functions to report on and keep in check other branches of government.

Agenda setting is one of the most explored theories of news and public opinion (McCombs & Shaw, 1993). In brief, the theory argues that the prominence of news stories on particular issues causes people to perceive the issue as important. For example, at different periods during history, the Gallup poll has routinely asked respondents to identify the most important or pressing issues facing the country. Media agenda setting would suggest that poll responses reflect how much media attention news outlets give to these issues at different times in history (e.g., health, crime, international security). Overall, the agenda-setting function of media has received a wealth of support.

BOX 9.1 WHAT MAKES SOMETHING NEWSWORTHY?

News outlets can only cover so much news each day because of resource restrictions on time (e.g., how many hours a journalist has to write each day), space (e.g., physical space in a newspaper), and money (e.g., how many writers and editors an outlet can afford to employ), among others. As a result, news sources must choose which stories to report. But what makes something newsworthy?

Basic journalistic guidelines offer six factors that can influence the extent to which something is considered newsworthy. Although this list is not exhaustive, it covers some of the major factors that many news outlets consider when determining what to report.

- *Timing*: News outlets are interested in covering current events: new makes the news. A past event or long-term issue is unlikely to receive top coverage in the news unless some new information is uncovered.
- *Proximity*: Consumers tend to be more interested in issues and events that happen close to home. People care more about everyday news regarding local high schools, local elections, or local restaurants than about similar news from a different state or country.
- *Conflict/Controversy*: Information about violence, conflict, or controversy tends to be newsworthy because it keeps us updated about problems and issues.
- *Impact/Relevance*: One reason people seek out news coverage is so that they are up to date about things that affect them. Major roadwork in your area might receive a great deal of local news coverage because it could affect your drive time to work or school.

- *Prominence*: The prominence of the people involved in a story can influence newsworthiness. The marriage of Prince Harry and Meghan Markle received international attention, but the thousands of marriages by "commoners" that occurred on the same day received little, if any, attention.
- *Human Interest*: We like to read stories about other people. These stories are a little unusual in that they can "break" the rules of newsworthiness. The timing, proximity, and impact factors can be less influential when we discuss human interest stories.

Understanding how and why news is constructed is an essential part of being a media literate consumer.

Two variants of agenda setting that have received much less attention are **intermedia agenda setting** and **public agenda setting** (Roselyn Du, 2017; Seethaler, 2017). Intermedia agenda setting refers to the idea that news coverage of a given topic by some news outlets may affect the extent to which other news outlets also cover the issue. For example, if *The New York Times* prominently covers the topic of unsafe drinking water, other outlets may opt to cover the same topic. **Public agenda setting** refers to the idea that the public's concerns or discussions about issues heightens the likelihood that the media will cover those issues. For example, public outcry about the pharmaceutical industry may give rise to greater news coverage about this issue.

Agenda setting was initially developed during an era when there were few national television outlets, newspaper reading was common, and the commercial internet was nonexistent. Changes in the media landscape have resulted in numerous scholars posing questions about the mechanisms initially proposed. For example, individuals now have access to a very large variety of news outlets on the internet. As a result, rather than relying on a handful of news sources that often present similar issues, individuals now can easily peruse a variety of outlets that may focus on different topics. Likewise, people's news diets now frequently include articles or stories that were shared on social media. Finally, through the use of blogs, YouTube, and Instagram, individuals can create and distribute their own news stories in ways never imaginable in pre-internet times. Consequently, though some research suggests that agenda setting does occur even if via channels such as social media (Freezell, 2018), some scholars have called for an overhaul of traditional agenda-setting models, arguing instead for a more complex model of the interaction between mainstream news providers, the public, and "niche" media (Gruszczynski & Wagner, 2016).

It is important to understand that the initial formulation of agenda setting stressed that media affected public opinion by making salient which issues were important; that is, what to think *about*. However, an important extension to agenda-setting theory concerns **attribute agenda setting** (McCombs &

Reynolds, 1994). In brief, attribute agenda setting (or sometimes called **second-level agenda setting**) argues that the news media, in addition to reporting on some issues more than others, can also highlight certain attributes or characteristics of issues, thereby influencing not only *what* issues the public thinks are important, but also what attributes about the issue are noteworthy. This addition to traditional agenda setting is similar to the concept of **media framing** (Tewksbury & Schuefele, 2020). As described by one scholar,

> To frame is to select some aspects of a perceived reality and make them more salient in a communicating text, in such a way as to promote a particular problem definition, causal interpretation, oral evaluation, and/or treatment recommendation for the item described.
>
> *(Entman, 1993, p. 53)*

For example, in covering political activism concerning Black Lives Matter, two different media outlets framed the burning of a police precinct in extremely different ways. A Fox News headline of the story read "Minneapolis Third Precinct police station set on fire after rioters break in," and characterized George Floyd as "a black man who died while in police custody" (Calicchio, 2020, para. 1). In contrast, a *New York Times* headline read "Protests Against Police Escalate" and characterized George Floyd as killed by police (Leonhardt, 2020). From a framing perspective, these two different perspectives covering the same issue are likely to result in different ways of perceiving and understanding the protests, which, in turn, are likely to be associated with varying levels of support for public policy.

Exemplification theory offers an additional perspective on news-related effects. In brief, the theory notes that journalists often use examples (or exemplars) to illustrate broad or abstract issues as a way of "enlivening" the story or making it vivid (Zillmann & Brosius, 2000). For instance, a story about student finances may begin by describing a college student who had racked up credit-card debt and who needed to get food from a pantry in town. Even if the same story proceeded to state that most students are adept at managing their finances, exemplification theory would likely argue the vivid and salient example of the single student would be most influential in readers' perceptions of poverty among students. For example, in one study, readers read a news story about carjacking that explicitly stated that only 0.2% of car jackings result in fatalities (Gibson & Zillmann, 1994). However, when the story featured a salient example of a woman being killed, participants later estimated that significantly more car jackings were fatal (15.1%), an effect that persisted (and increased) over the course of several weeks.

Reinforcing spiral models are also informative for studies of news (Slater, 2007; 2015). In general, the phrase "spiral model" in media psychology refers to the interplay between the effects of media and individuals' selective exposure to media over time. For example, a person who enjoys good food may choose to watch a cooking show on television. Viewing the show then causes them to try a new recipe, and the enjoyment of the new recipe causes them to select more cooking shows to try, with this selection resulting in more cooking and eating. Although reinforcing spiral models can be applied to most any type of content (e.g., media violence and aggression; Slater, Henry, Swaim, & Anderson, 2003), its application to news content is particularly important in our politically fragmented time.

Reinforcing spiral models can aptly be applied to news and politics. A recent national survey of public opinion on social and political issues revealed wide differences between Democrats and Republicans on a host of different issues, including a 57% difference on gun policy, a 55% difference on racial issues, and a 48% difference on climate and environment issues (Pew Research Center, 2019). At the same time, additional research shows that since 1980, people who are partisan have increasingly identified with their own party and have greater feelings of hostility toward those in opposing political parties (Iyengar & Krupenkin, 2018). These results mirror an increased fragmentation in news consumption, with Republicans now relying heavily on Fox News for their news consumption, and Democrats relying on a more diverse but different set of news outlets: CNN, NBC, and ABC (Jurkowitz, Mitchell, & Walker, 2020). These two findings regarding polarization and news consumption are consistent with a reinforcing spiral model. As people become more fragmented in their political views, they are likely to choose media outlets that are consistent with their beliefs. This media exposure, then, reinforces or strengthens their political views. Importantly, too, the seemingly endless sources of news afforded by the internet, coupled with the tendency to share or post information to like-minded friends, suggests that internet and social media may serve to strengthen this type of spiral (Sunstein, 2001).

This summary of foundational theories of news illustrates that news outlets can set the public agenda, highlighting the issues that are thought to be important. They can also frame issues in different ways and make use of salient examples to illustrate stories, leading viewers to think about issues in terms of salient characteristics and to perceive social reality in ways that reflect exemplars that may not be representative. Finally, the interplay between news selection and public opinion is likely reinforcing, and can ultimately strengthen attitudes, sometimes resulting in fragmentation. Of course, all of these theories are constantly being revised to account for the vast changes in the media landscape, including official online news outlets, user-generated news content, and interactivity, including sharing and posting of stories. With this background in mind, we now turn to research on how news can not only inform, but can also serve to inspire its audience in positive and meaningful ways.

Positive News

Content and Exposure

News consumption may be the last media context in which anyone would expect transcendent depictions to occur. The news industry has often been accused of having a negativity bias, and past research on news editors' perceptions suggests that this accusation has some merit. For example, Galician and Pasternack (1987) found that among the 133 news directors in their sample, 61.7% agreed that bad news is more newsworthy than good news, 58.6% agreed that bad news attracts audiences more than good news, and 47.4% agreed that most people prefer stories about bad news. At the same time, 80.5% agreed that negative news stories reflect actual events in the world, and 57.1% disagreed that TV newscasts should try to balance positive and negative news. Similar results were obtained in a study of journalists who were asked to view and rate the importance of ten stories that were modified to present either positive or negative news (Bohle, 1986). Discarding responses of "no choice," participants selected the negative news as more important in nine of the ten stories.

With this characterization of news and negativity in mind, however, more and more news companies now also promote the dissemination of positive news. Popular newspapers and aggregators such as *USA Today, The Washington Post*, or *Huffington Post* now incorporate positive news sections. Likewise, in a study of perceptions of positive news, journalists rated stories that "bring hope to people when society is in a crisis," "promote desirable social values and norms," and "tell encouraging or touching stories" as having the highest news value (Leung & Lee, 2015).

Thus, it comes as no surprise that 77.6% of U.S. adults say they have been inspired by a news story before and 33% have been inspired in the last week (Janicke-Bowles et al., 2019). Further, research suggests that individuals are likely to tweet or share positive news stories, thereby increasing exposure among their followers, friends, and acquaintances. A content analysis by Ji et al. (2019) supports the notion that news can indeed be inspiring in nature. These researchers showed that 21.1% of *New York Times* articles that were the most emailed, tweeted, or posted on Facebook each day for the course of three months in the beginning of 2016 were inspirational in nature. Such articles also included significantly more positive emotional words (such as "good," "beautiful," "great") and were rated to be more interesting, surprising, and useful compared to non-inspiring articles. In terms of self-transcendent emotional elicitors (see Chapter 6), the inspiring articles contained an abundance of depictions of appreciation of beauty and excellence (61.8% of all articles), with examples including the author expressing great admiration for someone with an exceptional skill or awe at the wonders of a scientific discovery or nature. The second most often found self-transcendent depiction was hope (42.5% of all articles), followed by gratitude (30.1%).

Similar results have also been reported for websites specifically dedicated to presenting positive or good news. McIntyre (2016) content analyzed seven different news values present in *Good News Network, Happy News, Daryn Kagan, Odewire*, and *Huff Post Good News*. For purposes of comparison to mainstream news outlets, news stories from *The New York Times* were also coded.

A significantly larger percentage of stories on good-news outlets presented values of entertainment/oddity (67%) and emotional impact (46%) than did *The New York Times* (28% and 19% respectively), whereas the values of conflict (60%), power elite (68%), and timeliness (66%) were more common in *The New York Times* than in the good-news outlets (7%, 18%, and 43% respectively).

Inspiring materials are also common in political speeches often shown in the news and in political advertising (e.g., Irimieş & Irimieş, 2017). Politicians often deliver messages of hope, intersperse their arguments with moving and heart-warming exemplars, and focus on human virtues such as courage and generosity. Lamson and McGrath (2019) found that presidential candidate nomination speeches between the years of 1864 to 2016 which used more expressions that alluded to the transcendent character strengths of hope and kindness (but not incumbency) were more likely to win their candidates the popular vote and the election.

Finally, we note that a number of scholars have begun to explore specific types of news formats that hold great promise for providing viewers with transcendent experiences, particularly those of hope and gratitude. One such format is **restorative narratives** (Fitzgerald, Paravati, Green, Moore, & Qian, 2020; Tenore, 2015; see also Chapter 10). This format is often used to report on some crisis or emergency such as a hurricane, a health problem, or a devastating event. However, rather than focus exclusively on the negative effects of crises and the suffering that they cause, restorative narratives focus more on how people or communities show strength and resilience, providing a path toward a hopeful future. **Constructive journalism** is a similar concept, defined as "an emerging form of journalism that involves applying positive psychology techniques to news processes and production in an effort to create productive and engaging coverage, while holding true to journalism's core functions" (McIntyre & Gyldensted, 2017, p. 23). As McIntyre and Gyldensted explain, constructive journalism can take many forms, including a focus on solutions, restorative narratives, future-oriented stories (prospective journalism), and stories that highlight the challenges and opportunities that are afforded by conflict (peace journalism). These authors also offered various ways in which stories can be presented in a constructive way, drawing from literatures in positive psychology. The techniques include the journalist considering the well-being of the world when writing stories, evoking positive emotions in news stories, employing constructive interviewing techniques, focusing on solutions, and including PERMA (see Chapter 3) characteristics in stories.

To summarize, although news is often characterized by distressing content that highlights conflict, positive and inspiring stories are far from uncommon. A growing number of news outlets specifically focus on positive news, and journalistic trends show an increasing interest in presenting news that is constructive and restorative. Consequently, a large segment of individuals report having been inspired by something that they have seen in the news. Thus, we now turn to research on the effects of such exposure and audience responses and behaviors.

Effects of Positive News

Many of the outcomes associated with viewing inspiring or positive news content are ones observed in other types of media genres such as film, television programs, or short videos. These effects include a host of interconnected emotional, cognitive, and behavioral effects that point toward favorable outcomes associated with heightened well-being, connectedness, and compassion. Although many early studies on these effects were primarily focused on an audience member's response (more so than the elicitor of the response), it should be noted that the studies frequently used media messages to induce a response, including news messages.

Emotions

Feelings of positive affect, elevation, awe, and of being moved have received a growing amount of attention among scholars of entertainment. However, these feelings have also been observed in terms of audience reactions to news. Some studies have focused on positive affect per se and on audience enjoyment. For example, McIntyre and Gibson (2016) examined participants' responses to news stories framed as positive, negative, or as having a silver lining. Positive affect and greater enjoyment were highest for the positive news story, though not on an overall measure of well-being. Similarly, in two studies, stories that were framed in positive, constructive ways resulted in more positive affect and enjoyment, though importantly, they were not judged as lacking in journalistic values (Baden, McIntyre, & Homberg, 2018). Later research also examined similar effects in a more naturalistic setting (McIntyre, 2020). Participants were presented with a Google app that would provide the user with a news story using a constructive frame when the user stated, "Tell me something good." General affect was assessed prior to when the app was introduced to participants and again two weeks later. Those who opted to use the app reported significantly higher levels of positive affect at the end of the two weeks than at the beginning. They also reported higher agreement that mainstream news is too negative.

Additional studies have examined more complex affective responses, including the self-transcendent emotion elevation. For example, in one study, participants read a news story about the grace, resilience, and forgiveness of an Amish community following a mass shooting in their school (Aquino, McFerran, & Laven, 2011). Readers of the story reported significantly higher levels of elevation (measured in terms of awe, compassion, inspiration, and admiration) than did participants who read a pleasant story about watching a sunset. Research also shows that even political speeches can elicit elevation if the speaker includes moving or touching exemplars (Ellithorpe, Huang, & Oliver, 2019). Similar results have been obtained for restorative narratives (Fitzgerald et al., 2020). Participants read a story about a woman with a rare form of cancer that was presented as dire or that used a restorative narrative frame. Participants in the restorative-narrative condition reported higher levels of both positive and meaningful affect (e.g., hopeful, touched) and reported lower levels of fear and sadness.

Compassion, Connectedness, and Prejudice Reduction

In addition to eliciting positive and self-transcendent emotions, positive news can also affect perceptions of others in a host of favorable ways. Some research has examined individuals' perceptions of humanity, showing that after reading a moving or touching story, participants are more likely to hold a more positive view of humanity and to agree that people are generally good (Aquino et al., 2011). Indeed, some scholars have suggested that media exposure to positive content can cultivate a "kind-world syndrome," in which people are judged generally to be decent, upstanding, and kind (McIntyre, 2016; Oliver, Ash, & Woolley, 2012).

Additional research has examined how the consumption of positive news featuring specific groups of individuals can alter perceptions of the groups depicted. For example, Oliver, Dillard, Bae, and Tamul (2012) asked participants to read a news story that focused on health disparities among either elderly people, people in prison, or immigrants. These stories were either presented as policy stories or as narrative stories that included salient exemplars. People who read the narrative stories reported more compassion toward the characters depicted in the story, greater support for policy to assist people from the group, and even greater information seeking. Similar results were revealed in a study of people's responses to political speeches (Ellithorpe et al., 2019). When the speech included inspiring and heart-warming exemplars, participants felt more positively toward the individuals depicted and toward politicians in general.

In using meaningful media to instigate more favorable attitudes toward specific groups, it is important to keep in mind the variety of related emotions that may be aroused. For example, feeling empathy toward a group may involve admiration, closeness, or comradery. In particular, Bartsch, Oliver, Nitsch, and Scherr (2018) attempted to differentiate the roles of elevation, closeness, and pity on destigmatization. In their study, participants viewed an advertisement for the Paralympic Games that was edited to include music that elicited empathic feelings or emotionally neutral music. Empathic feelings were associated with heightened feelings of elevation, closeness to those with disabilities (e.g., admiration, connection), and pity for those with disabilities (e.g., pity, sympathy). Importantly, whereas elevation and closeness were associated with greater destigmatization, pity was associated with greater stigmatization. These results highlight the complexity of reactions that meaningful media elicit, and serve as a cautionary tale that not all responses may result in the favorable outcomes desired.

Finally, some scholars have explored the idea that the experience of elevation and its accompanying feelings of connectedness with humanity may ultimately serve to reduce prejudice to frequently marginalized groups who may not have been explicitly depicted in the media stimulus employed. Generally, the reasoning behind this research is that feelings of connectedness with humanity necessarily includes *all* of humanity, including groups that may routinely be stigmatized or oppressed (see Oliver et al., 2015). Further, given that elevation is thought to counteract any feelings of disgust that one may have toward some oppressed groups, the experience of media-induced elevation should work against these prejudicial feelings. Lai, Haidt, and Nosek (2014) employed this reasoning to examine the role of elevation in diminishing homophobic sentiment toward gay men. Participants viewed inspiring videos taken from news and nonfiction (a talk show) that were unrelated to sexual orientation, videos that were amusing though not elevating, or a control. In contrast to videos that elicited positive affect or a control, the inspiring videos elicited elevation and also reduced negative attitudes toward gay men, measured both explicitly and implicitly.

Altruism and Generosity

Given the feelings of connection that inspiring stories may elicit, it comes as no surprise that a host of research has also examined how self-transcendent emotions may heighten motivations to be a better person or to help others (see Algoe & Haidt, 2009). Some of these studies have focused on participants' self-reported behavioral intentions. For example, Baden and colleagues (2018) found that after reading constructive news stories about a solution-framed environmental issue or one focused on peace, participants reported greater intentions to act on the issue in the story, such as talking with family and friends about this issue, changing one's behavior to be more environmentally friendly, and donating to charity. Similar results were observed in a study that involved participants reading a restorative narrative about cancer (Fitzgerald et al., 2020). Not only were participants more positive and hopeful in comparison to those who read a more dire story, they also expressed more altruistic motivations (e.g., willingness to help, volunteering) that were positively mediated by positive and meaningful affect, but negatively mediated by fear, sadness, and anger.

Other studies have examined actual behavioral changes. For example, Aquino and colleagues (2011) first primed participants about their moral identity via a crossword-puzzle task and then had them read an inspiring news story. Later, when playing a game that involved the choice of how much money to give to a competitor in the game, those participants who were primed and who read the inspiring story gave significantly more money than those not primed or those who read a simple positive story about a sunset. In a subsequent study, the researchers found that people who scored high on a measure of moral identity and who viewed an inspiring video donated more of the money they received for their research participation to a charity.

Elevating content also appears to mitigate more antisocial tendencies. Freeman, Aquino, and McFerran (2009) noted that social dominance orientations are frequently associated with more anti-Black attitudes and, hence, lower tendencies to display altruistic behaviors toward African Americans in particular. However, across several studies, these authors showed that reading an elevating news story that prominently featured human kindness served to alleviate these tendencies. Whereas social dominance was associated with lower charitability to Black-focused organizations among participants in the control condition, this relationship was negated after reading elevating news stories.

Interest and Curiosity

In addition to demonstrating the effects of positive news on prosocial tendencies, additional scholarship has explored how uplifting or meaningful news may inspire greater interest in the topic depicted and, hence, greater information seeking. Bartsch and Schneider (2014) developed a **dual-process model** to explain how eudaimonic (compared to hedonic) entertainment that touches on a political or newsworthy topic can stimulate interest in the topic. Specifically, the authors argued that eudaimonic content often elicits negative or mixed-valence and that it is moderately arousing. These variables were all predicted to heighten more elaborate or reflective processing, which should enhance interest in the topic depicted. In their research, participants viewed scenes from either *The Kite Runner* (about the Taliban) or *Sin Nombre* (about a criminal gang of youths). After viewing and rating their perceptions of the video, they were given the opportunity to read a news story about the issue depicted in the video clip. Feeling moved by the video (e.g., mixed affect, etc.) predicted higher reflectiveness after viewing, with reflective thoughts then leading to higher indicators of interest when reading the news stories (e.g., ratings of interest, reading times). These results were then replicated using an experimental manipulation of a television magazine program. These authors concluded "thought-provoking … entertainment may not only serve to raise political awareness among otherwise indifferent audience groups but may also motivate intrinsic learning processes in the context of entertainment education" (p. 392).

Similar results were also observed with talk show audiences. Roth, Weinmann, Schneider, Hopp, and Vorderer (2014) assessed viewers' motivations for viewing political television talk shows, their experiences when viewing, and the extent to which they felt informed as a function of viewing. Overall, controlling for demographic characteristics and motivations for viewing, eudaimonic experiences were significant predictors of feeling informed. Of course, feeling informed is not synonymous with *being* informed, though the results of this study point to the importance of meaningful experiences in news contexts as a means of potentially sparking interest and heightening careful processing of the information presented.

Sharing, Liking, and Commenting

Prior to the internet, news audiences were generally only the receivers of information. With the exception of talking with friends or writing a letter to the editor, individuals were generally not involved in the creation or dissemination of news. Of course, in today's media landscape, individuals have ample opportunity to create news (e.g., blogs, citizen journalism), to comment on news, and to share news via social media. With this backdrop in mind, a growing number of researchers have begun to examine aspects of news that predict social sharing, as well as the effects of user comments on audience reception.

In an earlier study of social sharing of news, Berger and Milkman (2012) content analyzed news stories from *The New York Times* to examine factors that predict when stories go viral. Although positively valenced stories were more frequently shared than negatively valenced stories, stories that were arousing were also heavily shared, including stories that were associated with awe, as well as stories that were associated with anger or anxiety.

In contrast, other scholarship suggests that positive and self-transcendent content may play a more important role in social sharing than previously thought. In a recent study of social sharing of *New York Times* articles, Ji et al. (2019) employed both human coding and machine coding to examine the predictors of news stories that were retransmitted via e-mail, Twitter, and Facebook. Among the thousands of articles examined, 22.0% were characterized as inspirational, and among the most shared stories, 29.0% were inspirational in nature. An examination of the words appearing in the inspirational stories showed a prevalence of words related to growth, kindness, hope, and love. Further, the topics of the inspirational stories spanned a range of issues, including politics, science/health/technology, music, and sports.

The importance of self-transcendent emotions has also been reported for additional types of nonfiction content. Tellis, MacInnis, Tirunillai, and Zhang (2019) examined advertisements to see what types of content characteristics predict greater and lesser social sharing. Important to research on transcendent emotions, their results showed that advertisements that were dramatized and that included "cute" portrayals (e.g., babies, animals) elicited greater warmth, amusement, and inspiration. These affective reactions, in turn, were significant predictors of greater social sharing.

In addition to having the ability to share media content, news sites also frequently allow viewers to comment on the stories and to respond to others' comments. In this sense, users' reactions to stories can "frame" how the story is interpreted and can provide a gauge of public sentiment. Of course, not all comments are positive or constructive. Indeed, a content analysis of online news discussions found that 10% contained posts coded as aggressive, 34% as controversial, and 40% as negative (Ziegele, Breiner, & Quiring, 2014). Fortunately, 10% of posts were also coded as indicating humor.

To examine the effect of user comments on readers' perceptions, Waddell and Bailey (2017) conducted an experiment that involved participants reading an inspiring or non-inspiring news story that was accompanied by user comments that were civil in tone, uncivil, or were absent from the story. Although the inspiring news story elicited higher levels of elevation overall, comments per se (civil or uncivil) appeared to dampen this effect. In contrast, civil comments indirectly predicted feelings of universal orientation (e.g., feelings of connectedness with humanity) via bandwagon perceptions (i.e., that other people would like and share the story). These authors concluded that "media effects traditionally associated with inspiring media can also be induced by comments that suggest others have been inspired" (p. 547).

Summary

The landscape of news is frequently characterized as hostile, conflictual, and negative. However, many news stories reflect hope, gratitude, kindness, and inspiration. Not only do large portions of the population report encountering such content, a growing body of work demonstrates that positive news stories can elicit positive and self-transcendent affect, feelings of connectedness, motivations for greater altruism, and can reduce prejudicial feelings toward oppressed or stigmatized groups. Applied to foundational theories of news, this body of work suggests that many news stories can set the agenda for more peaceful and harmonious interpretations of issues, that they can frame stories in constructive or restorative ways, and that they can include moving and uplifting exemplars. Further, given the tendency for individuals to share positive news stories with others and to feel greater connectedness when they perceive that others are also inspired by positive news, we are hopeful that inspiring and uplifting stories that go viral can represent a reinforcing spiral model that serves to spread kindness and gratitude.

References

Algoe, S. B., & Haidt, J. (2009). Witnessing excellence in action: The "other-praising" emotions of elevation, gratitude, and admiration. *Journal of Positive Psychology*, 4, 105–127. doi:10.1080/17439760802650519.

Aquino, K., McFerran, B., & Laven, M. (2011). Moral identity and the experience of moral elevation in response to acts of uncommon goodness. *Journal of Personality and Social Psychology*, 100, 703–718. doi:10.1037/a0022540.

Baden, D., McIntyre, K., & Homberg, F. (2018). The impact of constructive news on affective and behavioural responses. *Journalism Studies*, 20, 1940–1959. doi:10.1080/1461670x.2018.1545599.

Bartsch, A., Oliver, M. B., Nitsch, C., & Scherr, S. (2018). Inspired by the paralympics: Effects of empathy on audience interest in para-sports and on the destigmatization of persons with disabilities. *Communication Research*, 45, 525–553. doi:10.1177/0093650215626984.

Bartsch, A., & Schneider, F. M. (2014). Entertainment and politics revisited: How non-escapist forms of entertainment can stimulate political interest and information seeking. *Journal of Communication*, 64, 369–396. doi:10.1111/jcom.12095.

Berger, J., & Milkman, K. L. (2012). What makes online content viral? *Journal of Marketing Research*, 49, 192–205. doi:10.1509/jmr.10.0353.

Bohle, R. H. (1986). Negativism as news selection predictor. *Journalism Quarterly*, 63, 789–796.

Calicchio, D. (2020, May 28). Minneapolis Third Precinct police station set on fire after rioters break in. *Fox News*. Retrieved from https://www.foxnews.com/us/minneap olis-third-precinct-police-station-set-on-fire-after-rioters-break-in.

Ellithorpe, M. E., Huang, Y., & Oliver, M. B. (2019). Reach across the aisle: Elevation from political messages predicts increased positivity toward politics, political participa-tion, and the opposite political party. *Journal of Communication*, 69, 249–272. doi:10.1093/joc/jqz011.

Entman, R. M. (1993). Framing: Toward clarification of a fractured paradigm. *Journal of Communication*, 43, 51–58. doi:10.1111/j.1460-2466.1993.tb01304.x.

Fitzgerald, K., Paravati, E., Green, M. C., Moore, M. M., & Qian, J. L. (2020). Restora-tive narratives for health promotion. *Health Communication*, 35, 356–363. doi:10.1080/ 10410236.2018.1563032.

Freeman, D., Aquino, K., & McFerran, B. (2009). Overcoming beneficiary race as an impediment to charitable donations: Social dominance orientation, the experience of moral elevation, and donation behavior. *Personality and Social Psychology Bulletin*, 35, 72–84. doi:10.1177/0146167208325415.

Freezell, J. T. (2018). Agenda setting through social media: The importance of incidental news exposure and social filtering in the digital era. *Political Research Quarterly*, 71, 482–494. doi:10.1177/1065912917744895.

Galician, M.-L., & Pasternack, S. (1987). Balancing good news and bad news: An ethical obligation? *Journal of Mass Media Ethics*, 2, 82–92. doi:10.1080/08900528709358298.

Gibson, R., & Zillmann, D. (1994). Exaggerated versus representative exemplification in news reports: Perception of issues and personal consequences. *Communication Research*, 21, 603–624. doi:10.1177/009365094021005003.

Gruszczynski, M., & Wagner, M. W. (2016). Information flow in the 21st century: The dynamics of agenda-uptake. *Mass Communication and Society*, 20, 378–402. doi:10.1080/ 15205436.2016.1255757.

Irimieș, L., & Irimieș, C. (2017). Effective communication in politics: Barack Obama's inspirational speeches. *Journal of Media Research*, 10, 122–129. doi:10.24193/jmr.29.10.

Iyengar, S., & Krupenkin, M. (2018). The strengthening of partisan affect. *Political Psy-chology*, 39, 201–218. doi:10.1111/pops.12487.

Janicke-Bowles, S. H., Raney, A. A., Oliver, M. B., Dale, K. R., Jones, R. P., & Cox, D. (2019). Exploring the spirit in U.S. audiences: The role of the virtue of transcendence in inspiring media consumption. *Journalism & Mass Communication Quarterly*. Advanced online publication. doi:10.1177/1077699019894927.

Ji, Q., Raney, A. A., Janicke-Bowles, S. H., Dale, K. R., Oliver, M. B., Reed, A., Seibert, J., & Raney II, A. A. (2019). Spreading the good news: Analyzing socially shared inspirational news content. *Journalism & Mass Communication Quarterly*, 96, 872–893. doi:10.1177/1077699018813096.

Jurkowitz, M., Mitchell, A., & Walker, M. (2020, January 24). U.S. Media polarization and the 2020 election: A nation divided. *Pew Research Center*. Retrieved from https://www.journalism.org/2020/01/24/u-s-media-polarization-and-the-2020-election-a-nation-divided/.

Lai, C. K., Haidt, J., & Nosek, B. A. (2014). Moral elevation reduces prejudice against gay men. *Cognition & Emotion*, 28, 781–794. doi:10.1080/02699931.2013.861342.

Lamson, W. R. J., & McGrath, R. E. (2019). Speaking of character: Character strength references in movies and presidential nomination speeches. *The Journal of Positive Psychology*. Advanced online publication. doi:10.1080/17439760.2019.1689415.

Leonhardt, D. (2020, May 29). Protests against police escalate. *New York Times*. Retrieved from https://www.nytimes.com/2020/05/29/briefing/minneapolis-twitter-coronavir us-your-friday-briefing.html.

Leung, D. K. K., & Lee, F. L. F. (2015). How journalists value positive news: The influence of professional beliefs, market considerations, and political attitudes. *Journalism Studies*, 16, 289–304. doi:10.1080/1461670x.2013.869062.

McCombs, M., & Reynolds, A. (1994). How the news shapes our civic agenda. In J. Bryant & M. B. Oliver (Eds.), *Media effects: Advances in theory and research* (3rd ed., pp. 1–16). New York: Routledge.

McCombs, M. E., & Shaw, D. L. (1993). The evolution of agenda-setting research: Twenty-five years in the marketplace of ideas. *Journal of Communication*, 43, 58–67. doi:10.1111/j.1460-2466.1993.tb01262.x.

McIntyre, K. (2016). What makes "good" news newsworthy? *Communication Research Reports*, 33, 223–230. doi:10.1080/08824096.2016.1186619.

McIntyre, K. (2020). "Tell me something good": Testing the longitudinal effects of constructive news using the google assistant. *Electronic News*, 14, 37–54. doi:10.1177/1931243120910446.

McIntyre, K., & Gyldensted, C. (2017). Constructive journalism: Applying positive psychology techniques to news production. *The Journal of Media Innovations*, 4, 20–34. doi:0.5617/jomi.v4i2.2403.

McIntyre, K. E., & Gibson, R. (2016). Positive news makes readers feel good: A "silver-lining" approach to negative news can attract audiences. *Southern Communication Journal*, 81, 304–315. doi:10.1080/1041794x.2016.1171892.

Oliver, M. B., Ash, E., & Woolley, J. K. (2012). Responses to media portrayals of moral beauty. In R. Tamborini (Ed.), *Media and the moral mind* (pp. 93–108). New York, NY: Routledge.

Oliver, M. B., Dillard, J. P., Bae, K., & Tamul, D. J. (2012). The effect of narrative news format on empathy for stigmatized groups. *Journalism & Mass Communication Quarterly*, 89, 205–224. doi:10.1177/1077699012439020.

Oliver, M. B., Kim, K., Hoewe, J., Ash, E., Woolley, J. K., & Shade, D. D. (2015). Media-induced elevation as a means of enhancing feelings of intergroup connectedness. *Journal of Social Issues*, 71, 106–122. doi:0.1111/josi.12099.

Pew Research Center. (2019, December 17). In a politically polarized era, sharp divides in both partisan coalitions. *Pew Research Center*. Retrieved from https://www.people-press.org/2019/12/17/in-a-politically-polarized-era-sharp-divides-in-both-partisan-coalitions/.

Roselyn Du, Y. (2017). Intermedia agenda-setting effects. In P. Rössler, C. A. Hoffner, & L. van Zoonen (Eds.), *The international encyclopedia of media effects* (pp. 1–13). Hoboken, NJ: John Wiley & Sons.

Roth, F. S., Weinmann, C., Schneider, F. M., Hopp, F. R., & Vorderer, P. (2014). Seriously entertained: Antecedents and consequences of hedonic and eudaimonic entertainment experiences with political talk shows on TV. *Mass Communication and Society*, 17, 379–399. doi:10.1080/15205436.2014.891135.

Seethaler, J. (2017). Political agenda-building. In P. Rössler, C. A. Hoffner, & L. van Zoonen (Eds.), *The international encyclopedia of media effects* (pp. 1–12). Hoboken, NJ: John Wiley & Sons.

Slater, M. D. (2007). Reinforcing spirals: The mutual influence of media selectivity and media effects and their impact on individual behavior and social identity. *Communication Theory*, 17, 281–303. doi:10.1111/j.1468-2885.2007.00296.x.

Slater, M. D. (2015). Reinforcing spirals model: Conceptualizing the relationship between media content exposure and the development and maintenance of attitudes. *Media Psychology*, 18, 370–395. doi:10.1080/15213269.2014.897236.

Slater, M. D., Henry, K. L., Swaim, R. C., & Anderson, L. L. (2003). Violent media content and aggressiveness in adolescents: A downward spiral model. *Communication Research*, 30, 713–736.

Sunstein, C. R. (2001). *Republic.com*. Princeton, NJ: Princeton University Press.

Tellis, G. J., MacInnis, D. J., Tirunillai, S., & Zhang, Y. W. (2019). What drives virality (sharing) of online digital content? The critical role of information, emotion, and brand prominence. *Journal of Marketing*, 83, 1–20. doi:10.1177/0022242919841034.

Tenore, M. J. (2015). The case for restorative narratives. *Kosmos*. Retrieved from https://www.kosmosjournal.org/article/the-case-for-restorative-narratives/.

Tewksbury, D., & Schuefele, D. A. (2020). News framing theory and research. In M. B. Oliver, A. A. Raney, & J. Bryant (Eds.), *Media effects: Advances in theory and research* (4th ed., pp. 51–68). New York, NY: Routledge.

Waddell, T. F., & Bailey, A. (2017). Inspired by the crowd: The effect of online comments on elevation and universal orientation. *Communication Monographs*, 84, 534–550. doi:10.1080/03637751.2017.1369137.

Ziegele, M., Breiner, T., & Quiring, O. (2014). What creates interactivity in online news discussions? An exploratory analysis of discussion factors in user comments on news items. *Journal of Communication*, 64, 1111–1138. doi:10.1111/jcom.12123.

Zillmann, D., & Brosius, H. B. (2000). *Exemplification in communication: The influence of case reports on the perception of issues*. Mahwah, NJ: Lawrence Erlbaum Associates.

Additional Readings

Berger, J. (2011). Arousal increases social transmission of information. *Psychological Science*, 22, 891–893. doi:10.1177/0956797611413294.

Heimbach, I., & Hinz, O. (2016). The impact of content sentiment and emotionality on content virality. *International Journal of Research in Marketing*, 33, 695–701. doi:10.1016/j.ijres-mar.2016.02.004.

Holt, L. F. (2013). Writing the wrong: Can counter-stereotypes offset negative media messages about African Americans? *Journalism & Mass Communication Quarterly*, 90, 108–125. doi:10.1177/1077699012468699.

10

NARRATIVE PERSUASION

Source: Shutterstock 342526523

Communication technologies like mass broadcasting and the internet have fundamentally changed the way we share information. With a quick internet search, we can find new recipes, learn how to change a tire, and discover almost anything we could want to know about history and the world around us. New technology makes it easier than ever to access and share information across cultures, space, and time. Of course, humans were sharing information with each other long before these technologies existed, even in preliterate societies where access to and knowledge of the written word was scarce. One vehicle for communicating knowledge, cultural values, and history that has persisted through it all is storytelling. Around the world and for millennia, people have shared knowledge through stories. Although storytelling traditions and technologies have evolved, stories themselves remain powerful tools for knowledge communication and persuasion.

Stories, or narratives as we often call them, provide a unique vehicle for conveying information. This chapter will explore the reasons why narratives can be an especially useful tool for persuasion and how specific narratives can be used to promote positive and prosocial outcomes through a process known as narrative persuasion. Broadly speaking, the term **narrative persuasion** refers to the impact of mediated narrative messages on the beliefs, attitudes, or behaviors of audience members.

Overview of Persuasion and Narratives

The study of persuasion is often traced back to interest in the effectiveness of political speeches in Ancient Greece. Historically, persuasion has been differentiated from other forms of communication based on the *intentions* of the messenger. That is, although any message may impact an audience, persuasive messages—such as advertisements, public service announcements, campaign speeches—are specifically designed and intended to do so. For some narrative persuasion scholars, this distinction remains important. They contend that narrative persuasion can occur with stories (or certain parts of stories) that are created with the express purpose of affecting specific beliefs, attitudes, or behaviors. Other scholars focus more on persuasion as a process rather than a content type. As such, many researchers now argue that the impacts of narrative persuasion can be intended or unintended by the message creators. We do not necessarily take a position on this matter. But because our interest is the adoption or reinforcement of beliefs, attitudes, and behaviors that are beneficial in nature, the following discussion focuses on intentional efforts to facilitate those outcomes through narratives.

As a form of communication, though, what makes a narrative different from a political speech or rhetorical argument? Scholars have defined narratives in various ways, with entire works dedicated to understanding exactly what constitutes a narrative. Many definitions converge on three particular elements that all narratives contain: (1) a specific structure, which features (2) characters and (3) some form of conflict (e.g., Green & Brock, 2000; Hinyard & Kreuter, 2007). Moyer-Gusé and Dale (2017) contend that the structure—specifically, that narratives must contain a beginning, middle, and end—is the most essential feature of narratives. The structure has important implications for the way narratives are cognitively and emotionally processed, with audience members needing to piece together the story as it progresses. Political speeches and rhetorical arguments can certainly include narratives, but they are inherently different because they follow a different structure.

Narrative structure, characters, and conflict promote narrative engagement. An important aspect of narrative engagement is the feeling of being a part of the story world. You have surely experienced this phenomenon when reading your favorite book or watching your favorite television show. The real world seems to fade away as you are completely absorbed into the story. This experience of being pulled into a story world is known as transportation; it is discussed in-depth below. Further, because narratives involve characters (whether real or fictional), our relationships with them can also influence the persuasive effects of narratives. For instance, the extent to which audience members perceive themselves to be similar to characters can make narratives more or less effective at spreading their message. Ultimately, narrative engagement can lead to narrative persuasion. We now examine several theories and key concepts related to narrative persuasion.

Key Narrative Persuasion Theories and Concepts

Narrative persuasion research assumes an *attentive* audience, at least to some extent. That is, paying attention to a message on some level is thought to be a precondition for learning from or being persuaded by it. But audiences can be in different attentional states when consuming media content. Potter (2012) identified four such states: automatic, attentional, transported, and reflexive. In the **automatic** state, you are not paying attention to a piece of content, even though you perceive and recognize that it is present. For instance, you might listen to music on your drive to school or work but your attention is (ideally) on driving. You "know" that the music is on, but you are not attending to it. In the **attentional** state, you are aware of and paying some attention to the message. An example of this would be sitting down to watch your favorite show or read a book. The **transported** state takes this level of attention one step further and implies that you are absorbed into the message, that you lose track of the time and place around you. And finally, the **reflexive** state involves being aware of the message and of your own thinking about the message. During this state, you might be considering the effects of the message on you or your decisions about why you chose a particular piece of content. Potter (2012) described the reflexive state as being "hyperaware of the message and of your own processing of the message" (p. 23). Researchers typically examine and theorize about audiences in the attentional and transported states.

Furthermore, most theories of narrative persuasion presume that narratives can (and do) persuade. As a result, the theories primarily seek to describe and explain *how* (rather than *if*) narratives can change attitudes or behaviors among audience members.

Transportation Imagery Model

The concept of **transportation** was introduced above. Green and Brock (2000) described the state of transportation with the example of being so engrossed in a book that the reader does not notice another person coming into the room.

The state occurs on varying levels as readers, viewers, listeners, users, or players become cognitively and emotionally engaged in a narrative to the point that they lose track of the world around them; that is, all mental processes are focused on the events occurring in the story. In fact, highly transported people are so absorbed that they become less aware or critical of information presented in the message that contradicts real life. As a result, the more people are transported into a story world the more they report higher levels of story-consistent attitudes—even ones that may not be based on or supported by real-world facts—than those who experience less or no transportation. The **transportation imagery model** (TIM) (Green & Brock, 2002) explains this process.

Generally speaking, we hold beliefs and attitudes because we think they are correct; we act the way we do for the same reasons. When someone tries to persuade us otherwise, a tendency is to argue with them, to think through all of the ways their argument is wrong or flawed. In persuasion studies that process is known as **counterarguing**. The TIM states that transportation leads to narrative persuasion by reducing counterarguing. Being transported into the story world means that we become less aware of the material world. As a result, information presented in the story world is less likely to be compared to and contrasted with real-world information. Thus, transported media users are less likely to argue with beliefs, attitudes, and behaviors presented in the story, even if they might otherwise do so in the real world. The lack of counterarguing increases the likelihood that the beliefs, attitudes, and behaviors presented in the story will be adopted by the user. Put another way: Transportation mitigates the effects of counterarguing by making the media user less aware of possible counterarguments.

Consider that the organization where you intern is trying to change attitudes toward employee recycling by including short narratives about its importance in the company newsletter. The TIM suggests that creating a story that results in a high level of transportation among readers would result in more story-consistent attitudes (e.g., recycling is important, easy to do, helpful for the environment, everyone's responsibility, what a good employee does) than a narrative that does not lead to transportation. Employees who are highly transported into such a narrative—even those who do not currently recycle—should be more likely to adopt the pro-recycling messages because they were less likely to counterargue with them while reading.

Many story- and audience-related factors can affect the level of transportation experienced during narrative reception. Of particular importance to the issue of counterarguing is the multifaceted concept of perceived realism (Green, 2004). In developing the extended transportation imagery model, Van Laer and colleagues (2014) highlighted the role of two facets of perceived realism in transportation: (1) the extent to which the narrative is created in a way that encourages readers and viewers to develop strong imagery, and (2) the extent to which the events in the story could actually occur. Busselle and Bilandzic (2008) further emphasized the importance of realism in the narrative persuasion process when developing their model of narrative comprehension and engagement. **Narrative realism** is the extent to which information in the story is consistent with previous information in the narrative, whereas **external realism** is the extent to which the information is consistent with real-world facts. For instance, if a character in a television show hates spiders but is seen interacting with them later with no problem and no explanation, narrative realism would be low. If that spider could talk, external realism would be low. When either of these types of realism are low, it can disrupt narrative engagement, transportation, and narrative persuasion. Audience-related factors can also influence the level of transportation experienced, including transportability (i.e., how likely an individual is to be transported, measured as an individual-difference variable; Mazzocco, Green, Sasota, & Jones, 2010), need for affect (Appel & Richter, 2010), and story familiarity (Van Laer, De Ruyter, Visconti, & Wetzels, 2014), among other factors.

Extended Elaboration Likelihood Model

In addition to transportation, identification with characters plays an important role in narrative persuasion. **Identification** with a character involves taking on the role or perspective of a character (Cohen, 2001). It is similar to transportation in that it involves being absorbed in the story, but identification is specifically associated with experiencing the story world through characters and their perspectives, motivations, and roles. Identification plays a key part in narrative persuasion as explained by the **extended elaboration likelihood model** (E-ELM) (Slater & Rouner, 2002). The E-ELM model builds on a long-standing explanation of the (non-narrative) persuasion process known as the elaboration likelihood model (ELM) (Petty & Cacioppo, 1986), altering it to be applicable to narratives.

As an intrinsically motivated behavior, narrative reception through media use is naturally rewarding. When we consume narratives, we want to stay involved with them, we want to experience transportation, and we want to identify with characters. Think of the last time you went to the movies and someone's cell phone rang in the middle. You were likely annoyed at the distraction because you wanted to stay engrossed in the film, not be drawn back into the real world. Because of this motivation to remain transported in a story world in which we identify and engage with characters, Slater and Rouner (2002) argued that narratives provide an opportunity for persuasion that is unique from traditional message forms. Higher levels of transportation and identification with characters are associated with higher levels of attitudes that are consistent with the story, primarily because of reduced counterarguing (per the TIM).

Entertainment Overcoming Reactance Model

As noted above, persuasive messages sometimes contain information that is inconsistent with our current beliefs, attitudes, and behaviors. One natural response is to engage in counterarguing, though transportation can suppress that response. Another is to experience reactance. **Reactance** is the threatened feeling that occurs when it seems like someone or something is trying to take away our freedom to choose and make our own decisions. It can occur when we perceive that a message is trying to convince us to act or think a certain way. Self-determination theory (see Chapter 3) states that the need for autonomy is a key aspect of well-being. When people think that their autonomy is threatened, they experience reactance, which can actually make them hold on to the attitude more firmly or engage in the behavior even more. For instance, many people ignore medical advice and continue to engage in harmful health behaviors. Fogarty (1997) explains that this may be due to feelings of reactance.

Reactance plays a key role in the **entertainment overcoming resistance model** (EORM) (Moyer-Gusé, 2008). According to the model, narratives may overcome natural reactance responses in audiences by diminishing the appearance of an overt persuasive goal. Most media users know that an advertisement or other persuasive message is trying to convince them of something, which can trigger reactance. However, the unique structure of and mental processing required for narratives suppresses reactance because users are less likely to be aware of persuasive attempts in the story. For instance, if a character in a television drama decides to quit smoking in order to improve their health, viewers are less likely to process this as an intentional attempt to persuade them to also quit smoking (even if the storyline was intentionally inserted in consultation with the Centers for Disease Control) than if they saw an anti-smoking advertisement during the commercial break.

Building on the E-ELM, the EORM also argues that identification with characters plays a key role in the persuasiveness of a narrative, particularly messages intended to curb risky behaviors. In general, people tend to underestimate their vulnerability to certain threats. For instance, few people think about the risks of being in a car crash when they drive because many people believe it will not happen to them. However, the EORM states that when we identify with a character who experiences negative effects of a situation or decision, we may adjust our expectations about how likely we are to experience that same threat (i.e., perceived invulnerability). In one study, Moyer-Gusé and Nabi (2010) explored the effects of a narrative featuring an unplanned pregnancy on reactance, counterarguing, and perceived invulnerability. Two weeks after viewing the narrative, character identification predicted a decrease in perceived invulnerability, meaning participants who experienced identification with the pregnant character reported greater intention to practice safe sex in the future.

Emotional Flow

One final important theoretical perspective on narrative persuasion was introduced by Nabi and Green (2015). **Emotional flow** is conceptualized as the emotional shifts that occur throughout a piece of content. Picture a river that twists and turns as it flows through the land. The emotions we experience throughout a message may similarly twist, turn, and flow as we make our way through it. In the non-narrative literature, emotional flow has been shown to impact the persuasiveness of messages. For instance, Rossiter and Thornton (2004) found that advertisements that start with a fear appeal then shift to relief were more effective than advertisements that start with and increase the levels of fear throughout.

Nabi and Green (2015) argued that emotional flow might also contribute to persuasion through narratives. We might feel elated at a favorite character's good fortune, only to feel saddened when their storyline suddenly takes a turn for the worse. The sadness you experience at the sudden misfortune experienced by a favorite character (identification) may keep you more engaged in a story (trans-portation) because you want to see how the story turns out (and if things will get better). Thus, emotional flow can play a key role in engagement with a story and ultimately affect narrative persuasion (per the TIM, E-ELM, and EORM).

Together, these theories identify a variety of factors that can influence the extent to which narratives are persuasive, particularly transportation and identifi-cation. These factors are further influenced by story- (e.g., realism, emotional flow) and audience-related (e.g., transportability, need for affect) factors. Although many factors determine the persuasiveness of narratives, researchers agree that they can be powerful tools to change beliefs, attitudes, and behaviors. In the next section, we explore some of the contexts in which scholars have used narratives to persuade people to change their thoughts and behaviors.

Narratives in Action

Narratives and Health Information

The longest and richest tradition of scholarly research on narrative persuasion is known as entertainment-education (E-E). **Entertainment-education** is a "theory-based communication strategy for purposefully embedding educational and social issues in the creation, production, processing, and dissemination process of an entertainment program, in order to achieve desired individual, community, institutional, and societal changes" (Wang & Singhal, 2009, pp. 272–273). Suc-cessful E-E efforts can be found across the globe (in particular in Mexico, India, and several countries in Africa and South America), leveraging a variety of media formats (though radio and television serials or episodes are most common), tack-ling issues ranging from farming techniques to domestic violence prevention (for more see Singhal & Rogers, 2012). For our purposes, the long line of E-E efforts designed to adjust health-related behaviors and beliefs are of primary interest.

For instance, Vaughan and colleagues (2000) examined the effects of an entertainment-education radio show on safe-sex practices in Tanzania.

The program was intentionally designed to prevent the spread of HIV, including plot points about the role of condom use in preventing the spread of sexually transmitted infections. Characters on the show provided both positive (e.g., good health decisions led to positive outcomes) and negative (e.g., lack of condom use led to infection) models. The results showed that listening to the radio program was associated with both a reduced number of sexual partners and an increase in condom use among listeners. Similar studies were conducted in St Lucia and Ethiopia, among other locations, with similar positive results.

An oft-addressed health issue in E-E programming is cancer. In one study, Wilkin and colleagues (2007) examined a storyline related to breast cancer embedded in a Spanish-language telenovela, with the researchers examining its effects on viewers' knowledge about and behavioral intentions related to the disease. The researchers found that calls to a cancer hotline increased when the phone number was featured during the program. Furthermore, watching the show was associated with greater knowledge about breast cancer and higher intention to encourage mammograms among women.

Similarly, Hether and colleagues (2008) examined the effects of storylines from *ER* and *Grey's Anatomy* on viewers' knowledge of, attitudes toward, and behaviors regarding breast cancer. Both storylines focused on characters who tested positive for the so-called "breast cancer susceptibility gene" (BRCA1) and had to decide whether or not to have preventative surgery as a result. Participants responded to a questionnaire before and after the episodes aired, and results were analyzed for those who watched only one of the shows and those who watched both. Although viewing just one of the shows was associated with positive outcomes (e.g., improved knowledge, changed attitudes), participants who viewed both showed the greatest changes in knowledge, attitudes, and behaviors. This suggests that repeated exposure to positive health messages in entertainment narratives can be influential and beneficial.

Another common area of narrative persuasion research deals with attitudes and behavioral intentions toward organ donation. In one study, Morgan, Movius, and Cody (2009) examined the effects of viewing an episode from several popular television programs (*CSI:NY, Numb3rs, House*, and *Grey's Anatomy*) that contained a storyline on organ donation. The results showed that emotional involvement with the story played an important role with regard to knowledge and motivation to donate. Additionally, participants' beliefs about organ donation aligned with the information presented in the show, even when the particular episode contained inaccurate information or myths (e.g., that a black market for organs exists to serve rich people in the United States). The findings demonstrated that, although narratives can have real-world effects on attitudes, knowledge, and behaviors, the content of the narratives matters. Content creators must ensure that narratives contain correct information, lest they accidentally steer audiences in the wrong direction with their storylines.

BOX 10.1 WHY DO WE SEE SO MUCH RESEARCH ABOUT *ER* AND *GREY'S ANATOMY?*

Medical dramas have long been popular among U.S. audiences, evidenced by two long-running shows: *ER* and *Grey's Anatomy*. *ER* aired for 15 seasons and included 331 episodes; as of publication of this book, *Grey's Anatomy* had been contracted for a 17th season. These popular medical dramas follow the personal and professional lives of the doctors, nurses, and staff at their respective hospitals. The dramas are not only popular among general audiences but among researchers as well, as episodes from the shows have been used as stimuli in many entertainment-education studies. Why are these shows used so often in narrative persuasion research?

First, *ER* and *Grey's Anatomy* are compelling, immersive narratives. As dramas, the shows are designed to draw the viewer into the story world, a key feature of narratives that encourage transportation. As we explored in the chapter, transportation plays a vital role in narrative persuasion. Viewers who recall the episode of *Grey's Anatomy* where Meredith (a leading female character) puts her hand on a live bomb to stop it from exploding likely also recall being so gripped by the action on screen, so entirely immersed in the experience, that they lost track of the world around them. The story design makes transportation likely, which makes these kinds of shows appealing to researchers.

A second reason why these shows are chosen is because they are popular. People enjoy the shows, which is helpful when you are requiring participants to view something for a study. Enjoying a show typically means that you will have a positive experience. Were researchers to choose shows that people actively dislike, they may find that lower levels of transportation and identification occur among audience members. Popularity also means that a lot of people have seen the show, which has implications for the size of potential effects. As a result, it is important that researchers explore the effects of widely viewed medical storylines so that we understand how attitudes toward medical issues and behaviors may be influenced by these narratives.

A third reason why these shows are frequently chosen is because they include important storylines that fit researchers' interests. When you design a study on narrative persuasion, it can be difficult to find appropriate stimuli. If you want to study the effects of a breast cancer or safe-sex narrative, you need a narrative that addresses these issues. One option is to find or write a story that addresses these issues. This is a great option for those who are interested in studying text-based narratives, and it gives the researcher a lot of freedom to develop a stimulus that matches their goals exactly. However, problems arise when researchers are interested in studying visual narratives like television, advertisements, or movies. Most researchers do not have access to media creation tools on the scale of professional television shows; so, we have to choose from available content. Because *ER* and *Grey's Anatomy* have aired hundreds of episodes, there is a good chance that whatever health-related issue a researcher is interested in has been covered on the show. It is an imperfect solution because the researcher cannot control the narratives, but the external validity offered by using an existing, popular show is a valuable trade-off.

Finally, another reason that these shows are used by researchers is that the health information contained in them is—for the most part—scientifically accurate. Researchers with the "Hollywood, Health & Society" (HH&S) program housed in The Norman Lear Center at the University of Southern California work hand-in-hand with the entertainment industry to provide information and access to experts on issues related to health, security, and safety. In fact, between 2012 and 2017, HH&S assisted on more than 1,100 storylines in hundreds of shows that aired across broadcasting and cable television and streaming services. Two shows that they routinely assisted: *ER* and *Grey's Anatomy*.

Developing and Influencing Attitudes Toward Others

Several communication and psychology theories have been used to examine the way we learn things about the world around us, including cultivation theory and social cognitive theory (see Chapter 2). The theories and the supporting evidence confirm that, in addition to learning through first-hand experience and through modeled real-world behaviors, people can (and do) learn about the world through media. One specific instance of this involves learning about other people. For instance, it is possible that you may have never met someone from a particular religious group or country, or someone of a specific sexual orientation or gender identity. However, you may still know things about these groups of people from (fictional and nonfictional) media content. Many researchers have examined the ways that narratives can be used to positively influence our attitudes and our actions toward other people.

A key concept within this line of research is the idea of the "other." An "other," or an **outgroup member**, is someone who is a member of a different group than you in some way. An outgroup member might be of a different gender identity, race, or attend a different university, among other characteristics. In general, humans tend to group themselves according to a wide variety of categories, identifying individuals as **ingroup members** if they share even one characteristic (or as outgroup members if they differ in some way). For instance, because of sports and other competitions, many universities in the U.S. have rivals. Despite the fact that students share religion, race, gender identity, countries of origin, and majors at both schools, many consider students at the rival school to be outgroup members solely because of their school affiliation. A student who attends The Ohio State University would likely consider a student at the University of Michigan to be an outgroup member (and vice versa).

The **contact hypothesis** states that positive contact between outgroup members can lead to more positive attitudes toward the outgroup, provided four conditions are met: (1) the individuals involved in the contact are of equal status; (2) they share a common goal; (3) they cooperate with each other; and (4) the contact between them is viewed as acceptable (e.g., it is legal or sanctioned by whoever is in power; see Allport, 1954). Although generations of scholars have examined the ways that positive, real-world interpersonal interactions can be used to alter our attitudes toward others, several issues with the approach exist. First, the ideal conditions required for the interactions to lead to positive effects as stated by the contact hypotheses are rare (Dixon, Durrheim, & Tredoux, 2005). The second is that intergroup interaction can be associated with feelings of anxiety (Greenland & Brown, 1999). As a result, researchers began to examine ways that media could be used as a substitute for interpersonal contact to alter attitudes toward others.

One way that narratives might be used to change attitudes is by allowing users to build relationships in a "safe" environment with characters who are different from them. As we explored in Chapter 2, the human brain processes media content as if it were real. Building on this idea, research suggests that humans experience interactions with media characters as if they were real, leading to real-world effects. For instance, television viewers may experience a **parasocial interaction** (PSI) with a character in a series that makes them feel like they know the character (Horton & Wohl, 1956; see also Chapter 4). You may have experienced PSI when you see the actor who plays your favorite character on a show appear on a different show as a different character, and you think for a moment "that's not how so-and-so behaves." Even though we realize that the character is not real, it still feels like we know them and how they behave. It feels like we have a (one-way) interaction with them.

The **parasocial contact hypothesis** capitalizes on this feeling of interaction and is used to explain one reason why positive portrayals of outgroup members in media content might lead to more positive attitudes toward those individuals in audiences. In a series of studies, Schiappa, Gregg, and Hewes (2005) examined whether narratives could be used to change attitudes toward outgroup members. In one study, participants viewed the first season of the television show *Six Feet Under*, which focuses on a family which owns a funeral home and contains a storyline where a major character (David) grapples with his identity and ultimately comes out as gay. After viewing Season One, general attitudes toward lesbians and gay men, among other items, were measured. The results showed that parasocial contact with David was associated with increasingly positive attitudes toward gay men.

The parasocial contact explanation for shifting attitudes toward outgroup members requires that the user experience a *positive* parasocial interaction with a character. However, similar positive outcomes might be experienced when users observe characters interacting with each other, taking the viewer's personal experiences out of the equation. The **mediated intergroup contact** approach argues that we can learn from positive models of intergroup interaction and develop more positive attitudes toward others through this experience (Ortiz & Harwood, 2007). This approach builds on social cognitive theory (see Chapter 2) and contends that an ingroup member who has a positive interaction with an outgroup member can serve as a positive model for intergroup interaction. This is different than the parasocial contact hypothesis in that the relationship exists between two characters in the narrative, not between the viewer and a character. Research in this area shows that character identification plays an important role in the extent to which mediated intergroup contact can affect positive attitudinal change (Moyer-Gusé, Dale, & Ortiz, 2019).

Although a great deal of research has supported the argument that narratives can be used to positively change attitudes toward others, the approaches mentioned above all require that positive portrayals of outgroup members actually be shown in the narrative. Doing so might require a counter-stereotypical portrayal or a positive intergroup interaction, but the success of the narratives in affecting positive change hinges on the presence of positive portrayals. But the reality is that many groups are underrepresented in media, and others are often shown in a negative light. Because of this fact, researchers began to explore other ways that media might be used to alter attitudes toward others.

One way that narratives can be used to change attitudes toward others is by eliciting self-transcendent emotions (see Chapter 6). For instance, experiencing elevation can make one feel closer to others and humankind in general. Oliver and colleagues (2015) hypothesized that perhaps elevating media could be used to change attitudes toward other people, even in the absence of a specific, positive intergroup message. The study revealed that watching inspirational videos that elicited elevation was associated with feeling closer to humanity, which was in turn associated with more positive attitudes toward diverse others. The researchers concluded that feeling closer to humanity in general led to an expansion of the participants' perceived ingroup. We tend to favor ingroup members, and by expanding the ingroup to include "humanity," participants felt more positively toward people who may have been previously considered outgroup members. Ellithorpe, Huang, and Oliver (2019) additionally found that the elevating messages can have a positive effect when included in political speeches. Exposure to such messages was associated with higher levels of positivity toward both politics and the speaker, along with increased perceived closeness with political others. Experiencing elevation while viewing footage from the Paralympic Games has also been associated with decreased stigmatization of persons with disabilities (Bartsch, Oliver, Nitsch, & Scherr, 2018).

With their unique persuasive powers, narratives can impact attitudes toward others in positive ways. However, nothing about narrative persuasion requires the outcomes to be positive. Narratives are defined by their structure and characteristics, just as easily influencing negative attitudes as well. Those wishing to encourage unhealthy behaviors or promote hate are equally able to leverage narratives in the same way as those who wish to positively change behaviors and promote acceptance. Because of this, researchers have begun to study the use of narratives in propaganda that encourages extremism and what can be done to counter these efforts.

In one study, Frischlich and colleagues (2018) examined counter-narratives opposing violent extremism. Participants viewed extremist propaganda videos, as well as videos designed to counter violent extremism. The results showed that narrativity was influential for *both* the propaganda and counter-narrative videos. Narrativity was associated with increased appeal of the videos and identification with the individuals featured. Identification was subsequently related to cognitive inducement, suggesting that identification with individuals in both of the videos influenced the way that viewers processed this content.

Ultimately, narratives can be used to influence the way we think about and our attitudes toward other people, whether the narrative is specifically designed to promote positive attitudes or not. The addition of self-transcendent emotions as an avenue for attitude change opens up a wider range of narratives for examination, no longer limiting researchers to studying content solely including positive portrayals of outgroup members or interactions. Although positive portrayals can certainly be used to influence attitudes, narratives that elicit self-transcendent emotions may also lead to positive effects.

Hope, Underdogs, and Restorative Narratives

Another self-transcendent emotion that offers promising benefits is hope (see Chapter 6). **Hope** is the feeling of wanting a specific outcome that may be unlikely to happen. Various researchers have found that hope and elicitors of hope are commonly found in media content, including traditional media forms such as movies and television and newer media such as YouTube videos and Facebook. One particular type of story that may elicit hopeful feelings is that of the underdog. **Underdog narratives** are stories that feature an unlikely character working to overcome a difficult obstacle. As Prestin (2013) explained, underdogs are disadvantaged characters who face barriers with "tenacity, persistence, and effort" (p. 322). In her study of underdog narratives, Prestin found that viewing stories featuring underdog narratives led to higher levels of hope and greater motivation to work toward goals. Although outside of the specific realm of narratives, Chadwick (2015) examined the persuasiveness of hope appeals within climate change messages. In the study, feelings of hope predicted both interest in addressing climate change and perceived message effectiveness. Together, these studies show that hope offers a particularly interesting route for influencing attitudes via narratives.

Restorative narratives offer a specific context for examining positive effects. **Restorative narratives** are a form of journalism and storytelling that focuses on hope and resilience rather than on the shortcomings and insufficiencies of people (see also Chapter 9). They have been shown to consistently elicit elevation and hope among readers and viewers. Fitzgerald and colleagues (2019) compared restorative narratives to negative narratives in a health context. In this study, participants were randomly assigned to read either a restorative or a negative narrative about a woman with a rare form of cancer. The narratives were the same except that the restorative narrative featured a hopeful outlook and the negative one featured a hopeless outlook focused on negative outcomes. People who read the restorative narrative were more likely to think that it was important to help people with rare diseases and that they would help those with the specific form of cancer described in the story.

Ray and colleagues (2019) further tested the effects of restorative narratives on communicating important health and resilience information. This study examined an online program at Florida State University designed to encourage and develop resilience—particularly, emotional and academic coping skills—among students. Participants watched at least two videos containing students talking about problems they encountered during college and how they used institutional resources to address and overcome these problems. When students thought the videos were high in restorative quality, they tended to believe that the content in the video would be useful in handling problems they might encounter in the future. They were also more likely to use the site again and recommend it.

Although research into the effects of underdog and restorative narratives is relatively new, this line of research offers a promising way to promote desired outcomes through narratives. By using underdog narratives, we may be able to encourage individuals to work harder toward achieving their own goals. By using restorative narratives featuring stories of overcoming obstacles and hope, we might encourage people to adopt positive health behaviors, help those who are suffering from health problems, seek out resources to help themselves, as well as a host of other outcomes.

Summary

Scholars have developed several theoretical models—TIM, E-ELM, EORM—that explain how narratives can promote positive belief, attitude, and behavioral change. Narratives are identifiable based on several characteristics, including their structure (which includes a beginning, a middle, and an end) and their inclusion of characters who face some sort of conflict. When we are transported into a narrative, we are less likely to counterargue with a message and less likely to experience reactance. Because of this, narratives can persuade us in a way that traditional messaging may not be able to. Identification with characters in a narrative can also affect the persuasiveness of a narrative by causing the viewer or reader to take on that character's perspective. Narrative persuasion has been studied in many different settings, including health-related, intergroup, self-transcendent, and restorative contexts. Whether we hope to educate people, encourage positive health behaviors, or change attitudes toward outgroup members, narratives can be an effective way to communicate many different kinds of information.

References

Allport, G. W. (1954). *The nature of prejudice*. Reading, MA: Addison-Wesley.

Appel, M., & Richter, T. (2010). Transportation and need for affect in narrative persuasion: A mediated moderation model. *Media Psychology*, 13, 101–135. doi:10.1080/15213261003799847.

Bartsch, A., Oliver, M. B., Nitsch, C., & Scherr, S. (2018). Inspired by the Paralympics: Effects of empathy on audience interest in para-sports and on the destigmatization of persons with disabilities. *Communication Research*, 45, 525–553. doi:10.1177/0093650215626984.

Busselle, R., & Bilandzic, H. (2008). Fictionality and perceived realism in experiencing stories: A model of narrative comprehension and engagement. *Communication Theory*, 18, 255–280. doi:10.1111/j.1468-2885.2008.00322.x.

Chadwick, A. E. (2015). Toward a theory of persuasive hope: Effects of cognitive appraisals, hope appeals, and hope in the context of climate change. *Health Communication*, 30, 598–611. doi:10.1080/10410236.2014.916777.

Cohen, J. (2001). Defining identification: A theoretical look at the identification of audiences with media characters. *Mass Communication & Society*, 4, 245–264. doi:10.1207/S15327825MCS0403_01.

Dixon, J., Durrheim, K., & Tredoux, C. (2005). Beyond the optimal contact strategy: A reality check for the contact hypothesis. *American Psychologist*, 60, 697–711. doi:10.1037/0003-066X.60.7.697.

Ellithorpe, M. E., Huang, Y., & Oliver, M. B. (2019). Reach across the aisle: Elevation from political messages predicts increased positivity toward politics, political participation, and the opposite political party. *Journal of Communication*, 69, 249–272. doi:10.1093/joc/jqz011.

Fitzgerald, K., Paravati, E., Green, M. C., Moore, M. M., & Qian, J. L. (2020). Restorative narratives for health promotion. *Health Communication*, 35, 356–363. doi:10.1080/10410236.2018.1563032.

Fogarty, J. S. (1997). Reactance theory and patient noncompliance. *Social Science & Medicine*, 45, 1277–1288. doi:10.1016/S0277-9536(97)00055-5.

Frischlich, L., Rieger, D., Morten, A., & Bente, G. (2018). The power of a good story: Narrative persuasion in extremist propaganda and videos against violent extremism. *International Journal of Conflict and Violence (IJCV)*, 12, a644. doi:10.4119/UNIBI/ijcv.644.

Green, M. C. (2004). Transportation into narrative worlds: The role of prior knowledge and perceived realism. *Discourse Processes*, 38, 247–266. doi:10.1207/s15326950dp3802_5.

Green, M. C., & Brock, T. C. (2000). The role of transportation in the persuasiveness of public narratives. *Journal of Personality and Social Psychology*, 79, 701–721. doi:10.1037/0022-3514.79.5.701.

Green, M. C., & Brock, T. C. (2002). In the mind's eye: Transportation-imagery model of narrative persuasion. In M. C. Green, J. J. Strange, & T. C. Brock (Eds.), *Narrative impact: Social and cognitive foundations* (p. 315–341). Mahwah, NJ: Lawrence Erlbaum Associates.

Greenland, K., & Brown, R. (1999). Categorization and intergroup anxiety in contact between British and Japanese nationals. *European Journal of Social Psychology*, 29(4), 503–521. doi:10.1002/(SICI)1099-0992(199906)29:4-503:AID-EJSP941-3.0.CO;2-Y.

Hether, H. J., Huang, G. C., Beck, V., Murphy, S. T., & Valente, T. W. (2008). Entertainment-education in a media-saturated environment: Examining the impact of single and multiple exposures to breast cancer storylines on two popular medical dramas. *Journal of Health Communication*, 13, 808–823. doi:10.1080/10810730802487471.

Hinyard, L. J. & Kreuter, M. W. (2007). Using narrative communication as a tool for health behavior change: A conceptual, theoretical, and empirical overview. *Health Education & Behavior*, 34, 777–792. doi:10.1177/1090198106291963.

Horton, D., & Wohl, R. R. (1956). Mass communication and para-social interaction. *Psychiatry: Journal for the Study of Interpersonal Processes*, 19, 215–229. doi:10.1080/00332747.1956.11023049.

Mazzocco, P. J., Green, M. C., Sasota, J. A., & Jones, N. W. (2010). This story is not for everyone: Transportability and narrative persuasion. *Social Psychological and Personality Science*, 1, 361–368. doi:10.1177/1948550610376600.

Morgan, S. E., Movius, L., & Cody, M. J. (2009). The power of narratives: The effect of entertainment television organ donation storylines on the attitudes, knowledge, and behaviors of donors and nondonors. *Journal of Communication*, 59, 135–151. doi:10.1111/j.1460-2466.2008.01408.x.

Moyer-Gusé, E. (2008). Toward a theory of entertainment persuasion: Explaining the persuasive effects of entertainment-education messages. *Communication Theory*, 18, 407–425. doi:10.1111/j.1468-2885.2008.00328.x.

Moyer-Gusé, E., & Dale, K. (2017). Narrative persuasion theories. In P. Roessler, C. Hoffner, & L. Van-Zoonen (Eds.), *International encyclopedia of media effects*. Boston, MA: Wiley-Blackwell.

Moyer-Gusé, E., Dale, K. R., & Ortiz, M. (2019). Reducing prejudice through narratives: An examination of the mechanisms of vicarious intergroup contact. *Journal of Media Psychology*, 31, 185–195. doi:10.1027/1864-1105/a000249.

Moyer-Gusé, E., & Nabi, R. L. (2010). Explaining the persuasive effects of narrative in an entertainment television program: Overcoming resistance to persuasion. *Human Communication Research*, 36, 25–51. doi:10.1111/j.1468-2958.2009.01367.x.

Nabi, R. L., & Green, M. C. (2015). The role of a narrative's emotional flow in promoting persuasive outcomes. *Media Psychology*, 18, 137–162. doi:10.1080/15213269.2014.912585.

Oliver, M. B., Kim, K., Hoewe, J., Chung, M. Y., Ash, E., Woolley, J. K., & Shade, D. D. (2015). Media-induced elevation as a means of enhancing feelings of intergroup connectedness. *Journal of Social Issues*, 71, 106–122. doi:10.1111/josi.12099.

Ortiz, M., & Harwood, J. (2007). A social cognitive theory approach to the effects of mediated intergroup contact on intergroup attitudes. *Journal of Broadcasting & Electronic Media*, 51, 615–631. doi:10.1080/08838150701626487.

Petty, R. E., & Cacioppo, J. T. (1986). The elaboration likelihood model of persuasion. *Advances in Experimental Social Psychology*, 19, 123–205. doi:10.1016/S0065-2601(08)60214-2.

Potter, W. J. (2012). *Media effects*. Thousand Oaks, CA: Sage.

Prestin, A. (2013). The pursuit of hopefulness: Operationalizing hope in entertainment media narratives. *Media Psychology*, 16, 318–346. doi:10.1080/10410236.2014.916777.

Ray, E. C., Arpan, L., Oehme, K., Perko, A., & Clark, J. (2019). Testing restorative narratives in a college student resilience project. *Innovative Higher Education*, 44, 267–282. doi:10.1007/s10755-019-9464-4.

Rossiter, J. R., & Thornton, J. (2004). Fear-pattern analysis supports the fear-drive model for antispeeding road-safety TV ads. *Psychology & Marketing*, 21, 945–960. doi:10.1002/mar.20042.

Schiappa, E., Gregg, P. B., & Hewes, D. E. (2005). The parasocial contact hypothesis. *Communication Monographs*, 72, 92–115. doi:10.1080/0363775052000342544.

Singhal, A., & Rogers, E. (2012). *Entertainment-education: A communication strategy for social change*. New York, NY: Routledge.

Slater, M. D., & Rouner, D. (2002). Entertainment—education and elaboration likelihood: Understanding the processing of narrative persuasion. *Communication Theory*, 12, 173–191. doi:10.1111/j.1468-2885.2002.tb00265.x.

Van Laer, T., De Ruyter, K., Visconti, L. M., & Wetzels, M. (2014). The extended transportation-imagery model: A meta-analysis of the antecedents and consequences of consumers' narrative transportation. *Journal of Consumer Research*, 40, 797–817. doi:10.1086/673383.

Vaughan, W., Rogers, E., Singhal, A., & Swalehe, R. (2000). Entertainment-education and HIV/AIDS prevention: A field experiment in Tanzania. *Journal of Health Communication*, 5(sup1), 81–100. doi:10.1080/10810730050019573.

Wang, H., & Singhal, A. (2009). Entertainment-education through digital games. In U. Ritterfeld, M. Cody, & P. Vorderer (Eds.), *Serious games: Mechanisms and effects* (pp. 271–292). New York, NY: Routledge.

Wilkin, H. A., Valente, T. W., Murphy, S., Cody, M. J., Huang, G., & Beck, V. (2007). Does entertainment-education work with Latinos in the United States? Identification and the effects of a telenovela breast cancer storyline. *Journal of Health Communication*, 12, 455–469. doi:10.1080/10810730701438690.

Additional Readings

Appel, M., & Richter, T. (2007). Persuasive effects of fictional narratives increase over time. *Media Psychology*, 10, 113–134. doi:10.1080/15213260701301194.

Appel, M., & Richter, T. (2010). Transportation and need for affect in narrative persuasion: A mediated moderation model. *Media Psychology*, 13, 101–135. doi:10.1080/15213261003799847.

Bilandzic, H., & Busselle, R. (2013). Narrative persuasion. In J. P. Dillard & L. Shen (Eds.), *The Sage handbook of persuasion: Developments in theory and practice* (2nd ed., 200–219). Thousand Oaks, CA: Sage.

De Graaf, A., Hoeken, H., Sanders, J., & Beentjes, J. W. (2012). Identification as a mechanism of narrative persuasion. *Communication Research*, 39, 802–823. doi:10.1177/0093650211408594.

Joyce, N., & Harwood, J. (2014). Improving intergroup attitudes through televised vicarious intergroup contact: Social cognitive processing of ingroup and outgroup information. *Communication Research*, 41, 627–643. doi:10.1177/0093650212447944.

Moyer-Gusé, E., Chung, A. H., & Jain, P. (2011). Identification with characters and discussion of taboo topics after exposure to an entertainment narrative about sexual health. *Journal of Communication*, 61, 387–406. doi:10.1111/j.1460-2466.2011.01551.x.

Ramasubramanian, S. (2013). *Intergroup contact, media exposure, and racial attitudes. Journal of Intercultural Communication Research*, 42, 54–72. doi:10.1080/17475759.2012.707981.

Ratcliff, C. L., & Sun, Y. (2020). Overcoming resistance through narratives: Findings from a meta-analytic review. *Human Communication Research*. Advanced online publication. doi:10.1093/hcr/hqz017.

11

EDUCATIONAL AND PROSOCIAL MEDIA FOR CHILDREN

Source: Shutterstock 1749892721

One of the first published references to "positive media psychology" appeared in a 2016 article by Dutch communication scholars Rebecca de Leeuw and Moniek Buijzen in which they challenged researchers to begin examining how media can contribute to the psychological well-being of children and adolescents. As a group of authors, we wholeheartedly agreed and have also been advocating for this work as well. To date, though, such examinations are few and far between; perhaps by the next edition of this text, enough scientific evidence will have accumulated to address this particular set of issues.

But that does not mean that children have been overlooked in the media-for-good movement. In fact, some of the earliest research on the beneficial effects of media can be traced to studies on children's educational and prosocial television.

We think this rich research tradition deserves a place under the broad positive media psychology umbrella. In this chapter, we provide an overview of this important work.

In doing so, we distinguish children's content that is designed for education from that which is designed for prosocial development. In truth, much of the content that has been produced for children and examined by researchers contains elements of both. Also, because the majority of the research on the benefits of children's media has been conducted on television content, it will be the main focus of the chapter.

Brief History of Children's Media

Local stations across the United States aired shows targeting children from the earliest days of television. Most contained a combination of storytelling, puppets, skits, music, and special guests. One notable example was *The Children's Corner* that was produced by WQED in Pittsburgh beginning in 1954, with a young Fred Rogers as its puppeteer (see Box 11.1). But the 1960s saw the advent of cheap-to-produce cartoon series and profitable soap operas, both of which elbowed live-action children's programming nearly off the daytime airwaves. Seeking to fill the void that was left, the National Educational Television (NET) network—the precursor to today's Public Broadcasting Service (PBS) in the U.S.—aired the debut of *Misterogers' Neighborhood* on February 19, 1968. The series, which changed its name to *Mister Rogers' Neighborhood* in 1970, was arguably the first nationally broadcast prosocial children's television series in the U.S. NET (and then PBS) stations broadcast the first episodes of *Sesame Street* in 1969 and of *The Electric Company* (for "graduates" of *Sesame Street*) in 1971. Thus began the long-standing connection between PBS and educational and prosocial children's television; it also launched a first wave of academic studies on the effectiveness of the shows.

BOX 11.1 WON'T YOU BE MY NEIGHBOR?

The importance of Fred Rogers to the history of educational and prosocial children television cannot be overstated. He grew up in Latrobe, a hard-working and devout small town in Western Pennsylvania, which served as the inspiration for the televised neighborhood he ultimately created. He trained and served as a Presbyterian minister and was also an avid musician and puppeteer, aspects of his life that are well-reflected in his television work. *Mister Rogers' Neighborhood* celebrated the inherent value in children. He often said, "You are special and so is everyone else in this world." The show promoted self-worth, love, compassion, understanding, tolerance, care, appreciation of others; it taught children about their feelings, about the joy of learning, how to confront and embrace change and new experiences, how to deal with grief and death. *Mister Rogers' Neighborhood* was like no other show before or, in many ways, since. The final episode aired in 2001; Fred Rogers died in 2003. But his legacy and vision for children's television lives on through *Daniel Tiger's Neighborhood*, an animated show based on one of the puppets from the original program. The story of Fred Rogers was meaningfully captured in the award-winning documentary *Won't You Be My Neighbor?* (2018), and further celebrated in the fictionalized *A Beautiful Day in the Neighborhood* (2019; starring Tom Hanks as Mister Rogers). We recommend both films and encourage you to explore more about the work, life, and legacy of this pioneering television host, educator, and neighbor through the Fred Rogers Center for Early Learning and Children's Media (http://www.fredrogerscenter.org).

For the entirety of the 1970s and 1980s, PBS provided virtually all of the nationally available children's educational programming in the U.S. Things began to change in the 1990s for two major reasons. One was the increasingly widespread adoption of cable television, leading to the emergence of networks targeting children, most notably Nickelodeon, the Disney Channel, and (later) Noggin. The second was the Children's Television Act of 1990, which forced the FCC to develop and implement regulations for broadcast television stations in the U.S. for the airing of programming to meet the educational and informational (E/I) needs of children. Local stations were required to follow the new regulations or run the risk of losing their license upon renewal. In 1996, the Federal Communications Commission (FCC) imposed stricter (and clearer) regulations by requiring all broadcast stations to air a minimum of three hours per week of core E/I programming designed specifically to address the informational and educational needs of children 16 years and younger. Though not bound by the FCC regulations, many of the cable networks aimed at children ramped up their educational and prosocial offerings at this time as well, especially Nickelodeon with shows like *Blue's Clues, Gullah Gullah Island*, and *Dora the Explorer*. This led to a second wave of academic interest in children's programming.

Around the same time, the personal computing revolution was also surging. Educational and prosocial computer software (including games, puzzles, remedial lessons, advanced lessons, etc.) and hardware (like LeapFrog's LeapPad) were mass-marketed to parents for their preschoolers and young learners. In 1996, *Baby Einstein* was launched, ultimately offering a line of multimedia products geared to educating infants and toddlers. And, of course, today a host of streaming services (like YouTube Kids) offer channels and recommendation systems designed to deliver educational and prosocial media content anytime and anywhere.

In 2019, the FCC loosened the E/I restrictions on broadcasters. Stations are still required to air three hours of E/I content each week, but at least one third of it can now be in the form of specials and shorts (as opposed to recurring series) and a portion can also be delivered via multicast streams (rather than via the primary broadcast channel). Corporations owning lots of television stations had been lobbying for "relief" from the 1996 rules because, from their perspective, children's television does not attract enough advertising revenue. In contrast, media scholars, educators, policy makers, and other children's advocates criticized the move as devaluing a public interest and force of social good for the sake of profit.

Educational Children's Media

Theoretical Perspectives

Teaching children through media is a complicated task, requiring attention to myriad developmental, content-related, and situational factors. We could fill the entire book with discussions just on this one issue. But for the sake of brevity, we highlight two important perspectives now.

Piagetian Theory

The work of developmental psychologist Jean Piaget guided most of the early investigations into children's learning from educational media and still bears weight today. Piaget (1970) argued that children progress through a series of four stages in their intellectual development that correspond to broad changes in the structure of their logic or thinking, which, in turn, dictates the types of cognitive skills cultivated at a given point. Children from birth to age 2 are said to be in the *sensorimotor stage*, in which knowledge is primarily limited to motor activity and visual perception; near the end of the stage, the child begins to use mental images to represent objects and solve simple problems. Children between the ages of 2 and 7 are in the *preoperational stage*, characterized by a shift from a primarily sensorimotor mode of functioning to a conceptual-symbolic mode (e.g., speech, numbers, movement), the development of language and socialized behavior, and the constructing of an initial framework for higher-order reasoning and information-processing strategies. In the *concrete operational stage* (ages 7 to 11), the child moves beyond the egocentrism of the preoperational stage to a reality more shared with and understood through the perspective of others (decentration); more logical and conceptual thinking emerges, though abstract and hypothetical concepts often prove difficult. The final stage of development (age 12 through adulthood) is the *formal operational stage*, in which abstract logical reasoning, systematic planning, and moral reasoning emerge.

Classical Piagetian intellectual developmentalism has been enhanced by neo-Piagetian thought (e.g., Case, 1992; Demetriou, Shayer, & Efklides, 1994). Some of the major additions and alterations to the original theory include an emphasis on multiple substages of development, individual differences, and developing cognitive structures. In particular, Case (1985) argued for a departure from

Piaget's focus on a child's internal-logic function as a measure of development to a focus on the problem-solving function.

From a content-creation standpoint, Piagetian theory influenced writers and producers to develop (st)age-appropriate lessons and storylines; it also provided researchers with a framework to investigate learning effects. The earliest and largest set of educational programming was (and still is) geared toward preschool and early-primary-school-aged children (i.e., those in Piaget's preoperational stage). For example, many of the earliest television series (late 1960s and early 1970s) focused on supporting school preparedness, in particular pre-reading, pre-math, vocabulary, and language skills. The second major wave of children's educational programming (1990s to today), as well as many educational games, increasingly reflected the neo-Piagetian emphasis on problem solving and flexible thinking.

Capacity Model

In Chapter 2, we introduced the limited capacity model of motivated mediated message processing (LC4MP; Lang, 2000), which (among other things) argues that viewing television can be a cognitively taxing activity because it automatically demands some of our mental resources (to process content in line with our evolutionary response systems), in addition to the resources we intentionally dedicate to comprehending the content. This is taxing because our cognitive resources are thought to be limited. Based on similar assumptions about cognitive processing, Shalom Fisch, a developmental psychologist and former vice president for program research at Sesame Workshop (the producers of *Sesame Street*), developed a **capacity model of children's comprehension of educational content on television** (Fisch, 2000). It is the most comprehensive model explaining how children learn from educational programming to date.

Fisch's capacity model contends that, with educational programming, cognitive resources must be devoted to comprehending the **educational content** as well as the **narrative** (e.g., plot, sequence of events, characters). Thus, educational content requires the parallel processing of the "story" and the "lesson." In general, the processing of the narrative receives the lion's share of a viewer's dedicated resources because (a) television is typically engaged as an entertainment medium (especially by children) and (b) the narrative is inherently the more explicit element (i.e., the educational content is embedded in the narrative, not vice versa). Therefore, programming in which the educational content is intertwined with and intricately connected to the narrative should lead to greater learning. That is, a small **distance** between the narrative and educational content allows the cognitive processing of one to complement the other, supporting deeper processing of both and (theoretically) resulting in greater comprehension. A large distance means that the two contents compete for cognitive resources, a battle inevitably won by the narrative resulting in minimal processing of the educational content and less comprehension.

Numerous viewer characteristics also promote more efficient processing of the content: prior knowledge of the subject matter found in both the narrative and the educational content, well-developed understanding of the formal features of television and story schemas, interest, cognitive and other developmental factors, and reasoning abilities, to name a few. Similarly, the viewing situation impacts the learning process, particularly the child's motive for viewing (e.g., viewing to learn leads to greater comprehension) and adult co-viewing (especially if the adult reinforces or further explains the content). Finally, programming characteristics also alter learning, including the complexity and coherence of the narrative, clarity and explicitness of the educational presentation, fit of the story into existing schema, linearity and causal time order of the story, and the inclusion of clues about what is forthcoming (i.e., advanced organizers).

Although originally developed to explain the processing of television content, the capacity model applies well to how other forms of children's educational media—digital games, short online videos, interactive narratives, and even storybooks—might (or might not) lead to comprehension and learning. We now turn our attention to the empirical evidence for such learning through media.

Educational Content for Infants and Toddlers

The American Academy of Pediatrics recommends that parents avoid all forms of screen time for children under 24 months of age, except for video chatting. The recommendation includes content purportedly "designed" for infants, such as the television show *Teletubbies* and popular multimedia content such as *Baby Einstein.* Why? Put simply: Infants generally cannot learn from this content, due to underdeveloped cognitive, memory, and attention skills.

For example, studies show no advantage to infants of exposure to such video content on language or vocabulary skills (e.g., Krcmar, Grela, & Lin, 2007) or problem-solving abilities (e.g., Schmitt & Anderson, 2002). And even if infants do learn *something*, they lack the ability to transfer that knowledge to their lived experience (i.e., **transfer deficit**; Barr, 2010). For instance, imitation behaviors from television can begin to emerge as early as 6 months (Barr, Muentener, & Garcia, 2007), but the learning of those behaviors lags well behind that from live models, until at least age 3 (e.g., **video deficit effect**; Anderson & Pempek, 2005). Interactive forms of media—especially touch-screen tablets—may be slightly better at teaching under certain conditions (Kirkorian, Choi, & Pempek, 2016), but in general learning from a live model is much more effective. Moreover, exposure to *any* media during infancy is associated with lower cognitive and vocabulary development (e.g., Tomopoulos et al., 2010).

Educational Content for Preschoolers

As noted above, historically, a large proportion of children's educational television offerings have targeted preschool children (ages 2 to 6). The aim for most of these shows has been *school preparedness*, though this does not mean that they have solely promoted intellectual development. In general, programs have taken a "whole child" approach to learning. For example, in its first season, *Sesame Street* developed curriculum to address five areas of child development: reading and language; math and numbers; reasoning and problem solving; perceptions; and social, moral, and emotional growth (Fisch, 2014; see also Box 11.2).

The most effective educational programs are **curriculum-based**, with every segment of every episode designed in support of a set of predefined goals. For most programs (and games and other software), the goals and the content created in pursuit of them are heavily researched before the product is released to the public (i.e., **formative research**; typically conducted by in-house research staff but also, at times, academic scholars working as consultants), with the subsequent effects on learning and development also studied after the content has been released (i.e., **summative research**; often conducted by a third-party group for the sake of objectivity). The ultimate goal for most educational media content for preschoolers is *mastery* of a particular skill, which, given their developmental abilities, comes through *repetition* both within a particular episode and also through the re-airing of the same content multiple times (read about the novel approach to repetition introduced by *Blue's Clues* in Box 11.2).

BOX 11.2 TWO PIONEERING PROGRAMS: *SESAME STREET* AND *BLUE'S CLUES*

Still airing more than 50 years after its debut, *Sesame Street* is the longest running children's show of all time (for great histories and effects summaries, see Fisch & Truglio, 2001 and Fisch, 2014). Produced by Sesame Workshop, previously known as Children's Television Workshop (CTW), *Sesame Street* began with 130(!) episodes each season (compare that to the 8 or 10 you now get with your favorite Netflix or Hulu originals). Critically acclaimed from the outset, the show, its cast, and host of writers, musicians, choreographers, sound technicians, set designers, and art directors have won more Emmy Awards than any other program in television history. It is also beloved by audiences; a 1996 survey revealed that 95% of American preschoolers had watched the program at some point before the age of 3 (Fisch & Truglio, 2001). The show has appeared in more than 150 countries and 70 languages—as *Barrio Sésamo* in Spain, *Alam Simsim* in Egypt, *Zhima Jie* in China—typically coproduced with local experts to tailor the content to the cultural context.

Sesame Street literally created the model for all successful educational television shows that came after. It was the first to base its production on empirical, social scientific research: in developing curriculum, in pretesting segments and episodes, and in gauging the program's effects on viewers. This production process—known as the CTW Model—has been skillfully applied to additional CTW shows (e.g., *The Electric Company, 3–2-1 Contact*) and adapted by others outside the Sesame umbrella. Beyond production, Sesame Street broke barriers by appealing to *all* children. Recognizing that children from low income and (disproportionally) minority backgrounds were, on average, starting school with less-developed academic skills, the CTW team set out to create a story world that was welcoming and familiar. The set looked like a typical inner-city residential street in the U.S., with brownstone stoops, graffiti, garbage cans, and a small, local grocery. The cast was (and is) racially diverse, featuring the first Latina in a leading role on television (Sonia Manzano as Maria). Over the years, the show has featured children in wheelchairs (dancing ballet) and others with Down's syndrome; they have had Muppets with AIDS and autism. They helped children confront issues like homelessness, healthy eating, and scary thoughts. And, of course, they have helped prepare hundreds of millions of children worldwide to be more successful in their first years of school.

Blue's Clues was another ground-breaking children's television series. It premiered in 1996 as a part of the Nick Jr. programming block on the cable network Nickelodeon; it ran until 2006 and was relaunched as *Blue's Clues and You* in 2019. *Blue's Clues* was a "think along, play along" show that invited preschoolers to join a live-action host—initially Steve (played by Steven Burns), now his "cousin" Josh (played by Joshua Dela Cruz)—in an animated storybook world. The program was "created with a mission to empower, challenge, and build the self-esteem of preschoolers, all the while making them laugh" (Anderson et al., 2000, p. 180). Based on the CTW Model, *Blue's Clues* taught problem solving and flexible thinking skills, as children assist Steve in finding three clues left as paw prints by the animated puppy Blue. Finding the clues often required the completion of an educational game, with the ultimate goal of solving the problem or mystery associated with, for instance, what Blue wants to eat for lunch or what frightens Blue. Preschool audiences immediately fell for Blue and for the show; during the first several years, *Blue's Clues* was routinely the top-rated children's program on television.

Several aspects of the production make *Blue's Clues* a pioneer in the industry. First, the thinking-skills curriculum (as opposed to the typical "ABCs 123s") reflected the neo-Piagetian developmental approaches of the time. Second, the creators also leveraged contemporary learning and entertainment theories to maximize the effectiveness of their "play to learn" strategy. Third, one of the distinguishing features of each episode was the emphasis on and encouragement of direct interaction with Steve and Blue through active audience participation. Throughout the program Steve spoke directly to the audience, typically asking a question, pausing to allow the children to respond. In doing so, the preschoolers were not only audience members but also participants in the show, leading the viewing situation to approximate a true hands-on and direct-learning experience. Fourth, understanding that repetition leads to mastery, the creators developed a telecasting strategy like none other: They presented the same episode each day across a week. This allowed the viewers to rehearse the same skills across a five-day period, truly mastering concepts, leading to deep learning while they played.

Clips and full episodes of both shows are available across the internet. We encourage you to seek them out.

Sesame Street is the longest running children's show of all time. Unsurprisingly, it is also the most researched; more than 1,000 studies have examined its effectiveness (Fisch, 2014). The earliest ones were conducted by the Educational Testing Service (ETS), the same group that still administers standardized tests like the Graduate Record Examination (GRE) and the Test of English as a Foreign Language (TOEFL). After the first season, ETS tested nearly 1,000 3- to 5-year-olds, half of whom had been encouraged to watch the program across the 26-week season: the other half had not. Children who viewed the show more demonstrated greater gains (from pretest levels established just before the season aired) in a variety of areas, including alphabet, numbers, knowledge of body parts, shapes, classification, and sorting; the study was replicated after the second season with the same results (for a great overview, see Fisch, 2014). Encouragingly, the results were consistent across children at different ages, sex, geographic locations, and socioeconomic status. Furthermore, the findings seem to hold true across cultures. Mares and Pan (2013) conducted a meta-analysis evaluating 24 studies on the effects of *Sesame Street*, with more than 10,000 children in 15 countries. Overall, the result revealed a positive association between viewing the program and the basic literacy and numeracy knowledge noted above, as well as knowledge about the world (e.g., health, safety, culture) and social reasoning and attitudes (e.g., more positive attitudes toward outgroups, fewer stereotypical attitudes).

Moreover, the effects of *Sesame Street* appear to be long-lasting. As a part of the post-Season-2 study, the ETS researchers asked teachers to evaluate the school readiness of a subset of Season 1 participants (without telling the teachers about the children's earlier viewing habits). The teachers rated heavy viewers of the show as better prepared for school than their classmates who had previously watched less (or no) *Sesame Street*. Furthermore, in a famous "recontact" study among 570 high school students who either had or had not viewed *Sesame Street* as a child, researchers found the long-term effects of viewing the program to include higher grades in English, math, and science, more frequent use of books, higher academic self-esteem, and placing a higher value on academic performance (Huston, Anderson, Wright, Linebarger, & Schmitt, 2001).

Research on other educational television programs for preschoolers have shown similar (short-term) results. For instance, 3- and 4-year-olds demonstrated greater counting and vocabulary skills following the viewing of ten episodes of PBS' *Barney & Friends*, compared to nonviewers (Singer & Singer, 1998). Children who viewed *Blue's Clues* over a two-year period performed significantly better on problem solving and flexible thinking tasks than nonviewers (Anderson, et al., 2000). Many studies suggest that parental or teacher support can serve to further bolster these benefits.

Despite the availability of software and digital games designed to educate preschoolers ("learning technology"), unfortunately, little academic research has been conducted on their effectiveness. Tablet apps designed to boost early literacy skills (e.g., alphabet, writing) show some promise, though adult support and reinforcement appears to be crucial (e.g., Neumann & Neumann, 2014). Perhaps the greatest benefit of technology use with preschoolers is more basic: It familiarizes them with and begins to develop in them a disposition to learn from digital devices, skills that are increasingly necessary for learning throughout the rest of their lives (Plowman, Stevenson, Stephen, & McPake, 2012).

Educational Content for School-Aged Children

Once children enter a formal school setting, it becomes increasingly difficult to isolate the potential positive benefits of educational programming. Nevertheless, television series designed for specific learning purposes in the past have generally shown favorable results (for a nice overview, see Fisch, 2014). For instance, *The Electric Company* was created for young learners who had (perhaps) previously viewed *Sesame Street*; specifically, it sought to bolster reading skills in early primary school students. In a study of more than 8,000 students in grades 1 to 4, half of whom viewed *The Electric Company* in school for 6 months, researchers found that viewing the show was associated with better reading for meaning and various phonics-based skills. Similar positive effects were also observed for kindergarteners after viewing the PBS program *Between the Lions*, especially on emergent literacy skills (e.g., letter naming). Books featured on *Reading Rainbow* were more sought after by children in libraries and bookstores, though it is unclear whether the program actually promoted more reading.

Square One TV aimed to promote positive attitudes toward math and increased use of problem-solving strategies among 8- to 12-year-olds. Internal research suggested that the program was generally successful in doing so. Programs like *Bill Nye the Science Guy, Beakman's World, 3–2-1 Contact*, and *Cro* have been shown to improve attitudes toward and comprehension of science concepts, as well as to promote experimentation and hands-on activities associated with the content, among viewers in the 8- to 12-year age group. Unfortunately, (commercial) programs specifically targeting school-aged children with science and math learning are few and far between. In their absence, though, some hope is held for programs like *Mythbusters, Science is Stupid, Cosmos*, and *NOVA*, which, although targeted at adults, may offer informal learning opportunities for children as well.

Unfortunately, a less-than-clear picture has also been painted for educational software and games targeted at school-age children. Most of the academic research in the area has suggested how such games should be designed rather than how effective various titles may be; other work debates the potential benefits (or problems) of integrating games and other technologies into traditional classroom settings, without much large-scale empirical effects research supporting either claim. Use of augmented reality (AR; see Chapter 8) in educational settings appears to hold some promise for the teaching of some content (e.g., 3D spatial relations, kinesthetics), as it can better immerse learners in the virtual world. However, developmental skills and capacities may limit what younger children can learn via AR (Radu, 2014).

Prosocial Children's Media

The term *prosocial* can be applied to a variety of attitudes, motivations, intentions, and behaviors. One could argue that the previous section on educational and skill learning might broadly be thought of as prosocial. Others might suggest that content supporting an audience member's self-esteem, positive body image, and other personally helpful thoughts and actions is prosocial. We do not necessarily disagree with either of these perspectives. However, when it comes to prosocial children's media, most scholars focus their attention on content that is designed for learning in support of healthy social relationships, learning that is ultimately others-benefitting. Thus, the outcomes or effects of interests are generally **prosocial behaviors**, such as helping, friendly interactions, emotion management, inclusiveness, tolerance, altruism, as well as stereotype and aggression reduction.

In 1996, when the FCC established the regulation requiring three hours of educational and informational (E/I) programming each week for expediated broadcast television license renewals, they left the criteria for what "counts" as an E/I program quite broad. The programming discussed in the previous section that addresses the cognitive and intellectual needs of children is considered E/I. But, additionally, shows that address social and emotional needs for children meet the criteria. Because of this, a wide range of programs featuring some sort of moral or social lesson have "counted" as E/I over the years. In truth, many TV series— some designed for children, others not—depict characters treating others nicely, working together to solve problems constructively, inhabiting diverse and inclusive environments, and the like. As a result, the opportunity for informal learning of prosociality through television viewing is theoretically quite high. But the behaviors can be quite different from one another in terms of who performs them, who receives the benefit, for what motivation (e.g., pursing a positive vs. avoiding a negative outcome), and at what cost; this makes the empirical examination of the effects quite complicated.

Since the 1970s, content analyses have attempted to quantify the amount of prosocial content in media. Many have examined offerings specifically designed for children. For example, a study of 61 Disney films counted approximately one prosocial act (either verbal or physical) every minute on average (Padilla-Walker, Coyne, Fraser, & Stockdale, 2013). Woodard (1999) found that 50% of children's shows contained at least one social lesson, with that proportion much higher (77%) for shows targeting preschool children. But when the programs children actually view the most (according to Nielsen ratings) were examined, only four of the top 20 contained any sort of social lesson, and only two contained lessons with positive interactions or altruism.

The most comprehensive study of prosocial behavior on television to date was conducted by communication scholar Sandi Smith and colleagues (2006), who examined instances of sharing and helping in more than 1,750 hours of American broadcast and cable programming. Overall, 73% of shows contained at least one act of sharing and helping, with an average of 2.92 acts per hour. As one might expect, altruistic behaviors appeared in a higher proportion (78%) and at a higher rate (4.02 acts per hour) among children's shows (at least the ones found on basic cable).

Theoretical Perspectives

The basic idea behind prosocial children's media is quite simple: Have kids see, hear, read about, or play as characters who are kind, helpful, tolerant, and forgiving, and they will learn (and want) to do the same themselves. But as the rest of this volume has attested, the various psychological processes that support these relationships are quite complex. Three theoretical perspectives that help researchers understand that complexity are highlighted.

Theory of Mind

The first theoretical perspective related to learning from prosocial media that we should mention is not a theory in the classical sense, despite the appearance of the term in the name. Theory of mind (ToM) is a concept describing the ability to understand that other people have mental states (e.g., perceptions, beliefs, emotions, intentions, desires) that differ from your own, which impact, explain, and predict their behavior (e.g., Wellman, 1990). ToM is related to the ability to take another's perspective, and in turn it is associated with empathy. As such, ToM is thought to be a necessary component of comprehending the symbolic representation of prosocial behavior (e.g., why someone would help someone else, how someone would feel if they were helped), as well as motivating similar action.

It is assumed that children acquire theory of mind as a part of development; thus, one could speak of a child with more or less advanced ToM. Some disagreement exists among scholars about exactly when ToM emerges or becomes reflected in a child's cognitive reasoning. Some research indicates that rudimentary ToM can be found in infants; others discount those findings as reflecting an incomplete expression of the concept (Imuta, Henry, Slaughter, Selcuk, & Ruffman, 2016). The most commonly used measures of the concept consistently indicate that ToM emerges around age 4. Regardless, the development of ToM in a child has a direct impact on their ability to learn and replicate prosocial actions modeled in media content.

Social Cognitive Theory

As has been discussed at a few different points in the text, **social cognitive theory** (SCT; Bandura, 1986) is arguably the most-cited explanation for how we learn behaviors from media (see Chapter 2). Briefly, SCT explains how humans learn about behaviors by observing other people. Those observations can lead to the adoption of new behaviors (modeling), as well as to innovative thoughts leading to adaptations to the observed behaviors or novel behaviors that are similarly motivated (abstract modeling). In the field of children's television, SCT has been used to explain how children can learn and be motivated to act prosocially by watching characters do so. Generally speaking, behaviors are more likely to be modeled if the character is rewarded or positively reinforced for performing the behavior, if the character is realistic and similar to the viewer, and if the behavior can readily be imitated (Strasburger, Wilson, & Jordan, 2014). Further, by showing in which situations specific actions are acceptable and what consequences might result, children's prosocial content can shape the cognitive schema (see also schema theory, Fiske & Taylor, 1991) and behavioral scripts (see also script theory; Tomkins, 1978) in young users.

General Learning Model

A related perspective explaining how children (and adults) can learn prosocial behaviors from media is the **general learning model** (GLM; e.g., Buckley & Anderson, 2006; Swing & Anderson, 2008). Interestingly, the GLM was derived from research examining factors that may cause real-world antisocial behavior, namely aggression (general aggression model; Anderson & Bushman, 2002). Nonetheless, the GLM was initially developed to explain the immediate (proximate) and long-term (distal) behavioral effects from playing (particularly prosocial) digital games.

On the immediate level, playing a game that encourages and rewards prosocial behaviors can prompt similar behaviors in the short-term. Playing the game activates physiological arousal, emotions, and cognitions. Those processes exert influence on one another in ways that reward and punish the player, depending upon what happens onscreen. For example, in a game in which the player must protect a group of animals (prosocial cognitive script activated), a suspenseful mission (increasing arousal) to save an injured tiger cub can lead to great joy (emotional response), assuming it is successful. The positive outcome further influences the arousal, thoughts, and feelings of the player, impacting subsequent in-game decisions (e.g., helping actions that are rewarded should encourage similar ones). In other words, prosocial games activate prosocial cognitive and emotional scripts, providing players the opportunity to rehearse those scripts, and rewarding the successful enacting of those scripts within the game, thereby further reinforcing the use of the scripts. As a result, if given an opportunity to perform a similar behavior soon after playing (e.g., help a sibling with homework), the player should be more likely to do so because of the activated and rehearsed script (see also priming, Chapter 2; and broaden-and-build theory, Chapter 3).

The more one plays the prosocial game, the more often they should experience those short-term effects. Over time, long-term effects would be expected to emerge that would include changes to *precognitive and cognitive constructs* (e.g., perceptions, beliefs, scripts), *cognitive-emotional constructs* (e.g., attitudes, stereotypes), and *affective traits* (e.g., empathy). The more prosocial games that are played, the more additive (or even perhaps multiplicative) these effects become, leading ultimately to changes in the player's personality, which feeds back into subsequent learning encounters (Gentile et al., 2009), resulting in a spiral of prosocial learning and living.

Given the interactive nature of games (see Chapter 8), they do appear to be the media context in which the processes and outcomes explained in the GLM are most efficiently and effectively experienced. However, the principles of the model are sufficiently broad to explain behavioral effects from other forms of prosocial media as well.

Prosocial Effects from Television

Over the last several decades, scholars have explored the prosocial effects of television on children using a variety of methods, including surveys, single-exposure experiments, multiple-exposure longitudinal studies, and field experiments. To be honest: The vast majority of these studies were conducted following the first wave of children's programming in the 1970s and 1980s; recent prosocial media research has tended to focused on interactive games (see p. 191). Nevertheless, the findings from subsequent meta-analyses (e.g., Coyne et al., 2018; Mares & Woodard, 2005) have been quite consistent: Exposure to prosocial depictions on television are associated with an (albeit modest) increase in several positive outcomes in viewers, particularly altruism and helping, social interactions, and inclusivity. In fact, some evidence suggests that the positive effects of viewing prosocial television are as strong, and perhaps even stronger, than the negative effects associated with viewing media violence (a perennial concern for many parents and educators). Further, the observed positive effects appear to be stronger from encounters with passive prosocial media (like TV) than with (inter)active media (Coyne et al., 2018).

One of the most common representations of prosociality on television is kindness as expressed through helping behaviors. Mares and Woodard (2005) reported that, of the various outcomes examined across 34 studies, the effects of viewing prosocial television on altruism were the strongest, particularly among participants in experiments (which tended to measure the modeling effect of a concrete helping behavior). Many prosocial shows also emphasize positive and cooperative social interactions, especially friendly play. Evidence suggests that the effects of viewing such portrayals may take longer to emerge, as they appear to be much stronger in multi-exposure (as compared with single-exposure) studies. The same seems to be the case with representations and themes of inclusivity, particularly tolerance. For instance, attitudes toward other races were unchanged among viewers of *Sesame Street* after one year but were significantly more tolerant after a second year (Mares & Woodard, 2001). On the other hand, several studies have observed immediate stereotype reduction effects following prosocial portrayals, especially compared to participants in control conditions (Mares & Woodard, 2005).

Several factors appear to influence the processes associated with the behavioral benefits of viewing prosocial television. One is age, with the effects of viewing tending to increase most intensely for children between ages 3 and 7, with a steep decline thereafter. Another factor is empathy. Prot and colleagues (2014) found compelling evidence that empathy strongly mediates the observed relationship between prosocial media exposure and prosocial behaviors; that is, children at higher levels of empathy display greater effects. Moreover, the mediation effects seem to be independent of cultural context, as similarly strong results have been observed in samples from Eastern European, Eastern Asian, and Western countries. Effects are also pronounced when the lessons portrayed in the program are encouraged, reinforced, and elaborated upon by an adult, as well as supported by additional information, lessons, and related material. Unfortunately, the effects do not appear to necessarily be equal for all, as children from middle- to upper-class settings tend to demonstrate much stronger effects than those from lower socioeconomic situations (Mares & Woodard, 2001).

Finally, one common way of depicting a prosocial behavior in a program is to contrast it with an aggressive or some other antisocial act. The typical formula is an antisocial behavior is condemned, whereas a contrasting prosocial one is ultimately praised. Unfortunately, this narrative approach does not seem to work. In several studies, children—especially younger ones—are more likely to subsequently model or support the antisocial or less-than-ideal behavior rather than the prosocial one. For instance, Mares and Acosta (2008) showed 5- and 6-year-olds a cartoon featuring a three-legged dog, as a way to promote tolerance and decreased fear about disabilities. In the program, other dogs initially feared but later befriended the dog with three legs. Unfortunately, children viewing the program were more likely to say that the disability could make the other dogs sick, as compared to children viewing the same program with the dogs' fear responses removed. Similarly, in studies showing characters using aggression to punish wrongdoers in cartoons, children often end up exhibiting less cooperation in subsequent play activities (than those not seeing the aggression). Furthermore, children viewing narratives using the prosocial-trumps-antisocial-behavior trope consistently misunderstand or simply miss altogether the "moral of the story" (see Mares, Bonus, & Peebles, 2018). It appears that such narrative devices may be too abstract for many children to grasp the intended underlying prosocial lessons.

Prosocial Effects from Digital Games

Given the long history of prosocial children's television, it should not be surprising that it has received more scholarly attention than prosocial games. The lack of research in the area has been further exacerbated by the intense scrutiny placed on the potential negative effects of gaming. In fact, the earliest attention paid to gaming and prosociality actually focused on how playing violent games might be associated with a *lack* of helping behaviors and empathy; and, for what it is worth, it is (e.g., Anderson et al., 2010). Furthermore, the development of games specifically designed around prosocial themes were slow to appear commercially. Nonetheless, the past decade or so has seen an increase in the study of the prosocial effects of digital gaming.

Generally speaking, the positive effects from playing prosocial games are similar to those found after watching prosocial television. Initial support for the general learning model came from reported increases in helping behaviors after prosocial game play in school-aged children in Singapore and Japan (Gentile et al., 2009); similarly, short-term playing of a prosocial game led to increases in helping and decreases in hurtful behavior in an experimental setting in the U.S. (Saleem, Anderson, & Gentile, 2012). Prosocial gaming has also been associated with greater empathy (including empathic concern, perspective taking, and sympathizing abilities; e.g., Vieira, 2014), prosocial thoughts (e.g., Greitemeyer & Osswald, 2011), and positive affect (e.g., Whitaker & Bushman, 2012), as well as decreased accessibility of hostile thoughts (e.g., Greitemeyer & Osswald, 2009) and aggression (e.g., Greitemeyer, Agthe, Turner, & Gschwendtner, 2012). Furthermore, longitudinal studies indicate that these effects may be stable across time (Ihori, Sakamoto, Shibuya, & Yukawa, 2007).

Like television, prosocial actions in digital games often occur alongside or in response to antisocial (particularly, violent) ones. But unlike the television effects discussed above, the copresence of pro- and antisocial behavior does not appear to diminish the potential positive effects from games. Specifically, playing even violent digital games *cooperatively* (as opposed to competitively) can lead to decreased aggressive behavior (e.g., Jerabeck & Ferguson, 2013) and increased prosocial behavior (e.g., Greitemeyer, Traut-Mattausch, & Osswald, 2012). It should be noted, though, that this evidence comes from studies conducted with college-aged players. Research is needed to see if the same effects are possible with children. Also, for a better understanding of the features of digital games that might be responsible for these effects, we encourage the reader to see Chapter 8.

Complexity of Prosocial Behavior

As a whole, it appears that prosocial children's television and digital games can be quite beneficial. But, as was mentioned earlier, the prosocial behaviors displayed and learned can be quite complex and multidimensional. Coyne and colleagues (2018) highlighted this reality in the most recent meta-analysis of prosocial media effects, which, it should be noted, examined data from 72 studies involving various forms of media and both child and adult participants. For instance, prosocial media appear to be better at generating imitative rather than novel effects. That is, modeled helping behaviors are often adopted but do not appear to lead to increases in other forms of prosociality (e.g., charity, volunteering). Perhaps this is partly due to developmental issues (e.g., concrete operational vs. formal operational stages). Or perhaps it reflects something about the difficulty of prompting high- versus low-cost behaviors. Moreover, the effects are more often manifest in actions toward strangers rather than friends and family, which perhaps further underscores the empathy-bolstering effects of prosocial media. More research is needed to better understand the complicated psychology behind prosociality and media, especially among children.

Summary

Media can be used for a force of good, beginning with the youngest among us. Educational and prosocial programs and games can serve important roles in the early cognitive, emotional, and social development of children. As the media landscape continues to evolve, positive media psychologists, educators, parents, and policymakers must remain vigilant to protect and to grow the space for such content in the future.

References

Anderson, C. A., & Bushman, B. J. (2002). Human aggression. *Annual Review of Psychology*, 53, 27–51. doi:10.1146/annurev.psych.53.100901.135231.

Anderson, C. A., Shibuya, A., Ihori, N., Swing, E. L., Bushman, B. J., Sakamoto, A., Rothstein, H. R., & Saleem, M. (2010). Violent video game effects on aggression, empathy, and prosocial behavior in Eastern and Western countries: A meta-analytic review. *Psychological Bulletin*, 136, 151–173. doi:10.1037/a0018251.

Anderson, D. R., Bryant, J., Wilder, A., Santomero, A., Williams, M., & Crawley, A. M. (2000). Researching Blue's Clues: Viewing behavior and impact. *Media Psychology*, 2, 179–194. doi:10.1207/S1532785XMEP0202_4.

Anderson, D. R., & Pempek, T. (2005). Television and very young children. *American Behavioral Scientist*, 48, 505–522. doi:10.1177/0002764204271506.

Bandura, A. (1986). *Social foundations of thought and action: A social cognitive theory*. Englewood Cliffs, NJ: Prentice-Hall.

Barr, R. (2010). Transfer of learning between 2D and 3D sources during infancy: Informing theory and practice. *Developmental Review*, 30, 128–154. doi:10.1016/j.dr.2010.03.001.

Barr, R., Muentener, P., & Garcia, A. (2007). Age-related changes in deferred imitation from television by 6- to 18-month-olds. *Developmental Science*, 10, 910–921. doi:10.1111/j.1467-7687.2007.00641.x

Buckley, K. E., & Anderson, C. A. (2006). A theoretical model of the effects and consequences of playing video games. In P. Vorderer & J. Bryant (Eds.), *Playing video games: Motives, responses, and consequences* (pp. 363–378). Mahwah, NJ: Lawrence Erlbaum Associates.

Case, R. (1985). *Intellectual development: Birth and adulthood*. Orlando, FL: Academic Press.

Case, R. (1992). Neo-Piagetian theories of intellectual development. In H. Beilin & P. B. Pufall (Eds.), *Piaget's theory: Prospect and possibilities* (pp. 61–104). Hillsdale, NJ: Lawrence Erlbaum Associates.

Coyne, S. M., Padilla-Walker, L. M., Holmgren, H. G., Davis, E. J., Collier, K. M., Memmott-Elison, M. K., & Hawkins, A. J. (2018). A meta-analysis of prosocial media on prosocial behavior, aggression, and empathic concern: A multidimensional approach. *Developmental Psychology*, 54, 331–347. doi:10.1037/dev0000412.

Demetriou, A., Shayer, M., & Efklides, A. (Eds.) (1994). *Neo-Piagetian theories of cognitive development: Implications of application for education*. London, UK: Routledge.

Fisch, S. M. (2000). A capacity model of children's comprehension of educational content on television. *Media Psychology*, 2, 63–91. doi:10.1207/S1532785XMEP0201_4.

Fisch, S. M. (2014). *Children's learning from educational television: Sesame Street and beyond*. London, UK: Routledge.

Fisch, S. M. & Truglio, R. T. (Eds.) (2001). *"G" is for "growing": Thirty years of research on children and Sesame Street*. Mahwah, NJ: Lawrence Erlbaum Associates.

Fiske, S., & Taylor, S. (1991). *Social cognition* (2nd ed.). New York, NY: McGraw-Hill.

Gentile, D. A., Anderson, C. A., Yukawa, S., Ihori, N., Saleem, M., Ming, L. K., Shibuya, A., Liau, A., Khoo, A., Bushman, B. J., Huesmann, L. R., & Sakamoto, A. (2009). The effects of prosocial video games on prosocial behaviors: International evidence from correlational, experimental, and longitudinal studies. *Personality and Social Psychology Bulletin*, 35, 752–763. doi:10.1177/0146167209333045.

Greitemeyer, T., Agthe, M., Turner, R., & Gschwendtner, C. (2012). Acting prosocially reduces retaliation: Effects of prosocial video games on aggressive behavior. *European Journal of Social Psychology*, 42, 235–242. doi:10.1002/ejsp.1837.

Greitemeyer, T., & Osswald, S. (2009). Prosocial video games reduce aggressive cognitions. *Journal of Experimental Social Psychology*, 45, 896–900. doi:10.1016/j.jesp.2009.04.005.

Greitemeyer, T., & Osswald, S. (2011). Playing prosocial video games increases the accessibility of prosocial thoughts. *The Journal of Social Psychology*, 151, 121–128. doi:10.1080/00224540903365588.

Greitemeyer, T., Traut-Mattausch, E., & Osswald, S. (2012). How to ameliorate negative effects of violent video games on cooperation: Play it cooperatively in a team. *Computers in Human Behavior*, 28, 1465–1470. doi:10.1016/j.chb.2012.03.009.

Huston, A. C., Anderson, D. R., Wright, J. C., Linebarger, D. L., & Schmitt, K. L. (2001). Sesame Street viewers as adolescents: The recontact study. In S. M. Fisch & R. T. Truglio (Eds.), *"G" is for "growing": Thirty years of research on children and Sesame Street* (pp. 131–144). Mahwah, NJ: Lawrence Erlbaum Associates.

Ihori, N., Sakamoto, A., Shibuya, A., & Yukawa, S. (2007). Effect of video games on children's aggressive behavior and pro-social behavior: A panel study with elementary school students. *Proceedings of DiGRA 2007 Conference: Situated Play* (pp. 170–177). ISSN:2342–9666.

Imuta, K., Henry, J. D., Slaughter, V., Selcuk, B., & Ruffman, T. (2016). Theory of mind and prosocial behavior in childhood: A meta-analytic review. *Developmental Psychology*, 52, 1192–1205. doi:10.1037/dev0000140.

Jerabeck, J. M., & Ferguson, C. J. (2013). The influence of solitary and cooperative violent video game play on aggressive and prosocial behavior. *Computers in Human Behavior*, 29, 2573–2578. doi:10.1016/j.chb.2013.06.034.

Kirkorian, H. L., Choi, K., & Pempek, T. A. (2016). Toddlers' word learning from contingent and noncontingent video on touchscreens. *Child Development*, 87, 405–413. doi:10.1111/cdev.12508.

Krcmar, M., Grela, B., & Lin, K. (2007). Can toddlers learn vocabulary from television? An experimental approach. *Media Psychology*, 10, 41–63. doi:10.1080/15213260701300931

Lang, A. (2000). The limited capacity model of mediated message processing. *Journal of Communication*, 50, 46–70. doi:10.1111/j.1460-2466.2000.tb02833.x.

Mares, M. L., & Acosta, E. E. (2008). Be kind to three-legged dogs: Children's literal interpretations of TV's moral lessons. *Media Psychology*, 11, 377–399. doi:10.1080/15213260802204355.

Mares, M. L., Bonus, J. A., & Peebles, A. (2018). Love or comprehension? Exploring strategies for children's prosocial media effects. *Communication Research*. Advanced online publication. doi:10.1177/0093650218797411.

Mares, M. L., & Pan, Z. (2013). Effects of Sesame Street: A meta-analysis of children's learning in 15 countries. *Journal of Applied Developmental Psychology*, 34, 140–151. doi:10.1016/j.appdev.2013.01.001.

Mares, M. L., & Woodard, E. (2001). Prosocial effects on children's social interactions. In D. G. Singer & J. L. Singer (Eds.), *Handbook of children and the media* (pp. 183–203). Thousand Oaks, CA: Sage.

Mares, M. L., & Woodard, E. (2005). Positive effects of television on children's social interactions: A meta-analysis. *Media Psychology*, 7, 301–322. doi:10.1207/S1532785XMEP0703_4.

Neumann, M. M., & Neumann, D. L. (2014). Touch screen tablets and emergent literacy. *Early Childhood Education Journal*, 42, 231–239. doi:10.1007/s10643-013-0608-3.

Padilla-Walker, L. M., Coyne, S. M., Fraser, A. M., & Stockdale, L. A. (2013). Is Disney the nicest place on earth? A content analysis of prosocial behavior in animated Disney films. *Journal of Communication*, 63, 393–412. doi:10.1111/jcom.12022.

Piaget, J. (1970). *Genetic epistemology*. New York, NY: Columbia University Press.

Plowman, L., Stevenson, O., Stephen, C., & McPake, J. (2012). Preschool children's learning with technology at home. *Computers & Education*, 59, 30–37. doi:10.1016/j.compedu.2011.11.014.

Prot, S., Gentile, D. A., Anderson, C. A., Suzuki, K., Swing, E., Lim, K. M., Horiuchi, Y., Jelic, M., Krahé, Liuqing, W., Liau, A. K., Khoo, A., Petrescu, P. D., Sakamoto, A., Tajima, S., Toma, R. A., Warburton, W., Zhang, X., & Lam, B. C. P. (2014). Long-term relations among prosocial-media use, empathy, and prosocial behavior. *Psychological Science*, 25, 358–368. doi:10.1177/0956797613503854.

Radu, I. (2014). Augmented reality in education: A meta-review and cross-media analysis. *Personal and Ubiquitous Computing*, 18, 1533–1543. doi:10.1007/s00779-013-0747-y.

Saleem, M., Anderson, C. A., & Gentile, D. A. (2012). Effects of prosocial, neutral, and violent video games on children's helpful and hurtful behaviors. *Aggressive Behavior*, 38, 281–287. doi:10.1002/ab.21428.

Schmitt, K. L., & Anderson, D. R. (2002). Television and reality: Toddlers' use of visual information from video to guide behavior. *Media Psychology*, 4, 51–76. doi:10.1207/S1532785XMEP0401_03.

Singer, J. L., & Singer, D. G. (1998). Barney & Friends as entertainment and education: Evaluating the quality and effectiveness of a television series for preschool children. In J. K. Asamen & G. L. Berry (Eds.), *Research paradigms, television, and social behavior* (p. 305–367). Thousand Oaks, CA: Sage.

Smith, S. W., Smith, S. L., Pieper, K. M., Yoo, J. H., Ferris, A. L., Downs, E., & Bowden, B. (2006). Altruism on American television: Examining the amount of, and context surrounding, acts of helping and sharing. *Journal of Communication*, 56, 707–727. doi:10.1111/j.1460-2466.2006.00316.x.

Strasburger, V. C., Wilson, B. J., & Jordan, A. B. (2014). *Children, adolescents, and the media* (3rd ed.). Thousand Oaks, CA: Sage.

Swing, E. L., & Anderson, C. A. (2008). How and what do video games teach? In T. Willoughby & E. Wood (Eds.), *Children's learning in a digital world* (pp. 64–84). Oxford, UK: Blackwell.

Tomkins, S. S. (1978). Script theory: Differential magnification of affects. *Nebraska Symposium on Motivation*, 26, 201–236.

Tomopoulos, S., Dreyer, B. P., Berkule, S., Fierman, A. H., Brockmeyer, C., & Mendelsohn, A. L. (2010). Infant media exposure and toddler development. *Archives of Pediatrics & Adolescent Medicine*, 164, 1105–1111. doi:10.1001/archpediatrics.2010.235.

Vieira, E. T. (2014). The relationships among girls' prosocial video gaming, perspective-taking, sympathy, and thoughts about violence. *Communication Research*, 41, 892–912. doi:10.1177/0093650212463049.

Wellman, H. M. (1990). *The child's theory of mind*. Cambridge, MA: MIT Press.

Whitaker, J. L., & Bushman, B. J. (2012). "Remain calm. Be kind." Effects of relaxing video games on aggressive and prosocial behavior. *Social Psychological and Personality Science*, 3, 88–92. doi:10.1177/1948550611409760.

Woodard, E. H. (1999). *The 1999 state of children's television report: Programming for children over broadcast and cable television (Rep. No. 28)*. Philadelphia, PA: University of Pennsylvania, Annenberg Public Policy Center.

Additional Readings

de Leeuw, R. N. H., & Buijzen, M. (2016). Introducing positive media psychology to the field of children, adolescents, and media. *Journal of Children and Media*, 10, 39–46. doi:10.1080/17482798.2015.1121892.

de Leeuw, R. N. H., & Buijzen, M. (2017). Can media contribute to happiness in children and adolescents? In N. A. Jennings & S. R. Mazzarella (Eds.), *20 questions about youth and the media* (2nd ed., pp. 36–43). New York, NY: Peter Lang.

Padilla-Walker, L. M., Coyne, S. M., Collier, K. M., & Nielson, M. G. (2015). Longitudinal relations between prosocial television content and adolescents' prosocial and aggressive behavior: The mediating role of empathic concern and self-regulation. *Developmental Psychology*, 51, 1317–1328. doi:10.1037/a0039488.

12

INDIVIDUAL AND CULTURAL DIFFERENCES

Source: Shutterstock 305140991

Early work in media effects conceptualized media influence as a direct predictor of attitudes, beliefs, and behaviors (e.g., Harris & Sanborn, 2013). These "magic bullet" or "hypodermic needle" conceptualizations largely understood audience members to be passive receivers of information, with media exposure having a large and powerful influence. Of course, this type of conceptualization has largely been abandoned, as most studies in media psychology tend to reveal only small or moderate effects. In a typical experiment, if exposure to some media message accounts for 5% of the variance in resultant responses, then the remaining 95% of the variance is unaccounted for. What may account for this "unexplained" variation? In this chapter we address the "unexplained variation" in terms of individual and cultural differences. We begin by first discussing how individual differences are typically studied, providing our conceptualization of these differences. Thereafter, we consider how these variables function in the process of consuming and responding to positive media.

Studying and Conceptualizing Individual and Cultural Differences

Individuals vary on a limitless number of dimensions. Our backgrounds, education, tastes, experiences, and physiological characteristics are but a few of the many traits that make us unique. As a result of these traits, at least in part, we (1) do not share the same entertainment preferences, (2) may be exposed to different forms of entertainment, and (3) undoubtedly differ in terms of our responses to media offerings. Because of these variations, individual differences make studying media influence somewhat messy. Namely, because people may differ in so many ways that affect their responses to media, scholars face the difficult task of trying to control for these differences so as to be able to isolate the effects of media specifically.

BOX 12.1 TEMPORARILY BECOMING A DIFFERENT YOU

A major thrust of this chapter is to explore how our media choices are impacted by who we are. But sometimes, our media use is driven by a desire for us to be a *different version of ourselves*. The theory of **temporarily expanding the boundaries of the self** (TEBOTS) (Slater, Johnson, Cohen, Comello, & Ewoldsen, 2014) argues that we are drawn to narratives at times because they provide us the opportunity to temporarily let go of the demands of the personal and social self-image that we otherwise constantly seek to maintain. By getting immersed into a fictional narrative and identifying with the media characters' social roles, emotions, or identities, audiences can gratify the desire to temporarily expand the constraints of self-concept. Throughout our day-to-day lives we are constantly maintaining and defending our self-image. External stressors like work and relationship struggles can motivate people to expand the boundaries of their personal and social self by identifying with the characters and vicariously transcending their own self-concept.

In contrast to identification where the viewer takes on the identity of the character temporarily (Cohen, 2001; see also Chapter 4), during self-expansion the viewer stays aware of the self. Although TEBOTS does not make specific predictions about what type of narratives viewers engage in to temporarily expand the boundaries of the self, the research results seem to indicate that eudaimonic entertainment experiences are heightened when viewers' self-control is drained, such as after a long day at work (e.g., Johnson, Ewoldsen, & Slater; 2015) Thus, TEBOTS might help explain under what circumstances narratives could lead to the greatest eudaimonic (and hedonic) entertainment experiences.

In survey or correlational research (see Chapter 1), scholars often employ **control variables** (or covariates) to try to account for individual and cultural variation. For example, in studying how television viewing affects children's eating habits, a researcher may reason that traits such as parental education or household income may influence both television viewing *and* diet (e.g., Signorielli & Staples, 1997). Consequently, a researcher may opt to statistically control for these variables so that it is possible to examine the relationship between television viewing and diet that holds constant the other demographic variables that undoubtedly play a role.

In experimental research (see Chapter 1), rather than just measuring media exposure and resultant effects, scholars often manipulate some aspect of media content (e.g., the characters, the story outcome, the music), expose some groups to one version and other groups to a different version or versions, and then measure the effects of interest. Although experimentalists can also employ control variables in their statistical analyses, they typically employ **random assignment** to experimental conditions as a way of accounting for individual and/or cultural variation. That is, individuals who agree to take part in the study will be assigned to one of several different "versions" (or experimental conditions) randomly. Why not measure individual traits and match participants to ensure that these traits are equal across experimental conditions? Matching is often an option and is sometimes employed. However, experimental researchers typically realize that there are hundreds if not thousands of ways that people can differ, thereby making matching cumbersome if not impossible. Instead, experimentalists often opt to employ random assignment, as doing so will theoretically equalize the groups on a variety of differences without having to measure all potentially important individual characteristics.

Thus, for both survey and experimental research, variations between individuals are often thought of as potentially problematic, as they may obscure or even potentially bias studies of media influence. They also typically dwarf the size of the actual effects that can be unambiguously assigned to media. As a result, variations in the outcomes of media exposure due to individual (or within-group) differences are frequently identified as "noise," "error variance," or "unexplained variance."

Rather than conceptualize individual and cultural differences as "problems" in our research, this chapter treats them as opportunities to understand the nuances in how media messages and audience responses are interrelated. For example, individual differences often serve as important predictors of media exposure; some people may be attracted to some types of portrayals or genres rather than others. Individual differences can also be important **moderators** of media influence. In brief, a moderator refers to a variable that influences the relationship between a cause and an effect. For example, if a person argues that magazine reading causes disordered eating, but that the relationship depends on the gender of the reader, this argument is treating gender as a moderating variable: the effect of magazine reading on eating disorders *depends on* (or, is moderated by) gender. Finally, though rarely studied, individual differences may function as an outcome.

For example, a scholar may suggest that viewing some types of news programs results in heightened levels of authoritarianism. Although authoritarianism is generally considered to be a disposition or trait (and hence an individual difference), in this example it is functioning as an outcome.

With this background in mind, providing an unambiguous definition of individual and cultural differences is a daunting task. Part of the difficulty is that the list of potential differences is without bounds. Conceptually, every way that people vary from one another could conceivably be labeled as an individual difference, including attitudes, demographics, height, shoe size, diet, exercise, etc. However, many of these differences are likely inconsequential to how individuals select and respond to media. As a result, in this chapter we highlight the individual differences that appear to play important roles in media psychology and in positive media psychology in particular. Some of these variables include demographic characteristics, and some of them are enduring traits, attitudes, and dispositions that are typically stable over time.

The conceptualization of culture is equally challenging. As Kim and Eom (2020) pointed out, although many people operationalize culture in terms of nationality, this is perhaps too blunt a way of approaching this topic, as many nationalities share common features, and many people within a given culture differ on a host of characteristics. Hence, for purposes of this chapter, we adopt their perspective in understanding cultures as "groups of people who belong to certain shared contexts by which they are more likely to be exposed to similar cultural ideas, values, and practices" (p. 424). Using this perspective, nationality would certainly fit within this perspective, as would cultures within nationalities such as "girl culture," "hip hop culture," or "fan culture." Further, because culture varies between individuals, in this chapter, we also treat cultural differences as individual differences, as both concepts play important roles in media selection, response, and effects.

Individual Differences as Predictors of Preference for and Responses to Positive Media

It is evident that not everyone shares the same tastes in media. Some people find great pleasure in horror and thrillers, whereas others find such content deeply disturbing. A large body of scholarship has examined these types of differences, but given that positive media psychology is a relatively new trajectory of scholarship, the number of variables examined is somewhat more limited in scope. Nevertheless, a number of individual differences have been identified as important predictors of media selection and gratification.

Gender

Among demographic variables, gender—unfortunately, almost exclusively measured in communication and psychology as a binary, biologically determined concept to date—is likely one of the most studied traits used as a predictor of entertainment preference and exposure (see Oliver, 2000). Perhaps the focus on gender has reflected cultural norms concerning what men and women are interested in, as well as norms regarding the public display of emotion. For example, boys are generally taught that expressions of fear and sadness are inappropriate, whereas girls are generally taught that displays of anger or aggression are inappropriate (Brody & Hall, 2000). Consequently, media content that encourages "inappropriate" emotional reactions may be avoided or disliked.

Early work in meaningful media often focused on tragedy or sad films, perhaps as a reaction to prevailing scholarly norms that assumed that entertainment's primary function was to serve hedonic needs (Oliver, 1993). Given that tragedy stands in stark contrast to positively valenced fare such as comedy, studying non-hedonic content naturally gravitated to this particular type of meaningful media. However, sad films or tragedies are heavily targeted toward women, with colloquial phrases such as "chick flicks," "tragedies," or "tear jerkers" frequently used to refer to this genre. Understandably, then, studies of media preference have consistently found large gender differences in the liking of sad films. At the same time, however, the specific reasons for why these differences exist are not definitely clear.

One leading explanation is that these differences reflect the development of socialized gender norms that discourage male displays of sadness or vulnerability. Consistent with this interpretation, Oliver and Green (2001) found that gender differences in emotional responses to sad children's films (e.g., *Fox and the Hound, Lion King*) were very small among younger children (e.g., preschool) but became larger as children aged. This finding suggests that gender differences are a result, in part, of social development.

Of course, sad films or tragedies are only one type of meaningful media content. Contemplative dramas, stories of deep friendship, and portrayals of courage are but a few examples of the different types of content that people can find moving and inspiring. For example, inspiring videos are commonly available on social media that portray many elicitors of self-transcendent affect (Dale, Raney, Janicke, Sanders, & Oliver, 2017). Although these videos are not focused on sadness per se, they do appear to elicit feelings of warmth, love, gratitude, and hope, and sometimes tears. Nevertheless, in a study of selective exposure to these types of videos, females were significantly more likely than males to choose to view them and to spend a significantly longer time watching them (Oliver et al., 2017). Likewise, a national survey in the U.S. showed that a significantly larger percentage of women than men reported being inspired while listening to music, watching a movie or television show, reading a news story or a book, watching an online video, and using social media (Raney et al., 2018). Gender differences have even been observed in terms of inspiring memes, with significantly more women than men reporting receiving inspiring memes via social media and following groups that tend to post such memes (Rieger & Klimmt, 2019).

However, not all research on self-transcendent media has revealed gender differences. In developing measures of hedonic and eudaimonic motivations for media consumption, Oliver and Raney (2011) generally did not find large differences in media preference among males and females. Although this finding is somewhat surprising given the wealth of scholarship on gender differences, perhaps it reflects the idea that when meaningful content is not explicitly associated with one gender or avoids explicit attempts to elicit emotion (e.g., "This video will make you cry!"), gender differences may be minimized. Likewise, other research that has focused on the portrayals featured in many moving films has found that when the portrayals feature a more agentic rather than communication theme (e.g., a story about basketball team rather than about intimate relationships), gender differences are non-existent (Oliver, Weaver, & Sargent, 2000).

Of course, gender is not a binary construct. Increasingly scholars are exploring gender identity as a predictor of media use, showing that self-reported communal orientations (akin to femininity) are predictors of liking of moving films (e.g., Oliver, Sargent, & Weaver, 1998).

Age

Studies of age differences in preferences for meaningful media are somewhat rare. However, anecdotally, it seems that younger audiences enjoy some genres more so than older audiences, specifically for genres such as thrillers or horror. Similarly, some age-based differences have been observed for media technologies used for inspiration. For example, younger Americans (18- to 29-year-olds) report being touched and moved by online videos and social media more than older Americans (45 years plus), who tend to be more inspired by television, movies, and news stories (Janicke et al., 2019).

Socioemotional selectivity theory (Carstensen, Isaacowitz, & Charles, 1999) provides one framework to approach the question of age and meaningful media. The theory suggests that when individuals perceive that time is limited, they attempt to rid their environment of unpleasant experiences and, instead, seek more positive and meaningful experiences. The limit of time does not necessarily pertain only to age: holidays come to an end, college days come to an end, and careers come to an end at retirement. However, life endings are undoubtedly the most definitive, with the salience of limited time increasing with age.

Using this perspective, Mares, Oliver, and Cantor (2008) reasoned that younger adults would be more willing to experience negative emotions in their everyday lives than would older adults, with older adults more interested in experiencing mildly positive emotions. The results supported this reasoning and further showed that willingness to experience negative affect was associated with liking of entertainment with dark characteristics (e.g., creepy, scary, disturbing), whereas interest in experiencing positive affect was associated with liking of entertainment with uplifting characteristics (e.g., heart-warming, uplifting). Similar results were reported in a subsequent study in which participants read a series of brief descriptions of television programs (Mares, Bartsch, & Bonus, 2016). For each description, participants rated the emotions they thought the program would elicit, as well as their interest in viewing the program. The results showed that as the age of the participants increased, heart-warming affect was a better predictor of perceptions of meaningfulness.

Traits and Dispositions

Traits—also referred to as dispositions—have arguably received the most attention in terms of their role as predictors of the selection of positive media. For instance, some research has identified traits that are associated with the likelihood of being engaged by beauty. Diessner and colleagues (2008) tested an engagement with beauty scale containing three subscales: engagement with art, with nature, and with moral beauty (see also Diessner, Pohling, Stacy, & Güsewell, 2018). The engagement with moral beauty scale includes items such as "When perceiving an act of moral beauty I feel emotional, it 'moves me,'" such as feeling a sense of awe, or wonder or excitement or admiration or upliftment" (p. 329). Engagement with moral beauty has been associated with a host of other dispositions, including gratitude, spiritual transcendence, and satisfaction with life. In other words, people who tend to feel moved and touched when they encounter beauty also tend to be more grateful and satisfied with their lives; they also more often perceive and experience things greater than themselves. Those individuals are likewise more likely to seek out content that supports these traits.

Research in positive media psychology has identified many traits that are similar to those reported by Diessner and colleages (2008). For example, preferences for eudaimonic entertainment are positively associated with greater reflectiveness, need for cognition, intellectualism, need for affect, and searching for meaning in life (Oliver & Raney, 2011). In contrast, preferences for hedonic entertainment are positively associated with optimism, humor, playfulness, and spontaneity, and negatively associated with pessimism. Similar results have been obtained for being inspired across a variety of media platforms. Overall, inspiring media experiences are positively predicted by empathic concern, need for affect, and universality (Raney et al., 2018), as well as gratitude, searching for meaning, and spirituality (Janicke-Bowles et al., 2019). Additionally, research on selective exposure shows that choosing to view inspiring videos (in contrast to humorous or informative videos) is associated with higher levels of empathy, and lower levels of psychopathy, Machiavellianism, and narcissism (Oliver et al., 2017). Thus, the research indicates that people who like to think, feel, and orient themselves to others tend to seek out and appreciate media that makes them think about and feel for others.

Cross-Cultural Differences

A large body of literature has examined cultural differences in the experience and display of emotion. In his review of cross-cultural studies of emotions, including the words used to describe emotions, recognition of emotion, and dimensions of emotion, Russell (1991) concluded that although many similarities exist across cultures, differences do as well. Social norms, histories, and communities all play important roles in our emotional lives. It follows, then, that research on the selection and experience of inspiring media has demonstrated some consistency across different cultures, but some notable differences, too.

Perhaps one of the largest cross-cultural studies on self-transcendent emotion focused on the concept of **kama muta** (Fiske, Seibt, & Schubert, 2017; see also Chapter 6). In brief, kama muta—the Sanskrit term for "moved by love"—is a class of emotions that are elicited when seeing the sudden display of and intensification in a communal sharing relationship. For example, seeing a family reunited at the airport after being apart for many years might lead to one feeling choked up, tearful, or moved. Researchers in this area argue that kama muta as an emotional experience occurs across cultures. In this sense, it appears to be universal. On the other hand, the types of communal sharing relationships that give rise to this affect are heavily dependent on cultural norms. To examine the universal experience of kama muta, Zickfeld et al. (2019) gathered data across 19 countries (and 15 languages). The experience of kama muta was elicited either by showing the participants a video of a moving and touching portrayal or by having participants recall an event that they found moving. Overall, the research showed that the characteristics of kama muta (e.g., feeling moved, bodily sensations) were generally consistent across cultures.

Additional cross-cultural studies have reported similar findings in terms of motivations for consuming inspiring media and perceptions of such fare. For example, Igartua and Barrios (2013) translated Oliver and Raney's (2011) eudaimonic and hedonic media-preference scales for a Spanish audience, finding that they were reliable and that they predicted preferences for different genres in the ways hypothesized originally. Likewise, Schneider, Bartsch, and Oliver (2017) examined Oliver and Bartsch's (2010) measures of enjoyment, appreciation, and suspense in response to films, finding that the measures were generally comparable when translated for a German sample.

However, not all cross-cultural studies have demonstrated invariance in media–audience relationships. For example, Odağ, Hofer, Schneider, and Knop (2016) tested the measures of hedonic and eudaimonic media preferences among German and Turkish participants. Although the measures were associated with the same items, the weight of each item associated with their construct differed for the measure of eudaimonic preference, and the means of the items differed between cultures. In a later study, Odağ, Uluğ, Arslan, and Schiefer (2018) employed Hofstede's (1991) conceptualization of cultures in terms of individualist versus collectivistic values, and Markus and Kitayama's (1991) concept regarding self-construals—basically the extent to which we define ourselves independent of or interdependent with others—to explore how these variables predicted hedonic and eudaimonic media preferences. In so doing, the authors were able to examine both cross-cultural differences (in terms of country of birth) and within-cultural differences (in terms of self-construal). The authors found that hedonic preferences were predicted by higher interdependence self-construals and lower cultural individualism, whereas eudaimonic preferences were predicted by higher levels of independence self-construals. These authors interpreted these findings as suggesting that individualistic cultures and self-construals that value uniqueness may be drawn toward eudaimonic entertainment that grapples with "self-related existential concerns in pursuit of individual well-being" (p. 651). Likewise, collectivist cultures and self-construals that value harmony and unity may be drawn toward more light-hearted fare that serves the well-being of all members of the culture.

In their reviews of cultural differences and well-being, Kim (2017) and Kim and Eom (2020) highlighted three important cultural variations that have implications for the selection and gratification derived from meaningful media. These include the previously discussed cultural values of individualism and collectivism and the self-construals of independent and interdependent orientations. The third distinction involves analytic versus holistic thinking. These authors argued that Western cultures tend to employ analytic thinking, considering each object and its function alone, without context. Eastern cultures tend to employ holistic thinking, considering objects within a context and favoring cyclical, non-linear thinking and even contradictions (e.g., "good becomes bad and bad becomes good," Kim, 2017, p. 436). These cultural variations have implications for well-being and happiness, with Western cultures placing a greater emphasis on positive affect and individual well-being, and Eastern cultures placing a greater value on social well-being. Hence, according to these authors, in Eastern cultures, the expression of too much happiness by one individual may be seen as inappropriate, as it may make others feel bad about themselves. Consistent with this reasoning, Kim, Seo, Yu, and Neuendorf (2014) found that participants from South Korea were more likely than participants from the U.S. to report liking films that elicited mixed affect. Importantly, this preference was predicted by higher scores among South Koreans on a measure of "naïve dialecticism," or the tolerance and preference for seeming inconsistencies (e.g., "When two sides disagree, the truth is always somewhere in the middle," p. 534).

To sum: Selecting, viewing, and finding gratification in inspiring media is a common occurrence across many individual and cultural differences. At the same time, however, social norms, personality traits, and demographic characteristics play consequential roles in predicting who is most attracted to this type of media fare. Not everyone seems to like a "good cry," and our media preferences may shift over the course of our lifetime. We await future research that will undoubtedly add to our growing collection of the traits that predict preferences for self-transcendent portrayals.

Individual Differences and Moderators and Outcomes

Because individual traits and cultures are generally considered to be stable, they are typically employed as predictor variables (e.g., "What type of person from what type of culture enjoys media of a certain type?"). However, a small but growing body of work has also examined how they can serve as moderators, and even as outcomes, of media consumption. The final section considers both of these roles.

Individual Differences as Moderators

In a typical study of positive media, exposure to some uplifting content is predicted to elicit self-transcendent emotions, with these emotions then sometimes used to predict an additional outcome such as charitability or altruistic behaviors. However, exposure does not always induce self-transcendence nor does self-transcendence always result in predicted outcomes. In attempting to answer questions such as "For whom does positive media inspire?" or "For whom does self-transcendence spur subsequent actions?", scholars have explored individual traits that may help to explain the implied causal connections. In these instances, scholars are treating individual differences as moderating variables.

Personality characteristics are often explored as possible moderating variables. For example, Aquino, McFerran, and Laven (2011) reasoned that the experience of elevation that arises from viewing moral beauty may depend on an individual's moral identity. These authors argued that the more central moral characteristics are to one's self-concept, the more salient moral considerations may be in their processing of information. To test this hypothesis, individuals read either a news story about the resilience and forgiveness of an Amish community who had experienced a school shooting or a positive story about a sunset. Whereas all participants reported higher levels of elevation after reading the story about the Amish community than after the story about the sunset, this effect was particularly pronounced for those scoring higher on a measure of moral identity.

Individual differences can also moderate how elevation affects behavioral outcomes. In one study, the experience of elevation elicited from a moving video resulted in more charitable behavior in a game with an opponent, but particularly so for participants who scored high on a measure of engagement with moral beauty (Pohling, Diessner, Stacy, Woodward, & Strobel, 2019; see also Diessner, Iyer, Smith, & Haidt, 2013).

Just as research has demonstrated that some traits can serve to heighten self-transcendent emotions and resultant outcomes, research also indicates that some personality traits can serve to dampen such reactions. For example, Appel, Slater, and Oliver (2018) reasoned that traits that reflect a lack of empathy should diminish self-transcendent affective responses to eudaimonic entertainment. In particular, the scholars examined the moderating role of the so-called "dark triad" of personality characteristics—narcissism, Machiavellianism, and psychopathy—on brief videos that were eudaimonic or non-eudaimonic in tone. Although higher scores on elements of the dark triad did not strongly impact meaningful affect in response the eudaimonic videos, they did enhance perceptions of these videos as "corny" (e.g., silly, oversentimental, inauthentic).

Finally, we note that some scholars have examined the intersection between the characteristics of a media user and the type of content that elicits inspiration. For example, watching a moving love story may be more inspiring to romantics than pragmatists, whereas watching an inspiring athletic event may be more inspiring to pragmatists than romantics. This type of scenario was recently studied in the context of political advertisements from the 2016 U.S. presidential campaign (Seibt, Schubert, Zickfeld, & Fiske, 2019). Supporters of Donald Trump and Hillary Clinton viewed a moving advertisement for one of the two candidates and rated how much they were moved by the advertisement. Not surprisingly, Trump supporters were more moved by the Trump advertisement, whereas Clinton supporters were more moved by the Clinton one. Importantly, however, for *both* advertisements, feeling moved was associated with a greater self-reported likelihood of voting for the candidate depicted.

Individual Differences as Outcomes

We finally consider individual differences in a way that is rarely studied: as outcome variables. It is understandable that individual differences are rarely studied in this way, as traits are generally understood to be stable and enduring. For example, watching one 3-minute video is unlikely to fundamentally change a person's tastes, outlooks, or personality. Further, some individual differences such as one's age, culture, or race cannot be altered by outside influences. However, to the extent to which inspiring messages can be internalized, the possibility that their influence can be longer lasting exists.

To examine how repeated viewing can have long-term effects, Erickson and colleagues (2018) conducted three studies to see how viewing short, inspiring videos may affect inspiring affect and prosocial tendencies over the course of 7, 10, or 12 days across a 30-day period. Not surprisingly, people who viewed the inspiring videos reported higher levels of elevation immediately after viewing. Importantly, though, positive affect, greater feelings of affiliation with others, and feelings of elevation had a sustained impact as well. Because none of the exposures lasted longer than a month, the authors concluded, "Our results cannot speak to long-term character change … but suggest reasons to test elevation as a component of interventions to shape character" (p. 652) (see also Nabi & Prestin, 2020).

Similar results were obtained in a recent study examining the effects of repeated exposure to media messages over the course of six weeks (Neubaum, Krämer, & Alt, 2020). Participants were assigned to view either violent, neutral, or elevating videos six times a week. Although the results showed no long-term effects of viewing on measures of flourishing or intended interaction with stereotyped groups, they did lead to higher levels of daily elevation. Daily elevation, in turn, was associated with longer term prosocial motivations and heightened perceptions that humans are basically good and kind. Although these motivations and perceptions were not considered traits per se, we think it is reasonable to suggest that should these variables become chronically activated, they may well become more stable aspects of a person's disposition, manifested for example in related character strengths (see Chapter 3).

In these studies of long-term exposure and effects, it may seem contrived to think that a person would be sent an inspiring video every day in "real life." However, in the actual, everyday use of media, it may not seem contrived to suggest that some people may choose to consume elevating content on a regular basis. Earlier in the chapter we discussed a selective-exposure study in which people could select to view videos that were inspiring, humorous, or informative (the control condition). At the end of the selection and viewing portion of the study, participants also completed measures assessing their feelings of connectedness with humanity and the extent to which they prioritized three sets of values: "meaningful" (e.g., being a better person), achievement (e.g., making a lot of money), and "fun" (e.g., being popular). The results showed that *even after controlling* for traits such as empathy, the selection and viewing of the inspiring videos (unlike the humorous or control videos) was positively associated with connectedness and meaningful values. Because these two variables are also similar to many of the predictors of *selecting* inspiring media offerings, we are hopeful that these results may imply a spiral of inspiration. People who are empathic select inspiring media, and the viewing of inspiring media elicits values that increase the likelihood of greater selection in the future. If this interpretation is correct, then long-term and repeated exposure may ultimately occur in natural (non-research related) contexts, thereby spreading self-transcendent states and the values that accompany them.

Summary

People come in all shapes, sizes, and experiences. These differences, although beautiful, sometimes make it difficult to isolate media effects; just as we all differ, so do our media diets and preferences. A host of traits lead us to choose and enjoy inspiring media, and some serve to heighten self-transcendent experiences. Further, hopeful research is beginning to emerge suggesting that consuming inspiring media may ultimately serve to shape and grow the dispositions that focus on other-connectedness and self-transcendence. Given that people undoubtedly reflect both traits they were born with and traits that are nurtured, a diet of inspiring depictions seems to be a decidedly healthy and uplifting option.

References

Appel, M., Slater, M. D., & Oliver, M. B. (2018). Repelled by virtue? The dark triad and eudaimonic narratives. *Media Psychology*, 22, 769–794. doi:10.1080/15213269.2018.1523014.

Aquino, K., McFerran, B., & Laven, M. (2011). Moral identity and the experience of moral elevation in response to acts of uncommon goodness. *Journal of Personality and Social Psychology*, 100, 703–718. doi:10.1037/a0022540.

Brody, L. R., & Hall, J. A. (2000). Gender, emotion, and expression. In M. Lewis & J. M. Haviland-Jones (Eds.), *Handbook of emotions* (2nd ed., pp. 338–349). New York, NY: The Guilford Press.

Carstensen, L. L., Isaacowitz, D. M., & Charles, S. T. (1999). Taking time seriously: A theory of socioemotional selectivity. *American Psychologist*, 54, 165–181. doi:10.1037//0003-066X.54.3.165.

Cohen, J. (2001). Defining identification: A theoretical look at the identification of audiences with media characters. *Mass Communication and Society*, 4, 245–264. doi:10.1207/S15327825MCS0403_01.

Dale, K. R., Raney, A. A., Janicke, S. H., Sanders, M. S., & Oliver, M. B. (2017). Youtube for good: A content analysis and examination of elicitors of self-transcendent media. *Journal of Communication*, 67, 897–919. doi:10.1111/jcom.12333.

Diessner, R., Iyer, R., Smith, M. M., & Haidt, J. (2013). Who engages with moral beauty? *Journal of Moral Education*, 42, 139–163. doi:10.1080/03057240.2013.785941.

Diessner, R., Pohling, R., Stacy, S., & Güsewell, A. (2018). Trait appreciation of beauty: A story of love, transcendence, and inquiry. *Review of General Psychology*, 22, 377–397. doi:10.1037/gpr0000166.

Diessner, R., Solom, R. D., Frost, N. K., Parsons, L., & Davidson, J. (2008). Engagement with beauty: Appreciating natural, artistic, and moral beauty. *The Journal of Psychology*, 142, 303–332. doi:10.3200/jrlp.142.3.303-332.

Erickson, T. M., McGuire, A. P., Scarsella, G. M., Crouch, T. A., Lewis, J. A., Eisenlohr, A. P., & Muresan, T. J. (2018). Viral videos and virtue: Moral elevation inductions shift affect and interpersonal goals in daily life. *Journal of Positive Psychology*, 13, 643–654. doi:10.1080/17439760.2017.1365163.

Fiske, A. P., Seibt, B., & Schubert, T. (2017). The sudden devotion emotion: Kama muta and the cultural practices whose function is to evoke it. *Emotion Review*, 11, 74–86. doi:10.1177/1754073917723167.

Harris, R. J., & Sanborn, F. W. (2013). *A cognitive psychology of mass communication* (6th ed.). New York, NY: Routledge.

Hofstede, G. (1991). *Cultures and organizations: Software of the mind.* New York, NY: McGraw-Hill.

Igartua, J.-J., & Barrios, I. (2013). Hedonic and eudaimonic motives for watching feature films. Validation of the Spanish version of Oliver & Raney's scale. *Communications*, 411–431. doi:10.1515/commun-2013-0024.

Janicke-Bowles, S. H., Raney, A. A., Oliver, M. B., Dale, K. R., Jones, R. P., & Cox, D. (2019). Exploring the spirit in U.S. audiences: The role of the virtue of transcendence in inspiring media consumption. *Journalism & Mass Communication Quarterly.* Advanced online publication. doi:10.1177/1077699019894927.

Johnson, B. K., Ewoldsen, D. R., & Slater, M. D. (2015). Self-control depletion and narrative: Testing a prediction of the TEBOTS model. *Media Psychology*, 18, 196–220. doi:10.1080/15213269.2014.978872.

Kim, J. (2017). Cultural differences in media and well-being. In L. Reinecke & M. B. Oliver (Eds.), *The Routledge handbook of media use and well-being* (pp. 434–447). New York, NY: Routledge.

Kim, J., & Eom, K. (2020). Cross-cultural media effects research. In M. B. Oliver, A. A. Raney, & J. Bryant (Eds.), *Media effects: Advances in theory and research* (4th ed., pp. 419–434). New York, NY: Routledge.

Kim, J., Seo, M., Yu, H., & Neuendorf, K. (2014). Cultural differences in preference for entertainment messages that induce mixed responses of joy and sorrow. *Human Communication Research*, 40, 530–552. doi:10.1111/hcre.12037.

Mares, M. L., Bartsch, A., & Bonus, J. A. (2016). When meaning matters more: Media preferences across the adult life span. *Psychololy and Aging*, 31, 513–531. doi:10.1037/pag0000098.

Mares, M. L., Oliver, M. B., & Cantor, J. (2008). Age differences in adults' emotional motivations for exposure to films. *Media Psychology*, 11, 488–511. doi:10.1177/009365092019004004.

Markus, H. R., & Kitayama, S. (1991). Culture and the self: Implications for cognition, emotion, and motivation. *Psychological Review*, 98, 224–253. doi:10.1037/0033-295x.98.2.224.

Nabi, R., & Prestin, A. (2020). Media prescriptions: Exploring the therapeutic effects of entertainment media on stress relief, illness symptoms, and goal attainment. *Journal of Communication*, 70, 145–170. doi:10.1093/joc/jqaa001.

Neubaum, G., Krämer, N. C., & Alt, K. (2020). Psychological effects of repeated exposure to elevating entertainment: An experiment over the period of 6 weeks. *Psychology of Popular Media*, 9, 194–207. doi:10.1037/ppm0000235.

Odağ, Ö., Hofer, M., Schneider, F. M., & Knop, K. (2016). Testing measurement equivalence of eudaimonic and hedonic entertainment motivations in a cross-cultural comparison. *Journal of Intercultural Communication Research*, 45, 108–125. doi:10.1080/17475759.2015.1108216.

Odağ, Ö., Uluğ, Ö. M., Arslan, H., & Schiefer, D. (2018). Culture and media entertainment: A cross-cultural exploration of hedonic and eudaimonic entertainment motivations. *International Communication Gazette*, 80, 637–657. doi:10.1177/1748048518802215.

Oliver, M. B. (1993). Exploring the paradox of the enjoyment of sad films. *Human Communication Research*, 19, 315–342. doi:10.1111/j.1468-2958.1993.tb00304.x.

Oliver, M. B. (2000). The respondent gender gap. In D. Zillmann & P. Vorderer (Eds.), *Media entertainment: The psychology of its appeal.* (pp. 215–234). Mahwah, NJ: Lawrence Erlbaum Associates.

Oliver, M. B., & Bartsch, A. (2010). Appreciation as audience response: Exploring entertainment gratifications beyond hedonism. *Human Communication Research*, 36, 53–81. doi:10.1111/j.1468-2958.2009.01368.x.

Oliver, M. B., Ferchaud, A., Bailey, E., Yan, H., Wang, R., Diddi, P., Raney, A. A., Janicke, S. H., Dale, K. R., & Wirth, R. (2017, November). *Predictors of selection of inspiring media and the resultant prosocial outcomes.* Paper presented at the meeting of National Communication Association, Dallas, TX.

Oliver, M. B., & Green, S. (2001). Development of gender differences in children's responses to animated entertainment. *Sex roles*, 45, 67–88. doi:10.1023/A:1013012401836.

Oliver, M. B., & Raney, A. A. (2011). Entertainment as pleasurable *and* meaningful: Identifying hedonic and eudaimonic motivations for entertainment consumption. *Journal of Communication*, 61, 984–1004. doi:10.1111/j.1460-2466.2011.01585.x.

Oliver, M. B., Sargent, S. L., & Weaver, J. B. (1998). The impact of sex and gender role self-perception on affective reactions to different types of film. *Sex Roles*, 38, 45–62. doi:10.1023/A:1018760427785.

Oliver, M. B., Weaver, J. B., & Sargent, S. L. (2000). An examination of factors related to sex differences in enjoyment of sad films. *Journal of Broadcasting & Electronic Media*, 44, 282–300. doi:10.1207/s15506878jobem4402_8.

Pohling, R., Diessner, R., Stacy, S., Woodward, D., & Strobel, A. (2019). Moral elevation and economic games: The moderating role of personality. *Frontiers in Psychology*, 10, 1381. doi:10.3389/fpsyg.2019.01381.

Raney, A. A., Janicke, S. H., Oliver, M. B., Dale, K. R., Jones, R. P., & Cox, D. (2018). Profiling the audience for self-transcendent media: A national survey. *Mass Communication and Society*, 21, 296–319. doi:10.1080/15205436.2017.1413195.

Rieger, D., & Klimmt, C. (2019). The daily dose of digital inspiration 2: Themes and affective user responses to meaningful memes in social media. *New Media & Society*, 21, 2201–2221. doi:10.1177/1461444819842875.

Russell, J. A. (1991). Culture and the categorization of emotions. *Psychological Bulletin*, 110, 426–450. doi:10.1037/0033-2909.110.3.426.

Schneider, F. M., Bartsch, A., & Oliver, M. B. (2017). Factorial validity and measurement invariance of the appreciation, fun, and suspense scales across US-American and German samples. *Journal of Media Psychology*, 31, 149–156. doi:10.1027/1864-1105/a000236.

Seibt, B., Schubert, T. W., Zickfeld, J. H., & Fiske, A. P. (2019). Touching the base: heart-warming ads from the 2016 US election moved viewers to partisan tears. *Cognition & Emotion*, 33, 197–212. Advance online publication. doi:10.1080/02699931.2018.1441128.

Seibt, B., Schubert, T. W., Zickfeld, J. H., Zhu, L., Arriaga, P., Simão, C., Nussinson, R., Fiske, A. P. (2017). Kama muta: Similar emotional responses to touching videos across the United States, Norway, China, Israel, and Portugal. *Journal of Cross-Cultural Psychology*, 49, 418–435. doi:10.1177/0022022117746240.

Signorielli, N., & Staples, J. (1997). Television and children's conceptions of nutrition. *Health Communication*, 9, 289–301. doi:10.1007/bf00290015.

Slater, M. D., Johnson, B. K., Cohen, J., Comello, M. L. G., & Ewoldsen, D. R. (2014). Temporarily expanding the boundaries of the self: Motivations for entering the story world and implications for narrative effects. *Journal of Communication*, 64, 439–455. doi:10.1111/jcom.12100.

Zickfeld, J. H., Schubert, T. W., Seibt, B., Blomster, J. K., Arriaga, P., Basabe, N., ... Fiske, A. P. (2019). Kama muta: Conceptualizing and measuring the experience often labelled being moved across 19 nations and 15 languages. *Emotion*, 19, 402–424. doi:10.1037/emo0000450.

Additional Readings

Bowleg, L. (2008). When Black + Lesbian + Woman ≠ Black Lesbian Woman: The methodological challenges of qualitative and quantitative intersectionality research. *Sex Roles*, 59, 312–325. doi:10.1007/s11199-008-9400-z.

Broussard, K., Warner, R., & Pope, A. (2017). Too many boxes, or not enough? Preferences for how we ask about gender in cisgender, LGB, and gender-diverse samples. *Sex Roles*, 78, 606–624. doi:10.1007/s11199-017-0823-2.

Ramasubramanian, S. (2016). Racial/ethnic identity, community-oriented media initiatives, and transmedia storytelling. *The Information Society*, 32, 333–342. doi:10.1080/01972243.2016.1212618.

Valkenburg, P. M., & Peter, J. (2013). The differential susceptibility to media effects model. *Journal of Communication*, 63, 221–243. doi:10.1111/jcom.12024.

13

LIVING WELL WITH MEDIA IN THE DIGITAL AGE

Source: Shutterstock 110537057

Media literacy is one of the goals of media psychology (see Chapter 2). It is a multidimensional concept describing the understanding that media content and technologies have the potential to influence our thoughts, emotions, physiology, and behaviors, either directly or indirectly. Decades of research have shown that people who know more about how to access and operate media, how media messages are created, how the media industries function and operate, how media messages and applications are intended, and how different content may lead to differing effects are better equipped and purposive media consumers. With knowledge and skill development, individuals can gain control over media influence (Potter, 2004). **Positive media literacy** is a movement that merges media literacy research arising from the field of media psychology with the insight about well-being and flourishing from the field of positive psychology. The purpose of the movement is—and, in many ways, the goal of this book has been—to communicate the scientific knowledge emerging from the field of positive media psychology so that people can strategically use media in mindful and purposive ways for their own benefit.

In this final chapter, we discuss positive media literacy, offering some additional insight and tips on how the power of media can be harnessed for personal and social good. To begin, though, we identify some challenges to doing so in the digital age.

Challenges to Living Well with Digital Media

Communication theorist Marshall McLuhan (1964) famously proclaimed "the medium is the message," which reflects the idea that all innovations in communication technology, regardless of how they are used, impact the structure and functioning of a society. The first two decades of the 21st century ushered in a new era of media technology, with the introduction and ubiquitous adoption of internet-supported digital devices—advanced laptops, tablets, smartphones, smartwatches, personal virtual assistants, the Internet of Things—and the myriad applications they support (especially social media and streaming services, but also the gig economy, casual games, on-demand entertainment, telecommuting, remote learning, etc.). It is undeniable that these devices have affected our social structure well beyond the content users consume or even produce. Fundamentally, the ways that we communicate with one another (e.g., more frequently, more briefly, using emojis, through memes) and the ways that we are entertained, informed, and persuaded have changed. Of course, many of the pre-21st century media technologies are still widely used: television, film, radio, printed newspapers and books, recorded music, console video games, etc. But their contents—both old and new—are increasingly digitized for convergence with and access from the latest devices.

The way internet-supported digital devices impact our understanding of and behavior in the world can be described by looking at the affordances that they provide (see Chapter 7). Affordances are the technological properties that enable specific user behaviors; they are the cues provided by the object that give us a sense of how to use it. Each digital device offers its own combination of affordances, providing users with unique media experiences. But broadly speaking, one affordance that all digital devices and the content and applications they support share is **accessibility** (i.e., how easy it is to engage in communication, regardless of time, place, or any other constraints; see Fox & McEwan, 2017). Compared to previous communication technologies, digital media devices are different because they (1) leverage artificial intelligence, using strategies to increase the likelihood that people will spend more time on them than they consciously want; (2) exert never-ending, 24/7 influence on people by simplifying use via portable and wearable technologies; (3) perpetuate social control like no other medium before by redefining the values of our social lives; and, (4) utilizing personalization as a means to increase engagement (Eisenmann, 2018).

One result is tremendous amounts of data about user preferences and choices collected and analyzed by technology companies and content providers. For example, simply based on an individual's social media profile and usage, researchers can reliably predict their Big Five personality traits, character strengths, any mental illnesses, and sexual orientation, just to name a few (e.g., Azucar, Marengo, & Settanni, 2018; Eichstaedt et al., 2018). Because of this, many scholars and social commentators have understandably highlighted privacy-related concerns from digital device use. Beyond privacy, though, several potential behavioral effects are worthy of our attention.

Problematic Media Usage

The accessibility affordance of digital devices is a well-researched area by scholars concerned with well-being. These days, digital media are no longer used at certain times of the day for a specific amount of time to retrieve information, entertain, or communicate with friends. Instead, most people are now **permanently online and permanently connected** (POPC) (Vorderer, Krömer, & Schneider, 2016). A state of POPC is defined by the constant use of electronic media for information and entertainment seeking, as well as a state of permanent communicative vigilance. Specifically, POPC refers to the use of digital media and engagement in online social interactions, while simultaneously being involved in other activities (e.g., social, cognitive, communicative, physical). Waiting on something or someone, using public transportation, or being home alone are the situations with the most frequent POPC.

Being permanently online and connected can potentially lead to pronounced negative effects, including problematic smartphone or social networking site use. These refer to a pattern of behavior associated with non-chemical behavioral dependency or addiction. Symptoms of behavioral dependency and addiction include an extreme focus of the user's life on usage, increased usage to achieve the same satisfaction, loss of interest in other activities, the inability to reduce the usage, and usage even in situations that might be dangerous (e.g., driving) or that might impact social or relational dynamics (e.g., phubbing), productivity, or academic performance (e.g., Billieux, 2012). Additionally, excessive smartphone use can result in **nomophobia** (no-mobile-phone-phobia) (King et al., 2013), which is the irrational fear one experiences when unable to use their device (e.g., the battery is dead, it was forgotten or lost).

BOX 13.1 HOW MUCH USE IS "PROBLEMATIC?"

The question of excessive technology use is a particularly important one for children and adolescents. Research suggests that any excessive time spent with screens, even for educational or occupational purposes, can be detrimental for the development of language acquisition, memory, and learning, leading to the development of psychopathological symptoms (e.g., Christakis, Ramirez, Ferguson, Ravinder, & Ramirez, 2018). But exactly how much use is "problematic?"

One study of 8- to 11-year-olds found that poorer cognitive development seemed to appear in any child engaging in more than two hours of screen time per day (including TV and smartphone use; Walsh et al., 2018). In a sample of 2- to 17-year-old Americans, Twenge and Campbell (2018) found that every additional hour of daily screen use for leisure (including TV, digital games, and electronic devices) beyond one was associated with lower curiosity, self-control, emotional stability, greater distractibility, and difficulty making friends. For 14- to 17-year-olds, moderate (four hours per day) and high (over seven hours per day) amounts of screen usage were associated with greater likelihood of being diagnosed with depression or anxiety, compared to those who used their screens only one hour per day. But Przybylski and Weinstein (2017) painted a more complex picture of the potential risks of screen time, showing that the amount of smartphone use before it hampers mental well-being differs on weekdays versus weekends. In 15-year-old English adolescents, up to two hours of use during the week led to an *increase* in mental well-being, in terms of happiness, life satisfaction, psychological, and social functioning. However, those factors of well-being suffered when use exceeded two hours. On the weekend, however, adolescent smartphone use did not impact well-being up to four hours of usage, with detrimental effects emerging when it was used longer.

With regard to college-aged individuals, one study suggested that 30 minutes per day of social media use might be an optimal time spent. Hunt, Marx, Lipson, and Young (2018) instructed a sample of college students to reduce their Facebook, Instagram, and Snapchat use to no more than ten minutes per platform per day for three weeks, compared to a control group which continued using their social media the same. The researchers found significantly reduced levels of loneliness and depression for the reduced-time group compared to the control group.

Another important factor seems to be the number of applications available to users. Primack and colleagues (2017) investigated the relationship between time spent and the number of platforms used among 19- to 32-year-old Americans. Participants accessing an extreme number of social media platforms (seven–11), compared to those accessing a few (zero–two), had significantly higher odds of suffering from depression and anxiety symptoms, controlling for the overall time spent on social media. Thus, one simple life-hack for digital flourishing might be to limit the number of social media platforms you use at a time. Additionally, being able to limit the number of check-ins for a specific platform per day seems to be similarly beneficial.

It is important to mention here that one of the important side effects of POPC is that the smartphone can be used as a crutch to avoid uncomfortable situations, boredom, and negative mental states. However, one of the most important predictors of well-being is **resilience**, which can only be achieved when people endure and challenge themselves to overcome short periods of discomfort. Thus, a crucial movement toward digital flourishing may also include a norm shift that makes smartphone technologies an "add-on" for enhancing productivity, entertainment, inspiration, connection, and information, and less of a mask to hide behind.

Many digital media devices and supported platforms are designed so that users spend prolonged and repeated time using them, despite the awareness that negative outcomes may result (e.g., texting and driving). One of the strongest design factors that can lead to problematic behavior is the inclusion of **rewards** that elicit the neurotransmitter dopamine, which is the physiological cause for people to re-engage in the same behaviors over time. Within social media, such rewards come in the form of *positive reinforcement* through likes or comments, *negative reinforcement* through the (perceivable) elimination of negative emotional states (e.g., boredom, anxiety) when using the platform, and *intermittent reinforcement* (e.g., only some content is perceived as rewarding). In addition to rewards, **triggers** (e.g., notifications) are used to encourage consumers to use devices and platforms repetitively. Further, devices and platforms are easy to access and navigate, with design strategies implemented that motivate the user to invest time and energy (e.g., recommended content to browse, profiles to visit). Each of these contribute to habit formation (Eyal, 2014), or using the device or platform in an unconscious way, further reinforcing possible problematic-use behaviors.

The scholarly discussion of problematic device and platform use has generally focused on six areas of potential impact: productivity, mental health, relationships, safety and privacy, physical health, and well-being (e.g., Baruh, Secinti, & Cemalcilar, 2017; Han, Lee, & Shin, 2019; Neophytou, Manwell, & Eikelboom, 2019). On an individual level, fear of ostracism and fear of missing out (FOMO) can at least partially explain the constant—and potentially problematic—use of such devices (Vorderer & Kohring, 2013). The acceleration of life on a societal level has been implicated, as well. To be fair: A direct causal link between digital media device use on negative mental health and well-being outcomes is not inevitable for all users, and generally speaking the observed effect sizes are small. Nevertheless, part of positive media literacy in the digital age is understanding the potential risks that may exist and acting (and thinking) mindfully to avoid them for the sake of well-being.

In Pursuit of Digital Flourishing

Well-being is a central concept in positive psychology (see Chapter 3). Recently, the concept of digital well-being (or wellness) has started to receive some attention by positive media psychology scholars. **Digital well-being** can be defined as "a state where subjective well-being is maintained in an environment characterized by digital communication overabundance" (Gui, Fasoli, & Carradore, 2017, p. 166). Although some scholars have adopted the term digital well-being, we actually prefer the term **digital flourishing**. From our perspective and based on the wider positive psychology literature, digital flourishing reflects a broader, multi-categorical approach to media technology and content use, one that involves more than just well-being.

Digital flourishing is characterized by mindful and intentional usage patterns that involve knowledge and skills about how to use media in a way that is most benefitting for one's self, self-efficacy (i.e., confidence to use media in a way that is most optimal), optimal levels of connectedness, potential for personal growth and resilience, and an absence of negative habitual use (e.g., distracted or mindless usage). Positive emotional and cognitive responsiveness (e.g., positive emotions, information seeking, reflectiveness, mindset) and a sense of feeling and doing well when using media are also characteristics of digital flourishing. Digital flourishing is a state where most mediated interactions one engages in are perceived as beneficial to the user, lead to behaviors that are beneficial for the psychological functioning of the individual and others, and where digital technologies are used to foster the individual's values and growth. In short, digital flourishing describes a state of thriving with media.

Admittedly, no simple formula for flourishing exists; many (subjectively perceived) paths lead to it. Therefore, it is not our intention to prescribe a media use diet or plan. We have no interest in telling the reader what to watch or listen to, which apps to use, or how many minutes of media to use per day. But for readers who seek to experience some of the positive effects of media discussed in the preceding chapters, we do offer a few suggestions based on the scientific record.

As noted above, media literacy involves the development of individual skills. A primary skill needed to develop digital flourishing in an environment of constant communication and information overabundance is mindfulness. **Mindfulness** can be defined as a state of non-judgmental awareness about the present moment. Mindful use of communication technologies allows for the creation of an intentional and purposive use pattern, with greater attention paid to interactions with technologies and content, with the user being aware while processing messages, conscious of their potential effects. Research has shown, for example, when instant messaging is used in a mindful way it can directly and positively support well-being (Bauer, Loy, Masur, & Schneider, 2017). Similarly, the mindful use of social media in the workplace has been shown to be positively related to health (Charoensukmongkol, 2016). To more generally discuss the potential role of mindfulness in media use, we remind the reader of the model of positive media use introduced in Chapter 1. Figure 13.1 depicts how mindfulness can impact each media use process in the pursuit of digital flourishing. Please note: The factors and characteristics identified in the model for each process are not intended to be exhaustive but rather representative. The model is offered primarily for heuristic purposes.

Mindful Media Use

Motivation

With the skill of mindfulness, audience members can become more aware of their automated and habitual use of media. Most of the time, media use is a leisure activity, something we do when we are not working. Of course, leisure time can be filled with countless activities: exercising, gardening, volunteering, painting, meditating, baking, crocheting, and so on. Turning to media during leisure is a choice, which typically includes a corresponding decision to *not* do something else. Being mindful of our motivations for using media involves a consideration of our choices by contemplating our past experiences, current states, norms, social factors, our near and future plans, and more.

One way to think about media use motivation is to conceptualize it as a mindset toward media. Within the context of social media, Lee and Hancock (2020) argued that a person's mindset—which involves beliefs, values, and

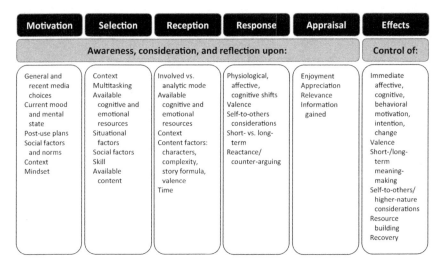

FIGURE 13.1 Mindful Media Use

expectations—shapes whether its use leads to positive or negative effects on well-being. For instance, approaching media use with the mindset that it is a *tool* that can help you accomplish goals should facilitate different impacts than approaching it from an *addiction* mindset. To approach the media motivation process with mindful awareness, we can ask ourselves: "Why do I want to engage with media right now?"

Consider the example of studying for an important exam. Music can be an inspiration and a distraction. If you turn it on when you start to study, it might do you well to be mindful of the role it is playing in each particular situation. Similarly, watching a few short YouTube videos can be a nice break and reward for hard work invested in studying, but it can also lead to hours of "wasted" time, especially with the recommendations serving a constantly updated list of enticements. Reflecting on this fact may help you manage your time better. If you know yourself to be easily tempted to check your phone (thereby interrupting your concentrated learning), then perhaps you should come up with strategies to deal with that reality before you sit down to study (e.g., put your phone in another room, turn off all notifications, temporarily remove access to certain apps).

Also, as discussed in several previous chapters, to derive positive well-being effects from media technology and content, it is important that usage is intrinsically rather than extrinsically motivated. Sometimes our media use—in particular, social media use—is motivated by external pressures to be online and available 24/7 (POPC), as well as by internalized pressures (like FOMO), both of which undermine self-determined behavior and can impede well-being. A purposeful use of technology that is self-determined is one that is more likely to lead to positive effects. For example, in waiting situations (e.g., on the bus, before class starts, at the doctor's office, before a meeting) where situational control is low, being able to use one's smartphone can impact recovery experiences positively, which in turn may increase cognitive performance (Rieger, Hefner, & Vorderer, 2017). Further, the use of entertaining media (e.g., online videos, digital gaming) when used intentionally in work situations can support recovery from stress and strain and increase energetic arousal and cognitive performance (e.g., Reinecke, Klatt, & Kraemer, 2011).

In contrast, constant interruptions via notifications or compulsive-checking habits are ways in which self-determined media use is impaired, often resulting in negative effects. For example, being interrupted while working can lead to significant levels of subjective stress, frustration, and mental exhaustion. Using the phone or being distracted by it while interacting with someone in a face-to-face situation (i.e., **phubbing**) has been shown to reduce relationship and life satisfaction, increase depressive symptoms, and promote social isolation (e.g., Roberts & David, 2016). Even the mere exposure of one's phone in a working situation can reduce cognitive performance (i.e., **mere presence phenomenon**). For those with high smartphone dependency, having the phone in one's field of vision while working on a task can greatly impair performance (Ward, Duke, Gneezy, & Bos, 2017).

In addition to mindfulness, **self-regulation** is a skill key for the development of digital flourishing that is particularly important in the media motivation process. Although most digital technologies promise instant gratifications, self-controlling one's mobile media use, for example, is a prerequisite for digital flourishing. Many digital apps are designed to support self-regulation with, for instance, time-blocking features. Roffarello and De Russis (2019) examined 42 digital well-being apps from the Google Play Store and found that most primarily provided tracking features for how much time people spend on their devices. More than one quarter of the apps also provided timers or blockers (i.e., tools that allow you to predetermine how much time you want to spend on a specific application or block their use completely for a set period of time). Thus, most of the digital well-being apps, according to the study, primarily supported self-monitoring (awareness) and self-regulation (tracking phone and app behavior and regulating phone and app use). Participants who used a typical digital well-being app for one week spent significantly less time on their phone (in particular on social media), indicating that such apps may be somewhat effective. Interestingly, the study also found that for app timers the majority of participants snoozed the timers, whereas only half of the participants snoozed the app blocker, indicating more restrictive features may be preferred by users who are trying to be more mindful about their media use motivations and behaviors.

Selection

Computer scientists often use the phrase "garbage in, garbage out" to mean that nonsensical input inevitably leads to nonsensical output. The same basic idea can be applied to digital flourishing. If you are seeking greater well-being, then the content you "ingest" matters. To select media technology and content in a mindful state, one should consider their current cognitive and emotional resources, situation, abilities, social context, and more. To approach the media selection process mindfully, we can ask ourselves: "What technology and content would be best for me to consume or engage with right now?"

Some uses and gratification researchers (see Chapter 4) have studied **gratifications sought** from media, which are ultimately compared with the **gratifications obtained** by the user (e.g., Palmgreen & Rayburn, 1982). Mindful media selection involves an awareness of the former, such that the latter can ultimately be properly determined. Having a firm grasp on the theories of content effects discussed in the earlier chapters is a great first step to developing a mindful media selection perspective.

As an example, to better understand what types of content are most promising to foster digital flourishing, it is helpful to revisit the two-factor model of entertainment (see Chapter 5). Entertaining media experiences can be categorized as being primarily hedonic or eudaimonic in nature. Thus, we can encounter content that brightens our day, makes us happy in the moment, and makes us feel delighted and uplifted, such as cute videos, funny memes, or inside jokes from a friend. Similarly, videos, news, or digital games about virtues in action in the lives of everyday people or supportive texts, snaps, or instant messages from a friend can provide meaning to our day, make us feel more connected, trigger empathy, promote strength and resilience, and reinstate our belief in the purpose of life. At the same time, content can also be distressing, anxiety-ridden, and anger-provoking, such as some news content or highly partisan threads on Twitter; such messages can detract from our hedonic and eudaimonic entertainment. Consequently, in order to increase digital flourishing, it is important to maximize exposure to content that you perceive to lead to hedonic and eudaimonic experiences. Of course, we acknowledge that this may be no easy task, as the amount of content to select from is staggering, with different effects on people across different situations, from different cultures and with different personality traits (Chapter 12).

The sources of content continue to evolve as well, which ensures that the media selection process will only become more complicated over time. For example, virtual reality (VR) is a powerful technology that can enable both types of entertainment experiences (see Chapter 8). It can provide users with perceptual cues that elicit strong emotional involvement, like wonder, awe, and gratitude; it can also deliver cognitive cues that provide the opportunity for the user to expand and even create new knowledge structures. Even a single exposure to VR can challenge a user's worldview so much so that real-world behavioral changes can be experienced. YouTube, TikTok, and similar video streaming platforms can be another source of flourishing. Online videos can foster moral development when the content contains models of moral values (Koh, 2014). Even funny cat videos that we stumble upon can have beneficial effects, including positive emotions and increased energy levels (Myrick, 2015). Moreover, most platforms allow users to design, create, and post their own content. When inspiring content is user-generated, research has shown greater elevation effects in the creator of the content than in consumers of it (Oliver & Raney, 2019). Importantly, the content we consume and distribute also has implications for other people's digital flourishing as well. Based on research on the transmission of happiness in social networks, we can infer that whatever content we share on our "wall" or newsfeed may directly affect the emotional state of our network friends. Thus, on the one hand it matters what type of content we select to consume. But on the other hand, in certain situations, users who generate their own content carry a responsibility because it also affects others.

Reception

On its face, it might seem counterproductive to be mindful when you are trying to be transported into a film or identify with a character. After all, being totally engrossed in the content is typically one of the primary goals of media use. But being narratively engaged or in a flow state does not mean that our minds shut off. Even with the most absorbing story, if something happens that seems to violate the rules of the story world—for example, in a serious drama, the family dog starts talking—then you pause, you shake your head, you wonder "what was that?" If you are reading a blog post and the writer misspells a word or uses a phrase or emoji incorrectly, then you might have a similar reaction.

The point here is that media use generally involves two modes of reception: involved and analytical (Vorderer, 1992; 1993). An **involved mode of reception** entails cognitive and emotional investment, transportation, character identification, absorption, and flow; it involves presence in the story world and engagement with the unfolding narrative. An **analytical mode of reception** is characterized by an awareness of the mediated nature of the experience, even if fleetingly or momentarily; it is more distant and (arguably) objective. When we notice the talking dog and the misspelled word, we are reflecting an analytical mode of reception. Similarly, when we acknowledge the beauty of a camera angle, the brilliance of an actor's performance, that they are playing one of our favorite songs in the background, we are reflecting an analytical mode of reception. As the examples imply, both modes of reception can and often do occur during the same media use experience; in fact, Klimmt and Vorderer (2003) suggested "that individuals' level of involvement oscillates between the prototypical poles of analytical and involved reception" (p. 348).

As we become more mindful during media use experiences, we further develop the scope and sensitivity of our analytical mode of reception. That is, mindful media use promotes analytical reception more frequently and in a wider range of situations. This then manifests in a multitude of ways: greater awareness of portrayals that violate our moral principles, reflect human goodness, represent diverse populations, give voices to those too often left voiceless, remind us of a past memory, to name just a few. Further, rather than detracting from our media experience, mindful analytical reception opens new avenues for enjoyment, appreciation, and positive effects.

Ample research has also shown that, in the context of social media, it matters if our use and reception is passive or active. Generally, passive use (e.g., scrolling) has been shown to decrease subjective well-being by eliciting envy via upward social comparisons. In contrast, using social media actively by expressing oneself, liking, working on one's own profile, and commenting on posts or seeking out specific information can enhance subjective well-being by building social capital and relatedness (Verduyn, Ybarra, Résibois, Jonides, & Kross, 2017).

Thus, to approach the media reception process mindfully, we can ask ourselves: "How am I approaching and preparing to use this particular media technology and content right now?"

Response and Appraisal

Mindful media use also involves an awareness of our responses. This can take place during reception, turning the analytical mode inward to consider what we are thinking and feeling and why. It can also occur as we conclude media use, informing our appraisals. Responses toward the media we consume, along with how we appraise our responses, directly feed into our media motivation, selection, and reception processes in the future. It is therefore helpful to reflect on each specific media encounter.

For instance, distracting oneself from a pressing task by scrolling through social media may lead to feeling better in the moment, but if it ultimately affects one's mental health (e.g., promoting jealousy toward others who always seem to be having more fun) then perhaps engaging with the technology in a different way or choosing another media activity for distraction would be more beneficial. Similarly, some online videos feature people with disabilities as inspirational simply because of their disability (i.e., inspiration porn). The videos are often created with good intentions and can stimulate empathy and pity in the viewer, but most people with disabilities and disability advocates say that such videos are demeaning and exploitative. Similar arguments have been made about "White savior films" (e.g., *The Blind Side, The Help, Freedom Writers*), which portray the success of Black and indigenous people of color (i.e., BIPOC characters) as completely dependent upon White characters. Being mindful of one's responses to and appraisals of such content are important. To approach the media response and appraisal processes mindfully, we can ask ourselves: "How is this media content and technology making me feel and think right now, and what do I think and feel about that?"

Becoming aware that the media we use impacts how we feel, how we think about the world, and how our brains operate should give us pause to reflect on how to strategically leverage technology and content in ways that support our values. For instance, many "free" digital applications (e.g., email, Facebook, smartphone games) are designed to capture as much of our attention as possible in order to deliver advertisements or to otherwise learn about us in order to better target us with advertisements in the future. In fact, industry leaders have coined the term **attention economy** to describe the currency exchanged from the attentive use of a specific application. The numerous new apps and tools that are released on the market daily fight for our attention, making it a rare commodity. We feel that fight in our own lives when we are torn between different tasks, tools, and content, which often leads to multitasking in ways that only stress us out even more. In such an environment, the technology company's agenda and values become our agenda and values. For mindful technology use that leads to digital flourishing, we should perhaps think about our values first and direct our awareness to technology use in support of those values.

Effects

A central aim of this book has been to illuminate the potential ways that media can lead to positive effects. But as has been mentioned throughout, media users are all different. What affects one may not affect another for countless reasons.

As a result, positive media psychologists cannot develop a formula that ensures particular beneficial outcomes of media use for each individual. However, from the research record, users can derive some "best practices" to guide their own positive media use. We offer an example for social media use in Box 13.2, largely based on the research presented in Chapter 7.

BOX 13.2 HOW CAN I MAXIMIZE THE BENEFITS OF SOCIAL MEDIA?

Social media can be a fun and fulfilling tool for connecting with others. However, research shows that *the way we use* social media can influence the effects. In order to maximize the benefits of social media, engaging in the following ways could improve your experience.

- *Be an active user.* Social media typically provides several options for usage: posting original content, engaging with content posted by others (e.g., liking, commenting, sharing), or passive consumption. Several studies have shown that active consumption is the most beneficial way to use social media (for an overview, see Verduyn et al., 2017). This includes both posting original content and engaging with content posted by others. So, when you use social media, you should reap the most benefits by engaging with and posting your own content rather than just scrolling through.
- *Connect with people you care about.* It can be difficult to keep in touch with family and friends, particularly when they are in a different city, state, or even country. Using social media to engage with them on a regular basis can be a good way to maintain meaningful relationships, a key aspect of well-being (see PERMA, Chapter 3).
- *Seek social support when needed.* One way to actively engage on social media is to seek out help when needed. If you are feeling particularly stressed about an upcoming assignment, for instance, you might benefit from sharing your struggle and seeking support on social media. This doesn't have to be a public blast from your account to be beneficial. You might seek out groups or accounts that post information about coping with the stresses of college life or share your struggles with a few close friends. Sharing your struggles (i.e., self-disclosure) and seeking peer support can help you to have a more positive social media experience.
- *Avoid negative comparisons.* What we typically see on social media is a highly curated version of someone's life, which can make it seem like they are doing better than us in some ways. When we see a perfectly decorated home or an expertly prepared meal, we might feel bad about ourselves in comparison. However, these kinds of comparisons can lead to harmful effects, and it is best to avoid envious comparisons. Instead, consider following people who inspire you to become a better version of yourself.

- *Monitor your screen time.* Studies have found that mental-health benefits can emerge when social media use is reduced to 10 minutes a day per account (e.g., Hunt et al., 2018). Monitoring one's screen time (via an app) can also reduce FOMO and anxiety. So, even if you are not ready to change much about your social media behavior just yet, you could start by simply tracking your weekly usage time.
- *Learn when you might need some time away.* As great as social media can be, it is also healthy to step away from them occasionally. If you find, for instance, that you are comparing yourself to others in a detrimental way, it might be best to reduce your usage of social media for a little while. Taking a break from social media can be a good way to reset and recharge.

Ultimately, though, any attempt to harness the power of media for good in your own life begins with you. It requires you to be aware that such effects are possible but not inevitable. It requires an acknowledgment that certain content and technology seem to promote certain effects for you at certain times and in certain situations. It requires contemplation on the various processes involved in media use, armed with an understanding of how the human body, mind, and spirit in general and your body, mind, and spirit specifically respond to stimuli in the environment. And it requires a hopeful outlook on media and on ourselves. The potential positive effects of media content are plentiful. Most of us are familiar with the joy that comes from watching a great movie, listening to our favorite song, and playing a mind-blowing new game. But media technologies and content can provide us with more than just joy. Mindful media use involves seeking out all of the positive ways that media technology and content can help you and your life flourish. To approach the media effects processes mindfully, we can ask ourselves: "What effects do I want or need to experience from this media encounter?"

Summary

Living well with media in the digital age requires literacy about the ways that media can impact our thoughts, emotions, and behaviors and awareness about one's own media habits. It requires self-regulated, autonomous, and goal-directed media use. It includes reflecting on use, whether enjoyable or not, appreciated or not, informative or not. Ultimately, living well with media in the digital age means different things for different people in different situations.

More research is needed to determine if a set of optimal "best practices" can be developed that would be helpful for a large number of users. As a starting point, it can be helpful to think about the content consumed, the purpose or intention of use, and the amount of time using it. Schools, universities, and workplaces should consider adopting policies for positive digital behaviors that promote productivity, connection, and learning instead of detracting from it. Within the physical and mental health field, positive media literacy should be addressed as an important factor in patient care. Thus, in addition to the need for reconsidering rules about technology use within families, friendships, and romantic partnerships, public and private institutions and businesses should start considering digital flourishing as an important part of their philosophy if they want to ultimately be positive agents of change in the digital age.

References

Azucar, D., Marengo, D., & Settanni, M. (2018). Predicting the Big 5 personality traits from digital footprints on social media: A meta-analysis. *Personality and Individual Differences*, 124, 150–159. doi:10.1016/j.paid.2017.12.018.

Baruh, L., Secinti, E., & Cemalcilar, Z. (2017). Online privacy concerns and privacy management: A meta-analytical review. *Journal of Communication*, 67, 26–53. doi:10.1111/jcom.12276.

Bauer, A. A., Loy, L. S., Masur, P. K., & Schneider, F. M. (2017). Mindful instant messaging: Mindfulness and autonomous motivation as predictors of well-being in smartphone communication. *Journal of Media Psychology*, 29, 159–165. doi:10.1027/1864-1105/a000225.

Billieux, J. (2012). Problematic use of the mobile phone: A literature review and a pathways model. *Current Psychiatry Reviews*, 8, 299–307. doi:10.2174/157340012803520522.

Charoensukmongkol, P. (2016). Mindful Facebooking: The moderating role of mindfulness on the relationship between social media use intensity at work and burnout. *Journal of Health Psychology*, 21, 1966–1980. doi:10.1177/1359105315569096.

Christakis, D. A., Ramirez, J. S. B., Ferguson, S. M., Ravinder, S., & Ramirez, J. M. (2018). How early media exposure may affect cognitive function: A review of results from observations in humans and experiments in mice. *Proceedings of the National Academy of Sciences*, 115, 9851–9858. doi:10.1073/pnas.1711548115..

Eichstaedt, J. C., Smith, R. J., Merchant, R. M., Ungar, L. H., Crutchley, P., Preoţiuc-Pietro, D. Asch, D. A., & Schwartz, H. A. (2018). Facebook language predicts depression in medical records. *Proceedings of the National Academy of Sciences*, 115, 11203–11208. doi:10.1073/pnas.1802331115.

Eisenmann, D. (2018, October 8). One to watch: Center for Humane Technology. Realign technology with humanity's best interest. *The Next Tech Thing.* http://thenexttechthing.blogspot.com/2018/10/center-for-humane-technology.html.

Eyal, N. (2014). *Hooked: How to build habit-forming products.* New York, NY: Penguin.

Fox, J., & McEwan, B. (2017). Distinguishing technologies for social interaction: The perceived social affordances of communication channels scale. *Communication Monographs*, 84, 298–318. doi:10.1080/03637751.2017.1332418.

Gui, M., Fasoli, M., & Carradore, R. (2017). "Digital well-being". Developing a new theoretical tool for media literacy research. *Italian Journal of Sociology of Education*, 9, 155–173. doi:10.14658/pupj-ijse-2017-1-8.

Han, H., Lee, S., & Shin, G. (2019). Naturalistic data collection of head posture during smartphone use. *Ergonomics*, 62, 444–448. doi:10.1080/00140139.2018.1544379.

Hunt, M. G., Marx, R., Lipson, C., & Young, J. (2018). No more FOMO: Limiting social media decreases loneliness and depression. *Journal of Social and Clinical Psychology*, 37, 751–768. doi:10.1521/jscp.2018.37.10.751.

King, A. L. S., Valença, A. M., Silva, A. C. O., Baczynski, T., Carvalho, M. R., & Nardi, A. E. (2013). Nomophobia: Dependency on virtual environments or social phobia? *Computers in Human Behavior*, 29, 140–144. doi:10.1016/j.compedu.2018.08.012.

Klimmt, C., & Vorderer, P. (2003). Media psychology "is not yet there": Introducing theories on media entertainment to the presence debate. *Presence: Teleoperators & Virtual Environments*, 12, 346–359. doi:10.1162/105474603322391596.

Koh, C. (2014). Exploring the use of Web 2.0 technology to promote moral and psychosocial development: Can YouTube work? *British Journal of Educational Technology*, 45, 619–635. doi:10.1111/bjet.12071.

Lee, A.Y., & Hancock, J. (2020, May). *Social media mindsets: The impact of implicit theories of social media use on psychological well-being.* Paper presented at the annual meeting of the International Communication Association, Gold Coast, AU.

McLuhan, M. (1964). *Understanding media: The extensions of man.* Cambridge, MA: MIT Press.

Myrick, J. G. (2015). Emotion regulation, procrastination, and watching cat videos online: Who watches Internet cats, why, and to what effect? *Computers in Human Behavior*, 52, 168–176. doi:10.1016/j.chb.2015.06.001.

Neophytou, E., Manwell, L. A., & Eikelboom, R. (2019). Effects of excessive screen time on neurodevelopment, learning, memory, mental health, and neurodegeneration: A scoping review. *International Journal of Mental Health and Addiction.* Advanced online publication. doi:10.1007/s11469-019-00182-2.

Oliver, M. B., & Raney, A. A. (2019). Emerging scholarship and a roadmap for emerging technologies. In J. A. Muniz-Velazquez & C.M. Pulido (Eds.), *The Routledge handbook of positive communication: Contributions of an emerging community of research on communication for happiness and social change* (pp. 111–119). New York, NY: Routledge.

Palmgreen, P., & Rayburn, J. D. (1982). Gratifications sought and media exposure an expectancy value model. *Communication Research*, 9, 561–580. doi:10.1177/009365082009004004.

Potter, W. J. (2004). *Theory of media literacy: A cognitive approach.* Thousand Oaks, CA: Sage.

Primack, B. A., Shensa, A., Escobar-Viera, C. G., Barrett, E. L., Sidani, J. E., Colditz, J. B., & James, A. E. (2017). Use of multiple social media platforms and symptoms of depression and anxiety: A nationally-representative study among US young adults. *Computers in Human Behavior*, 69, 1–9. doi:10.1016/j.chb.2016.11.013.

Przybylski, A. K., & Weinstein, N. (2017). A large-scale test of the goldilocks hypothesis: quantifying the relations between digital-screen use and the mental well-being of adolescents. *Psychological Science*, 28, 204–215. doi:10.1177/0956797616678438.

Reinecke, L., Klatt, J., & Krämer, N. C. (2011). Entertaining media use and the satisfaction of recovery needs: Recovery outcomes associated with the use of interactive and noninteractive entertaining media. *Media Psychology*, 14, 192–215. doi:10.1080/15213269.2011.573466.

Rieger, D., Hefner, D., & Vorderer, P. (2017). Mobile recovery? The impact of smartphone use on recovery experiences in waiting situations. *Mobile Media & Communication*, 5, 161–177. doi:10.1177/2050157917691556.

Roberts, J. A., & David, M. E. (2016). My life has become a major distraction from my cell phone: Partner phubbing and relationship satisfaction among romantic partners. *Computers in Human Behavior*, 54, 134–141. doi:10.1016/j.chb.2015.07.058.

Roffarello, A.M., & De Russis, L. (2019). The race towards digital wellbeing: Issues and opportunities. In *Proceedings of the 2019 CHI Conference on Human Factors in Computing*

Systems (pp. 1–14). New York, NY: Association for Computing Machinery. Twenge, J. M., & Campbell, W. K. (2018). Associations between screen time and lower psychological well-being among children and adolescents: Evidence from a population-based study. *Preventative Medicine Reports*, 12, 271–283. doi:10.1016/j.pmedr.2018.10.003.

Verduyn, P., Ybarra, O., Résibois, M., Jonides, J., & Kross, E. (2017). Do social network sites enhance or undermine subjective well-being? A critical review. *Social Issues and Policy Review*, 11, 274–302. doi:10.1111/sipr.12033.

Vorderer, P. (1992). *Fernsehen als Handlung: Fernsehfilmrezeption aus motivationspsychologischer Perspektive* [Watching television as action: Reception of TV movies from the perspective of motivational psychology]. Berlin: Edition Sigma.

Vorderer, P. (1993). Audience involvement and program loyalty. *Poetics*, 22, 89–98. doi:10.1016/0304-422X(93)90022-9.

Vorderer, P., & Kohring, M. (2013). Permanently online: A challenge for media and communication research. *International Journal of Communication*, 7, 188–196.

Vorderer, P., Krömer, N., & Schneider, F. M. (2016). Permanently online–Permanently connected: Explorations into university students' use of social media and mobile smart devices. *Computers in Human Behavior*, 63, 694–703. doi:10.1016/j.chb.2016.05.085.

Walsh, J. J., Barnes, J. D., Cameron, J. D., Goldfield, G. S., Chaput, J. P., Gunnell, K. E., … & Tremblay, M. S. (2018). Associations between 24 hour movement behaviours and global cognition in US children: a cross-sectional observational study. *The Lancet Child & Adolescent Health*, 2, 783–791. doi:10.1016/S2352-4642(18)30278-5.

Ward, A. F., Duke, K., Gneezy, A., & Bos, M. W. (2017). Brain drain: The mere presence of one's own smartphone reduces available cognitive capacity. *Journal of the Association for Consumer Research*, 2, 140–154. doi:10.1086/691462.

Additional Readings

Arpaci, I. (2019). Relationships between early maladaptive schemas and smartphone addiction: The moderating role of mindfulness. *International Journal of Mental Health and Addiction*. Advanced online publication. doi:10.1007/s11469-019-00186-y.

Banjo, O., Hu, Y., & Sundar, S. S. (2008). Cell phone usage and social interaction with proximate others: Ringing in a theoretical model. *The Open Communication Journal*, 2, 127–135. doi:10.2174/1874916X00802010127.

Booker, C. L., Kelly, Y. J., & Sacker, A. (2018). Gender differences in the associations between age trends of social media interaction and well-being among 10–15 year olds in the UK. *BMC Public Health*, 18, 321. doi:10.1186/s12889-018-5220-4.

Caird, J. K., Johnston, K. A., Willness, C. R., Asbridge, M., & Steel, P. (2014). A meta-analysis of the effects of texting on driving. *Accident Analysis & Prevention*, 71, 311–318. doi:10.1016/j.aap.2014.06.005.

Grue, J. (2016). The problem with inspiration porn: A tentative definition and a provisional critique. *Disability & Society*, 31, 838–849. doi:10.1080/09687599.2016.1205473.

Hofmann, W., Reinecke, L., & Meier, A. (2017). Of sweet temptations and bitter aftertaste: Self-control as a moderator of the effects of media use on well-being. In L. Reinecke & M.B. Oliver (Eds.), *The Routledge handbook of media use and well-being: International perspectives on theory and research on positive media effects* (pp. 211–222). New York, NY: Routledge.

Huang, C. (2017). Time spent on social network sites and psychological well-being: A meta-analysis. *Cyberpsychology, Behavior, and Social Networking*, 20, 346–354. doi:10.1089/cyber.2016.0758.

Kramer, A. D., Guillory, J. E., & Hancock, J. T. (2014). Experimental evidence of massive-scale emotional contagion through social networks. *Proceedings of the National Academy of Sciences*, 111, 8788–8790. doi:10.1073/pnas.1320040111.

Liu yi Lin, B.A., Sidani, J. E., Shensa, A., Radovic, A. Miller, E. Colditz, J. B., Hoffman, B. L., Giles, L. M., & Primack, B. A. (2016). Association between social media use and depression among US young adults. *Depression and Anxiety*, 33, 323–331. doi:10.1002/da.22466.

Madigan, S., Browne, D., Racine, N., Mori, C., & Tough, S. (2019). Association between screen time and children's performance on a developmental screening test. *JAMA Pediatrics*, 173, 244–250. doi:10.1001/jamapediatrics.2018.5056.

Mahapatra, S. (2019). Smartphone addiction and associated consequences: Role of loneliness and self-regulation. *Behaviour & Information Technology*, 38, 833–844. doi:10.1080/0144929X.2018.1560499.

Reinecke, L. (2018). POPC and well-being: A risk-benefit analysis. In P. Vorderer, D. Hefner, L. Reinecke, & C. Klimmt (Eds.), *Permanently online, permanently connected: Living and communicating in a POPC world* (pp. 2237–2243). New York, NY: Routledge.

Riva, G., Serino, S., Chirico, A., & Gaggioli, A. (2019). Positive technology. From communication to positive experience. In J. A. Muniz-Velazquez & C.M. Pulido (Eds.), *The Routledge handbook of positive communication: Contributions of an emerging community of research on communication for happiness and social change* (pp. 276–278). New York, NY: Routledge.

Schneider, F. M., Halfmann, A., & Vorderer, P. (2019). POPC and the good life: A salutogenic take on being permanently online, permanently connected. In J. A. Muniz-Velazquez & C.M. Pulido (Eds.), *The Routledge handbook of positive communication: Contributions of an emerging community of research on communication for happiness and social change* (pp. 295–304). New York, NY: Routledge.

Thomée, S., Härenstam, A., & Hagberg, M. (2011). Mobile phone use and stress, sleep disturbances, and symptoms of depression among young adults-a prospective cohort study. *BMC Public Health*, 11, 66. doi:10.1186/1471-2458-11-66.

INDEX

Entries in **bold** refer to text in boxes.

Printed in Great Britain
by Amazon

26674284R00143